Y0-AGJ-880

ŚĀKYAMUNI BUDDHA

SEATED ŚĀKYAMUNI BUDDHA WITH TWO ATTENDANTS

VENERABLE MASTER HSUAN HUA

FLOWER ADORNMENT SUTRA

CHAPTER FORTY

ENTERING THE INCONCEIVABLE
STATE OF LIBERATION BY MEANS OF
THE PRACTICES AND VOWS OF
SAMANTABHADRA BODHISATTVA

Buddhist Text Translation Society
UKIAH, CALIFORNIA

BASED ON
THE TANG DYNASTY
CHINESE TRANSLATION BY
TRIPITAKA MASTER PRAJNA OF KUBHA
796-798 CE

ENGLISH TRANSLATION BY
THE BUDDHIST TEXT
TRANSLATION SOCIETY

The Flower Adornment Sutra

CHAPTER FORTY
ENTERING the INCONCEIVABLE STATE of LIBERATION by MEANS of the PRACTICES and VOWS of SAMANTABHADRA BODHISATTVA

A COMMENTARY BY VENERABLE MASTER
HSUAN HUA

BUDDHIST TEXT TRANSLATION SOCIETY
UKIAH, CALIFORNIA

www.drba.org

©2020 Buddhist Text Translation Society
  Dharma Realm Buddhist University
  Dharma Realm Buddhist Association
  4951 Bodhi Way, Ukiah, CA 95482
  www.buddhisttexts.org
  www.drbu.edu
  www.drba.org

Buddhist Text Translation Society
4951 Bodhi Way, Ukiah, CA 95482

ISBN (hardcover): 978-1-64217-071-9

ISBN (ebook): 978-1-64217-072-6

Library of Congress Cataloging-in-Publication Data
Hsuan Hua, 1918-1995
    Flower adornment sutra (a commentary by Hsuan Hua). Chapter one, The wondrous adornments of the rulers of the worlds: based on the Tang dynasty Chinese translation by Tripiṭaka master Śikṣānanda of Khotan / English translation by the Buddhist Text Translation Society.—1st English ed.
        v. < > cm.
Includes bibliographical references and index.
    ISBN 0-88139-464-5 (v. 1)
1. Tripiṭaka. Sūtrapiṭaka.
Buddhāvataṃsakamahāvaipulyasūtra—Commentaries. I. Title: Wondrous adornments of the rulers of the worlds. II. Śikṣānanda, 652-710. III. Buddhist Text Translation Society. IV. Tripiṭaka. Sūtrapiṭaka.
Buddhāvataṃsakamahāvaipulyasūtra. English. Selections. V. Title.
    BQ1627.H78 2004
    294.3'85—dc21

                                                                    2003009264

Primary Translation by: Bhikshu Heng Shun
Reviewed by: Bhikshu Jin Yan and Dr. Gary Linebarger
Edited by: Dr. Wang Qingnan and John Pegan
Certified by: Bhikshuni Heng Hsien

CONTENTS

1.   SUTRA TEXT

TEXT WITH COMMENTARY

44. .... Introduction

105. .... To Worship All Buddhas

117. .... To Praise the Tathagatas

122. .... To Extensively Cultivate Making Offerings

141. .... To Repent of Karmic Obstacles and Reform

147. .... To Follow and Rejoice in Merit and Virtue

156. .... To Request the Turning of The Wheel of Dharma

159. .... To Beseech the Buddhas to Remain in the World

162. .... To Always Follow and Learn from the Buddhas

176. .... To Constantly Conform with Living Beings

188. .... To Transfer All Merit and Virtue

194. .... The Merit of these Practices and Vows

225. .... Verses

363. .... Epilogue

THE EIGHT GUIDELINES OF THE
BUDDHIST TEXT TRANSLATION SOCIETY

I.   A volunteer must free him/herself from the motives of personal fame and profit.

II. A volunteer must cultivate a respectful and sincere attitude free from arrogance and conceit.

III. A volunteer must refrain from aggrandizing his/her work and denigrating that of others.

IV. A volunteer must not establish him/herself as the standard of correctness and suppress the work of others with his or her fault-finding.

V.   A volunteer must take the Buddha-mind as his/her own mind.

VI. A volunteer must use the wisdom of Dharma-Selecting Vision to determine true principles.

VII. A volunteer must request Virtuous Elders in the ten directions to certify his/her translations.

VIII. A volunteer must endeavor to propagate the teachings by printing sutras, *śāstra* texts, and *vinaya* texts when the translations are certified as being correct.

Foreword

The Venerable Tripitaka Master Hua lectured on the last chapter of the *Flower Adornment (Avatamsaka) Sutra*, "Entering the Inconceivable State of Liberation By Means of the Practices and Vows of Samantabhadra Bodhisattva," during the 1969 summer cultivation and study session held at the Buddhist Lecture Hall in San Francisco. The lecture series ran for six weeks, from June 16th to July 25th, with a two-hour lecture delivered every day, six days a week. In addition to attending lectures, participants in the session devoted their time to language study, reviewing the lectures, meditation, and daily worship. The Venerable master's lectures, delivered in Chinese, are set forth in English translation in this volume.

On June 13, 1971, the Venerable Master again began lecturing the *Flower Adornment Sutra*. He began by explaining, in a series of three hundred and seventy-five lectures, Tang Dynasty National Master Qingliang's Preface and Prologue to the sutra. The Venerable Master Hua's explanation of the sutra text itself, began on November 12, 1972, and was completed on September 9, 1979. In all, the Venerable Master delivered nearly three thousand lectures, spanning more than eight years, on this "king of kings of Buddhist sutras."

Translators' Preface

The Venerable Master lectured on the *Great Expansive Buddha Flower Adornment (Avatamsaka) Sutra* for over eight years from 1971 to 1979. During that time he gave nearly 3000 public lectures on this most important Mahayana Sutra. The *Avatamsaka Sutra* is known as the king of kings of sutras, because it gives a very detailed map of the Bodhisattva's path to the "complete enlightenment" of a Buddha. The culmination of this path is expressed in the Practices and Vows of Samantabhadra Bodhisattva. Indeed, this chapter, entitled "Entering the Inconceivable State of Liberation By Means of the Practices and Vows of Samantabhadra Bodhisattva," describes the final stage of the youth Sudhana's quest to realize this ultimate state of spiritual awakening.

The chapter begins with the following words by Samantabhadra Bodhisattva:

> Good men! If all of the Buddhas of the ten directions continuously spoke of the merit and virtue of the Tathagata (Buddha) for kalpas (eons) as numerous as the smallest atomic particles in ineffably ineffable numbers of Buddha kshetra-lands, they would not be able to finish. If one aspires to perfect the gateway to the Tathagata's merit and virtue, one must cultivate ten kinds of great practices and vows.

Therefore, if any person wishes to truly walk the road to achieve the enlightenment of a Buddha, he or she must cultivate these ten practices of Samantabhadra Bodhisattva. And according to the *Shurangama Sutra*, when one discovers these practices and takes them to heart, Samantabhadra will personally assisted in one's quest.

> *Samantabhadra Bodhisattva arose from his seat, bowed at the Buddha's feet and said to the Buddha:*
>
> *"I have been a Dharma Prince with as many Tathagatas (Buddhas) as there are grains of sand in the Ganges. The Tathagatas of the ten directions tell their disciples who have the roots of a Bodhisattva to cultivate the practices of Samantabhadra, which are named after me.*
>
> *World Honored One, I use my mind to listen and distinguish all the knowledge and views of living beings.*
>
> *In other regions as many realms away as there are grains of sand in the Ganges, if there is a single living being who in his or her heart discovers the practices of Samantabhadra, I immediately mount my six-tusked elephant, creating hundreds of thousands of division-bodies to go to those places. Although their obstacles may be so heavy that they do not see me, I secretly rub their crown, protect and comfort them, and enable them to be successful."*

These passages of sutra text clearly show how fortunate we are to be able to read, study, and practice these incredible vows taught by Samantabhadra Bodhisattva.

In this second edition of "Entering the Inconceivable State of Liberation by Means of the Practices and Vows of Samantabhadra Bodhisattva" we were able to create a group including a couple of native Chinese speakers to listen to all of the original lectures in Chinese and then do a thorough review and modification of the English translation of the text and commentary. At the final stage of our work we asked the primary translator of the first edition to join us to do a final review of our work. With this more experienced team of translators and editors, we believe this new work is a significant improvement over the first edition that was published back in 1982. Our earnest wish is that this new edition will enable those who read it to plant the seeds that will eventually blossom into the Buddha's wisdom.

Sincerely, in Dharma,

(Bhikshu) Heng Shün

Member of the translation team that

included (Bhikshu) Jin Yan, Dr. Wang

Qingnan, and Dr. Gary Linebarger

August 7, 2019

VERSE FOR OPENING A SUTRA

The unsurpassed, profound, and wonderful Dharma
Is difficult to encounter in hundreds of millions of eons;
I now see and hear it, receive and uphold it,
And I vow to fathom the Tathāgata's true meaning.

Sutra
Flower Adornment Sutra

Chapter Forty
Entering the Inconceivable State of Liberation By Means of the Practices and Vows of Samantabhadra Bodhisattva

Translated on imperial command by the Tang Dynasty Tripitaka Master Prajna of Kubha

Entering the Inconceivable State of Liberation By Means of the Practices and Vows of Samantabhadra Bodhisattva, Chapter 40, Great Means, Expansive Buddha Flower Adornment Sutra (Taisho #293, Roll #40 of 40 Rolls)

(Translated on Imperial Command by the Tang Dynasty Tripitaka Master Prajna of Kubha 796-798 CE)

Introduction

At that time, after Samantabhadra Bodhisattva, Mahasattva finished praising the Tathagata's[1] supreme merit and virtue, he told all the Bodhisattvas and Sudhana, "Good men! If all of the Buddhas of the ten directions continuously spoke of the merit and virtue of the Tathagata for kalpas[2] as numerous as the smallest atomic particles in ineffably ineffable numbers of Buddha kshetra-lands,[3] they would not be able to finish. If

---

1. Tathagata, pronounced tə̩tägə'tə is one of the ten honorific titles of the Buddha. "Tatha" means "thus" or "such" and agata means to "return" or "come back."

2. Kalpa is a period of time in Buddhist cosmology equal to about 16 million human years.

3. Kshetra literally means "field." In Buddhism it refers to the field of influence of a Buddha. It refers to a system that includes billions of worlds.

one aspires to perfect the gateway to this merit and virtue, one must cultivate ten kinds of great practices and vows.

"What are the ten? The first is to worship all Buddhas. The second is to praise the Tathagatas. The third is to extensively cultivate making offerings. The fourth is to repent of karmic obstacles and reform. The fifth is to follow and rejoice in merit and virtue. The sixth is to request the turning of the wheel of Dharma. The seventh is to beseech the Buddhas to remain in the world. The eighth is to always follow and learn from the Buddhas. The ninth is to constantly conform with living beings. The tenth is to transfer all merit and virtue."

Sudhana asked, "Great Sage, what is the meaning of 'to worship all Buddhas' up to and including 'to transfer all merit and virtue?'"

1. To Worship All Buddhas

Samantabhadra told Sudhana, "Good man, to worship all Buddhas is explained like this. There are Buddhas, World Honored Ones, in the ten directions and the three periods of time, to the exhaustion of the dharma-realm and the reaches of space, that are as numerous as the smallest atomic particles in all Buddha kshetra-lands. Because of the power of Samantabhadra's practices and vows, I have a profound mind of faith in and understanding of them as if they were right before my eyes. With pure karma in body, speech, and thought, I always worship them.

In each and every place where there are Buddhas, I manifest ineffably ineffable number of bodies as numerous as the smallest atomic particles in a Buddha kshetra-land. Every single body worships all Buddhas everywhere, who are as numerous as the smallest atomic particles in ineffably ineffable numbers of Buddha kshetra-lands.

When the reaches of space come to an end, my worship will also come to an end. However, the reaches of space can never come to an end, therefore my worship has no end. In the same way, when the realms of living beings come to an end, when the karma of living beings comes to an end, and when the afflictions of living beings come to an end, my worship will also end. Since the realms of living beings up to and including their afflictions have no end, my worship has no end. It continues in thought after thought without cease. I never tire of this karma in body, speech, and thought.

2. To Praise the Tathagatas

Moreover, good man, to praise the Tathagatas is explained like this. In each of the smallest atomic particles in all the kshetra-lands in the ten directions and three periods of time, to the exhaustion of the dharma-realm and the reaches of space, there are Buddhas as numerous as the smallest atomic particles in all worlds. In each and every place where there are Buddhas, a vast ocean-wide assembly of Bodhisattvas surrounds them. Using a profound and supreme understanding, I should manifest knowledge and vision.

Each body has an eloquence that surpasses the subtle and wondrous tongue of Sarasvatī, the Goddess of Eloquence. Each tongue puts forth an inexhaustible ocean of sounds. From each sound comes an ocean of all words, which praise and exalt the ocean of all the merit and virtue of all the Tathagatas. To the ends of the boundaries of the future, these praises are continuous and unceasing. To the ends of the dharma-realm, there is no place they do not pervade.

In this way, when the reaches of space, the realms of living beings, the karma of living beings, and the afflictions of living beings come to an end, my praise will also end. However, because the reaches of space up to and including afflictions have no end, therefore this praise of mine is without end. It

continues in thought after thought without cease. I never tire
of this karma in body, speech, and thought.

3. To Extensively Cultivate Making Offerings

Moreover, Good Man, to extensively cultivate making offerings is explained like this. In each of the smallest atomic particles in all the Buddha kshetra-lands in the ten directions and three periods of time, to the exhaustion of the dharma-realm and the reaches of space, there are Buddhas as numerous as the smallest atomic particles in all worlds. In each and every place where there are Buddhas, an ocean-wide assembly of various kinds of Bodhisattvas surrounds them. Due to the power of Samantabhadra's practices and vows, I give rise to deep faith and understanding and manifest knowledge and vision.

I make offerings of superb and wonderful gifts to all of them. That is to say, I make offerings of clouds of flowers, clouds of garlands, clouds of celestial music, clouds of heavenly canopies, clouds of heavenly clothing, as well as all varieties of heavenly incense, including incense paste, burning incense, powdered incense, and other clouds of gifts such as these. Each offering is the size of Mount Sumeru, the king of mountains.

I burn all kinds of lamps. This includes butter lamps, oil lamps, and lamps of many fragrant oils. The wick of each lamp is as great as Mount Sumeru. The quantity of oil in each lamp is

like the waters of the great ocean. With all manner of gifts
such as these, I constantly make offerings.

Good man, of all offerings, the offering of Dharma is supreme.
That is to say, it is the offering of cultivating according to the
teachings, the offering of benefiting living beings, the offering
that gathers in living beings, the offering of undergoing suffering
on behalf of living beings, the offering of diligently cultivating
the roots of goodness, the offering of never forsaking the karma
of the Bodhisattvas, and the offering of never being apart from
the Bodhi-mind.

Good Man, the measureless merit and virtue created from
making the previous offerings, when compared to the merit
and virtue from a single thought of the offering of Dharma,
does not equal one one-hundredth, one one-thousandth, one
part in a hundred thousand kotis of nayutas, one part in a
kala, one part by reckoning, one part by calculation, one part
that can be demonstrated by comparison, or one part in an
upanishad. Why is this? Because all Tathagatas venerate the
Dharma. Because cultivating according to the teachings gives
birth to all Buddhas. If a Bodhisattva makes the offering of
Dharma, he will have made an offering to the Tathagatas
Cultivating in this way is a true offering. It is a vast and most
supreme offering.

In this way, when the reaches of space, the realms of living beings, the karma of living beings, and the afflictions of living beings come to an end, my making offerings will also end. However, because the reaches of space up to and including the afflictions of living beings can never end, therefore my making offerings is also without end. It continues in thought after thought without cease. I never tire of this karma in body, speech, and thought.

4. To Repent of Karmic Obstacles and Reform

Moreover, Good Man, to repent of karmic obstacles and reform is explained like this. The Bodhisattva reflects to himself, 'I, from beginningless kalpas in the past, because of greed, hatred, and delusion, have created measureless and boundless evil karma with my body, mouth, and mind. If this evil karma had a substance and form, it could not be contained within the reaches of space.

With my three karmas purified, before the assemblies of all Buddhas and Bodhisattvas in kshetra-lands throughout the dharma-realm that are as numerous as the smallest atomic particles, I now sincerely repent of and reform my offenses and will never create them again. I will always dwell in all the merit and virtue of the pure moral precepts.'

In this way, when the reaches of space, the realms of living beings, the karma of living beings, and the afflictions of living beings come to an end, my repentance will also end. However, the reaches of space up to and including the afflictions of living beings can never end. Therefore, my repenting and reforming is without end. It continues in thought after thought without cease. I never tire of this karma in body, speech, and thought.

5. To Follow and Rejoice in Merit and Virtue

Moreover, Good Man, to follow and rejoice in merit and virtue is explained like this. All the Buddhas, the Tathagatas, are as numerous as the smallest atomic particles in all the Buddha kshetra-lands of the ten directions and the three periods of time, throughout the dharma-realm and the reaches of space. From the time they first brought forth the Bodhi-mind for the sake of All-Wisdom, they diligently cultivated and amassed blessings without regard for their bodies and lives.

They did this throughout kalpas as many as the smallest atomic particles in ineffably ineffable numbers of Buddha kshetra-lands. During each kalpa they gave up their heads, eyes, hands, and feet, as many times as there are the smallest atomic particles in ineffably ineffable numbers of Buddha kshetra-lands.

In this way, they cultivated all the difficult ascetic practices, perfected the various paramitas, entered and realized each of the Bodhisattva grounds of wisdom, and accomplished the unsurpassed Bodhi of all Buddhas. Upon their Parinirvana, their sharira were divided and distributed. I follow and rejoice in all of their roots of goodness.

Moreover, I follow and rejoice in the merit and virtue of all the different types of beings in the six paths of existence and the four kinds of birth in all the worlds of the ten directions, even if it is as small as a single particle.

I follow and rejoice in all the merit and virtue of all the Shravakas, Pratyeka-Buddhas, Learners, and Those Beyond Learning in the ten directions and the three periods of time.

I follow and rejoice in the vast, great merit and virtue of all the Bodhisattvas, who in their quest for Unsurpassed, Right and Equal Bodhi, cultivate measureless difficult ascetic practices.

So it is that even if the reaches of space, the realms of living beings, the karma of living beings, and the afflictions of living beings come to an end, still my following and rejoicing in merit and virtue are without end. It continues in thought after thought without cease. I never tire of this karma in body, speech, and thought.

6. To Request the Turning of the Wheel of Dharma

Moreover, Good Man, to request the turning of the wheel of Dharma is explained like this. Within each and every smallest atomic particle in the Buddha kshetra-lands throughout the ten directions and the three periods of time, to the exhaustion of the dharma-realm and the reaches of space, there are vast Buddha kshetra-lands as many as the smallest atomic particles in ineffably ineffable numbers of Buddha kshetra-lands. In each and every land, in thought after thought, all Buddhas are accomplishing Equal and Right Enlightenment, their number as many as the smallest atomic particles in ineffably ineffable numbers of Buddha kshetra-lands. An ocean-wide assembly of Bodhisattvas surrounds each Buddha. Using all manner of skill-in-means with body, mouth, and mind, I earnestly request that they turn the wonderful wheel of Dharma.

So it is that even if the reaches of space, the realms of living beings, the karma of living beings, and the afflictions of living beings come to an end, my constant request that all Buddhas turn the wheel of proper Dharma is without end. It continues in thought after thought without cease. I never tire of this karma in body, speech, and thought.

7. To Beseech the Buddhas to Remain in the World

Moreover, Good Man, to beseech the Buddhas to remain in the world is explained like this. All Buddhas, Tathagatas, are as numerous as the smallest atomic particles in all Buddha kshetra-lands, throughout the ten directions and the three periods of time, exhausting the dharma-realm and the reaches of space. When they are about to enter Parinirvana, or when any Bodhisattva, Shravaka, One Enlightened to Conditions, Learner, and One Beyond Learning, including any Good Teacher wishes to enter Parinirvana, I ask them all not to enter Nirvana. I request that they remain in the world for as many kalpas as the smallest atomic particles in all Buddha kshetra-lands to benefit and delight all living beings.

So it is that even if the reaches of space, the realms of living beings, the karma of living beings, and the afflictions of living beings come to an end, my beseeching is without end. It continues in thought after thought without cease. I never tire of this karma in body, speech, and thought.

8. To Always Follow and Learn from the Buddhas

Moreover, Good Man, to always follow and learn from the Buddhas is explained like this. It is like Vairochana Tathagata of this Saha World, who, from the time he first brought forth the Bodhi-mind, vigorously advanced without retreat. He gave up ineffably ineffable numbers of bodies and lives. He peeled off his skin for paper, split his bones to fashion pens, and punctured his skin to draw blood for ink to write out Sutras stacked as high as Mount Sumeru. He revered the Dharma to such an extent that he did not even cherish his own body and life. How much the less did he cherish a king's throne, cities, towns, palaces, gardens, groves, or anything else at all. He also cultivated various kinds of difficult ascetic practices, up to and including that he accomplished the great Bodhi beneath the Tree.

Then he manifested all kinds of spiritual powers, gave rise to all kinds of transformations, made appear all kinds of Buddha bodies, and dwelled in all kinds of assemblies. Perhaps he dwelled amidst the assemblies in the Bodhimandas of all great Bodhisattvas. Perhaps he dwelled amidst the assemblies in the Bodhimandas of the Shravakas and the Pratyeka-Buddhas. Perhaps he dwelled amidst the assemblies in the Bodhimandas of Wheel-Turning Sage Kings, lesser kings, and their retinues.

Perhaps he dwelled amidst the assemblies in the Bodhimandas of kshatriyas, brahmans, elders, and lay people, up to and including dwelling amidst the assemblies in the Bodhimandas of the gods, dragons, others of the eightfold pantheon of spiritual beings, as well as humans, non-humans, and others. He dwelled in all kinds of assemblies such as these. His voice was full and perfect like a great thunderclap. He complied with the likes and desires of living beings and brought them to accomplishment, up to the time that he entered Nirvana.

In all these ways I will learn from the Buddhas. In the same way that I learn from the present World Honored One, Vairochana, so too I learn from all the Tathagatas in every particle in all Buddha kshetra-lands in the ten directions and the three periods of time, throughout the dharma-realm and the reaches of space. In thought after thought I will learn from them all.

So it is that even if the reaches of space, the realms of living beings, the karma of living beings, and the afflictions of living beings come to an end, still my learning from them is without end. It continues in thought after thought without cease. I never tire of this karma in body, speech, and thought.

9. To Constantly Conform with Living Beings

Moreover, Good Man, to constantly conform with living beings is explained like this. Throughout the oceans of kshetra-lands in the ten directions exhausting the dharma-realm and the reaches of space, all living beings have all kinds of differences. That is to say, there are those born from eggs, womb-born, moisture-born, born by transformation, as well as those who live in dependence upon earth, water, fire, or wind. There are also beings that dwell in space, or live in plants and trees.

This includes all the many kinds of living beings, with diverse bodies, shapes, appearances, lifespans, clans, names, and mental natures. This includes their many kinds of knowledge and views, desires and pleasures, intentional activities, and modes of deportment, clothing, and diets. They dwell in many different kinds of villages, towns, cities, and palaces. They include gods, dragons, others of the eightfold pantheon of spiritual beings, as well as humans, non-humans, and others. There are beings without feet, with two feet, four feet, or many feet, with form or without form, with thought or without thought, and not entirely with thought and not entirely without thought.

I will conform with all these many kinds of beings. I will make offerings to and serve them in various ways, just as I honor my own father and mother and serve my teachers, elders, Arhats, up to and including the Tathagatas equally without difference.

I will be a good doctor for those suffering from sickness. I will show the right road to those who have lost their way. I will be a beacon of light for those in the dark night. And I will enable the poor and destitute to uncover hidden treasures. The Bodhisattva impartially benefits all living beings in this manner.

Why? If a Bodhisattva conforms with living beings, then he conforms with and makes offerings to all Buddhas. If he honors and serves living beings, then he honors and serves the Tathagatas. If he makes living beings happy, he makes all Tathagatas happy. Why? Because all Buddhas, the Tathagatas, take the heart of great compassion as their substance. Because of living beings, they bring forth the heart of great compassion. From the heart of great compassion, the Bodhi-mind is born. And because of the Bodhi-mind, Equal and Right Enlightenment is accomplished.

This is like a great king of trees growing in the rocks and sand of a vast wasteland. If its roots get water, the branches, leaves, flowers, and fruits will all flourish. The Bodhi-tree king growing in the vast wasteland of birth and death (Samsara) is the same. All living beings are the roots of the tree and all Buddhas and Bodhisattvas are its flowers and fruit. By using the water of great compassion to benefit living beings, one can realize the flowers and fruit of the Buddhas' and Bodhisattvas' wisdom.

Why? If a Bodhisattva benefits living beings with the water of great compassion, he is able to attain Anuttara-Samyak-Sambodhi. Therefore, Bodhi depends upon living beings. If there were no living beings, no Bodhisattva could ever realize the Unsurpassed Proper Enlightenment.

Good Man, you should understand these principles in this way. When the mind is impartial towards living beings, one can accomplish perfect great compassion. By using the heart of great compassion to conform with living beings, one successfully makes offerings to the Tathagatas. In this way the Bodhisattva conforms with living beings.

So it is that even if the reaches of space, the realms of living beings, the karma of living beings, or the afflictions of living beings come to an end, my conforming with living beings is without end. It continues in thought after thought without cease. I never tire of this karma in body, speech, and thought.

10. To Transfer All Merit and Virtue

Moreover, Good Man, to transfer all merit and virtue is
explained like this. All of the merit and virtue from the first
vow, to worship all Buddhas, up to and including the vow
to conform with living beings, I transfer to all living beings
throughout the dharma-realm and the limits of space. I vow
to cause all living beings to always attain peace and happiness,
and to be without any sickness or suffering. I wish that they
will not succeed in doing any evil and that all the good karma
that they would like to do will quickly be achieved. I will close
the doors to the evil destinies and make known the right road
to becoming a human, a god, or realizing Nirvana. Suppose
there are living beings who, because they accumulated a lot of
evil karma, have evoked the retribution of all kinds of extreme
suffering. I will undergo all this suffering on their behalf. I
will enable all of these living beings to attain liberation and
to ultimately realize unsurpassed Bodhi. The Bodhisattva
cultivates transference in this way.

So it is that even if the reaches of space, the realms of living
beings, the karma of living beings, or the afflictions of living
beings come to an end, my transference of merit and virtue is
without end. It continues in thought after thought without
cease. I never tire of this karma in body, speech, and thought.

The Merit of These Practices and Vows

Good Man, these are the Bodhisattva, Mahasattvas' ten great vows in their entirety. If Bodhisattvas can conform to and enter these great vows, they will then be able to bring all living beings to maturity. They will be able to comply with Anuttara-Samyak-Sambodhi. And they will be able to perfect Samantabhadra's ocean of practices and vows. Therefore, Good Man, this is the way you should understand the meaning of these vows.

Suppose a good man or good woman were to fill up worlds as many as the smallest atomic particles in measureless, boundless, ineffably ineffable numbers of Buddha-lands throughout the ten directions with the seven extremely wonderful jewels as well as the most supreme peace and happiness known to gods and humans; and gave these to all the living beings in all those worlds; and made offerings of them to all the Buddhas and Bodhisattvas in all of those worlds; and did this continuously without cease for kalpas as numerous as the smallest atomic particles in all of those Buddha kshetra-lands. The merit and virtue acquired from this, when compared to the merit and virtue of a person who hears this king of vows pass by his ear but once, does not even equal one one-hundredth, one one-thousandth, or even one part in an upanishad.

Moreover, if a person, with a mind of deep faith in these great vows, receives and upholds, reads and recites them from memory, or even writes out a single four-line verse, he or she can quickly eradicate the karma of the five Avīci offenses. All of the world's illnesses that afflict the body and mind, as well as the various kinds of suffering and distress, up to and including all the bad karma equal in number to the smallest atomic particles in Buddha kshetra-lands will all be wiped away.

All the demon-armies, the yakshas, rākshasas, kumbhāndas, pishāchas, bhūtas, and so forth that drink blood and devour flesh, all these evil ghosts and spirits, will stay far away from this person. Or they will make a resolve to draw near and protect him.

Therefore, if a person recites these vows, he goes throughout the world without any obstruction, like the moon in the sky that emerges from clouds. All Buddhas and Bodhisattvas will praise him. All people and gods should venerate him. All living beings should make offerings to him.

This good man is well able to be reborn as a human and will perfect all of Samantabhadra's merit and virtue. Before long, he will be just like Samantabhadra Bodhisattva, obtaining a subtle and wonderful physical body replete with the thirty-two hallmarks of a great man.

If he is reborn among humans or gods, he will always live in a superior family.

He will totally destroy the evil destinies. He will be far apart from all bad friends. He will be able to vanquish all those on heterodox paths. He will be completely free from all afflictions. He's just like the lion king, able to subdue all beasts. Such a person is worthy of receiving the offerings of all living beings.

Further, when a person is on the verge of death, at the very last kṣaṇa-instant[4] of life, when all his sense-faculties deteriorate, all of his family departs from him, and all of his power and influence are diminished and lost; when his ministers, great officials, everything in his inner and outer court, his elephants, horses, carts, and precious jewels, hidden treasures, and all things such as these can no longer accompany him, then this king of vows alone will never leave him. At all times, these vows will be before him guiding him. In a single kṣaṇa-instant, he will be reborn in the Land of Ultimate Bliss."

Upon arriving there, he will immediately see Amitabha Buddha, Manjushri Bodhisattva, Samantabhadra Bodhisattva, the Bodhisattva Who Contemplates With Self-Mastery (Avalokiteshvara), Maitreya Bodhisattva, and others. The

---

4. Kṣaṇa is the smallest unit of time in Ancient Buddhist texts. The most common definition is that there are ninety kṣaṇas in a single thought.

physical features of these Bodhisattvas, who are all around
him, are dignified and majestic; their merit and virtue perfect.

This person will see himself born from a lotus flower and will
receive a prediction for future Buddhahood from the Buddha.
After receiving this prediction, for numberless quadrillions
of nayutas of kalpas throughout ineffably ineffable numbers
of worlds in the ten directions everywhere, with the power
of wisdom, he will accord with the minds of living beings and
bring them benefit.

Before long, he will sit in a Bodhimanda, vanquish the demon
armies, accomplish Equal and Proper Enlightenment, and turn
the wonderful wheel of Dharma. He will cause living beings
in worlds as many as the smallest atomic particles in Buddha
kshetra-lands to bring forth the Bodhi-mind. According with
their basic natures, he will teach and transform them until
they are brought to accomplishment. To the end of the oceans
of kalpas of the future, he will greatly benefit all living beings.

Good Man, if these living beings hear or have faith in this great
king of vows, or receive, uphold, read, recite from memory,
or extensively explain these vows for others, all the merit and
virtue they obtain can only be known by the Buddha, the
World Honored One, and by no one else.

Therefore, all of you who hear this king of vows should harbor no doubts. You should attentively accept these vows. After accepting them, you should be able to read them. After reading them, you should be able to recite them from memory. After reciting them from memory, you should be able to uphold them, and even write them out and extensively explain them for others. In a single thought, these people will be able to accomplish all of their practices and vows.

The blessings that one will amass are measureless and boundless. One will be able to rescue living beings from the great ocean of afflictions and suffering, causing them to make good their escape, so that all of them are reborn in Amitabha Buddha's Land of Ultimate Bliss."

At that time, Samantabhadra Bodhisattva Mahasattva, wishing to restate his meaning, contemplated everywhere in the ten directions and spoke these verses.

Verses

Before the lions among men[5] throughout the
worlds of the ten directions and the three periods of time,
    With a pure body, speech, and thought,
I worship them all, omitting none.

With the awesome spiritual power of Samantabhadra's
    practices and vows,
I appear everywhere before all Tathagatas.
One body manifests bodies as many as particles in a
    kshetra-land.
Each one worships Buddhas as many as particles in a
    kshetra-land.

In each particle there are Buddhas as numerous as particles,
And in each of these places there is an assembly of
    Bodhisattvas.
Each particle throughout the infinite Dharma Realm is the
    same.
I deeply believe they are all filled with Buddhas.

Each body using the ocean of all sounds
Everywhere gives voice to infinite and wonderful words

---

5. The "lions among men," Narasiṃhā in Sanskrit, refers to the Buddhas.

That throughout all kalpas of the future
Praise the deep ocean of the Buddhas' merit and virtue.

Using the most supreme and wonderful flower garlands,
Songs and music, incense pastes, parasols, and canopies,
And other most supreme adornments such as these,
I make offerings to all Tathagatas.

With the most supreme clothing and superior incense,
Powdered and burning incense, lamps, and candles,
Each one heaped as high as Wonderful High[6] Mountain,
I make offerings to all Tathagatas.

With a vast, great mind of supreme understanding,
I have deep faith in all Buddhas of the three periods of time.
With the power of Samantabhadra's practices and vows,
I make offerings to all Tathagatas everywhere.

All the evil karma I have created in the past,
Caused by beginningless greed, hatred, and delusion,
Produced by my body, speech, and thought,
I now repent and reform of it all.

All living beings in the ten directions,
Learners and Those Beyond Learning in the Two Vehicles,
And all Tathagatas and Bodhisattvas,

---

6. "Wonderful High" mountain or in Chinese 妙高 refers to Mount Sumeru.

I follow and rejoice in all their merit and virtue

All the Lamps of the World throughout the ten directions,
Those who first realized Bodhi,
I now request and beseech them all
To turn the wheel of the unsurpassed, wonderful Dharma.

If there are Buddhas who wish to enter Parinirvana,
I beseech them with utmost sincerity,
Wishing that they long remain in the world, for as many
    kalpas as there are particles in kshetra-lands.
To benefit and bring happiness to all living beings.

All of the blessings from worshipping, praising, and making
    offerings,
From beseeching the Buddhas to remain in the world and
    turn the Wheel of Dharma;
And from all the roots of goodness gained from following
    and rejoicing, and repentance and reform,
I transfer to living beings and to becoming a Buddha.

I follow and learn from all the Tathagatas
And cultivate the perfect practices of Samantabhadra.
I make offerings to all the Tathagatas of the past,
The Buddhas of the present throughout the ten directions,
And to all the Teachers of Gods and Humans of the future.
May all my aspirations be fulfilled.

I wish to learn from all the Buddhas of the three periods
   of time
And quickly attain great Bodhi.

In all the kshetra-lands throughout the ten directions,
Vast, pure, and wonderfully adorned,
The assemblies surround the Tathagatas,
As they sit beneath their royal Bodhi trees.

May all living beings in the ten directions
Be without worry and always have peace and happiness,
Obtain the Proper Dharma's profound benefit,
And may their afflictions be eradicated without remainder.

When I cultivate for the sake of Bodhi,
In all destinies I will gain the knowledge of past lives.
I will always renounce the householder's life and cultivate
   the pure moral precepts,
Unbroken, undefiled, and without outflows.

Gods, dragons, yakshas, kumbhandas,
Including humans, non-humans, and others,
In the languages of all living beings,
With every voice I will speak the Dharma.

I will diligently cultivate the pure paramitas,
And never forget the Bodhi-mind.

I will extinguish obstructions and defilements without
    remainder,
And will accomplish all the wondrous practices.

From all delusions, karma, and demonic states
Within the worldly paths, I will attain liberation.
This is like the lotus flower that is not sullied by the water,
Or like the sun and moon that do not stay fixed in the sky.

Completely eradicating all the suffering of the evil paths,
And equally bringing happiness to all living beings,
In this way passing through kalpas as numerous as particles
    in a kshetra-land
Always benefiting those in the ten directions without end.

I always conform with all living beings,
Exhausting all kalpas of the future.
Always cultivating the vast practices of Samantabhadra
Bringing to perfection the unsurpassed great Bodhi.

May all who practice the same way as myself,
In every place where we gather together,
Our karma of body, mouth, and mind the same,
Together we learn and cultivate all the same practices and
    vows.

All of the Good Teachers who benefit me,

Who elucidate for me the practices of Samantabhadra,
I wish that we will always gather together,
And that they will always be happy with me.

I vow to always see in person all the Tathagatas
And the assembly of disciples of the Buddhas that encircle
them.
I'll give vast and great offerings to all of them
To the end of future kalpas without ever becoming weary.

I vow to uphold the subtle and wonderful Dharma of all
Buddhas
And illuminate and make known all the practices of Bodhi,
And attain the ultimately pure path of Samantabhadra,
Always practicing to the end of future kalpas.

Within all states of existence,
I cultivate blessings and wisdom constantly and without
end.
By concentration, wisdom, skill-in-means, and liberation,
I will gain an endless treasury of merit and virtue.

In one particle are kshetra-lands as numerous as particles.
In each kshetra-land are inconceivable numbers of Buddhas.
Every Buddha dwells in the midst of their assemblies,
I see them always performing the practices of Bodhi.

Everywhere throughout the ocean of kshetra-lands in the
    ten directions,
On the tip of every hair in the ocean of the three periods of
    time,
Throughout the ocean of Buddhas and ocean of lands,
I cultivate in all of them passing through an ocean of kalpas.

The speech of all Tathagatas is pure;
Each word contains an ocean of all sounds
That conforms to what living beings like to hear.
Each sound flows forth from the Buddha's ocean of
    eloquence.

All Tathagatas of the three periods of time
With their inexhaustible ocean of languages
Constantly turn the wonderful Dharma wheel of principles
    and their tendencies.
With the power of deep wisdom, I can enter them
    everywhere.

I can deeply enter the future
And completely pass through all kalpas in a single thought.
Each and every kalpa of the three periods of time
In a single thought I enter them all.

In one thought I see in the three periods of time,
All the Lions Among Men,

And also constantly enter the states of the Buddhas
And their liberation like an illusion, and their awe-inspiring
    powers.

On the tip of an extremely fine hair,
Appear the adorned kshetra-lands of the three periods of
    time.
On a hair tip are the kshetra-lands of the ten directions as
    numerous as particles,
I deeply enter, beautify, and purify them all.

All of the illuminating Lamps of the World of the future
Who accomplish the path, turn the Wheel of Dharma, and
    awaken living beings
I go to visit and draw near to them all
As they complete the Buddha's work and manifest Nirvana.

I quickly complete the spiritual powers,
The power of thoroughly entering the Mahayana through
    the Universal Door,
The power of cultivating all merit and virtue through
    wisdom and practice,
The power of the awe-inspiring spirit to shield all with great
    kindness.

The power of supreme blessings to purify and adorn
    everywhere,

The power of wisdom that is unattached and without
    reliance,
The awe-inspiring power of samadhi, wisdom, and skill-in-
    means,
The power to universally accumulate Bodhi,

The power of purifying all good karma,
The power of eradicating all afflictions,
The power of subduing all demons,
The power to perfect all of Samantabhadra's practices.

I am able to adorn and purify everywhere the ocean of
    kshetra-lands,
And liberate the ocean of all living beings.
I'm well able to discern all Dharmas, like an ocean,
And can deeply enter into the ocean of wisdom.

I am able to purify everywhere the ocean of all practices,
And perfect the ocean of all vows.
I draw near and make offerings to the ocean of all Buddhas,
And cultivate without weariness for an ocean of kalpas.

All Tathagatas of the three periods of time,
And the practices and vows of most supreme Bodhi,
I make offerings to them all as I perfect and cultivate these
    practices.
Relying upon Samantabhadra's practices, I awaken to Bodhi.

All Tathagatas have an elder disciple
Whose name is the Venerated Samantabhadra.
I now transfer all my roots of goodness,
And I vow that all my wisdom and practices will be
    identical to his.

I vow that my body, mouth, and thought will always be pure
And that all of my practices and all kshetra-lands will also
    be the same.
Wisdom such as this is called Samantabhadra.
I vow in all ways to be the same as he is.

I will wholly purify Samantabhadra's conduct,
And all the great vows of Manjushri.
I will complete all of these activities without remainder.
Throughout all kalpas of the future, I'll never tire.

All of the practices I cultivate are without measure
And I attain measureless merit and virtue.
Amid measureless practices I peacefully dwell,
And thoroughly understand all spiritual powers.

Manjushri has courageous wisdom,
Samantabhadra's practices and wisdom are also the same.
I now transfer all roots of goodness.
To constantly cultivate with and learn from them all.

All Buddhas of the three periods of time praise
Such supreme and great vows as these.
I now transfer all roots of goodness,
In order to attain the preeminent practices of
    Samantabhadra.

I vow that when my life approaches its end,
All obstacles will be completely dispelled,
I will personally see Amitabha Buddha,
And be immediately reborn in his Land of Peace and Bliss.

After I'm reborn in that land,
I will then accomplish these great vows.
All of them will be completely perfected without remainder
Bringing benefit and happiness to the realms of all beings.

All in that Buddha's assembly are pure,
At that time I will be born from a supreme lotus flower,
I'll personally behold Measureless Light Tathagata
Who will appear and bestow upon me a prediction of
    Bodhi.

After receiving this prediction from the Tathagata,
With countless hundreds of kotis of transformation bodies,
My vast wisdom power that pervades the ten directions
Brings benefit everywhere to the realms of living beings.

To the ends of space or world-systems,
To the ends of living beings, their karma, or their afflictions,
But all things such as these have no end,
So too my vows ultimately will never end.

Suppose in all the boundless kshetra-lands of the ten
    directions,
One uses their multitude of jewels as adornments and
    offerings to the Tathagatas,
And gives the most supreme peace and happiness to gods
    and humans
Throughout kalpas as many as the smallest atomic particles
    in all kshetra-lands.

Suppose another person hears this king of supreme vows,
And as they pass by his ear but a single time is able to give
    rise to faith,
And his mind thirstily seeks supreme Bodhi,
The merit and virtue he gains will surpass that of the first
    person.

Always separating far from bad teachers,
And leaving forever all unwholesome paths,
Quickly seeing the Tathagata Measureless Light,
And perfecting Samantabhadra's most supreme vows.

This person well obtains a superior lifespan,
And is well able to attain rebirth in the human realm.
Before long this person will accomplish
These practices of Samantabhadra Bodhisattva.

In the past, owing to a lack of wisdom power,
I have done the five Avici offenses of extreme evil.
By reciting the great king of vows of Samantabhadra
In one thought they will all be wiped away.

His clan, family, race, or skin color,
His appearance and wisdom are all perfect.
All demons and those of heterodox paths cannot destroy
   him,
And for those in the three realms, he can become worthy of
   offerings.

He will quickly advance to the great Bodhi-tree king,
And seated there subdue the horde of demons,
Realize Equal and Right Enlightenment and turn the Wheel
   of Dharma,
And benefit all living beings everywhere.

If a person with respect to these vows of Samantabhadra,
Reads, recites, receives, upholds, and explains them,
One's reward can only be known by the Buddha,
And one will certainly attain the path of supreme Bodhi.

If a person recites these vows of Samantabhadra,
I'm only speaking about a small portion of one's roots
    of goodness,
In a single thought, everything will be perfected,
And one can accomplish the pure vows of living beings.

I practice the supreme conduct of Samantabhadra
And transfer all of its boundless and superior blessings,
Vowing that all living beings everywhere, who are sinking
    and drowning,
Will quickly go to the kshetra-land of Measureless
    Light Buddha!

Epilogue

At that time, after Samantabhadra Bodhisattva, Mahasattva, had finished speaking before the Tathagata these pure verses on the great king of vows of Samantabhadra, the youth Sudhana was overwhelmed with boundless joy. All the Bodhisattvas were extremely happy as well. And the Tathagata praised him, saying, "Very good! Very good!"

At that time, this supreme Dharma of the inconceivable state of liberation was spoken in the presence of the World Honored One and the Sagely Bodhisattvas, Mahasattvas with Manjushri Bodhisattva as their leader.

Also present were all the great Bodhisattvas and the six thousand Bhikshus who had matured in their practice, with Maitreya Bodhisattva as their leader, and all the great Bodhisattvas of the Worthy Kalpa who were led by Immaculate Samantabhadra Bodhisattva.

Assembled together were also all the great Bodhisattvas who will succeed to the position of a Buddha in one life and who were at the position of Anointment of the Crown, as well as all the remaining Bodhisattvas, Mahasattvas from the various different worlds of the ten directions, who were as numerous as the smallest atomic particles in an ocean of kshetra-lands.

All the great Shravakas were headed by the greatly wise Shariputra, Mahamaudgalyayana, and others. Also present were all the people, gods, and all the rulers of the worlds, as well as heavenly dragons, yakshas, gandharvas, asuras, garudas, kinnaras, mahoragas, humans, non-humans, and so forth. Upon hearing what the Buddha had said, all in the entire great assembly were extremely happy, faithfully accepted it, and put it into practice.

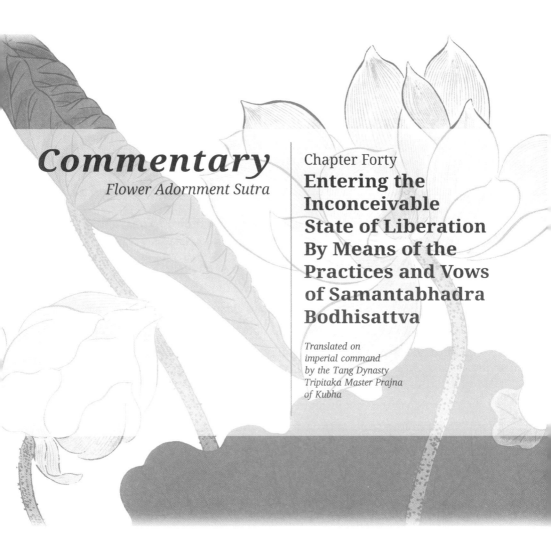

Commentary

Flower Adornment Sutra

Chapter Forty

Entering the Inconceivable State of Liberation By Means of the Practices and Vows of Samantabhadra Bodhisattva

Translated on imperial command by the Tang Dynasty Tripitaka Master Prajna of Kubha

Introduction

I believe that this is the first time this Sutra[1] is being explained in the United States. All of you are probably hearing it for the first time as well. Unfortunately, because of the limitations of time, I will not be able to explain the entire *Flower Adornment Sutra*. I will only expound on this one chapter on Samantabhadra Bodhisattva's Practices and Vows. Not even the title of this Sutra, *Great Means, Expansive Buddha Flower Adornment Sutra*, can be elucidated in detail. Why is this? I'm afraid that even if I were to explain this title for six weeks, I still would not be able to finish.[2]

First, I will discuss the origin of this Sutra.

The *Flower Adornment Sutra* is a king of Buddhist Sutras, and it is also the "king of kings" of Sutras. The *Wonderful Dharma Lotus Flower Sutra* is also a king of Buddhist Sutras, but it is not called the "king of kings" of Sutras. Therefore, among all the Mahayana Sutras spoken by the Buddha, the *Great Means, Expansive Buddha Flower Adornment Sutra* is the most extensive. However, the time it took for the Buddha to speak this Sutra was relatively short. Shakyamuni Buddha spoke the great *Flower Adornment*, this momentous Sutra, in twenty-one days.

This Sutra consists of eighty-one rolls. There are also versions of this Sutra in forty rolls and sixty rolls, which are not as complete. Even this

---

1. *Sutra* in Buddhism refers to a text containing the words spoken by the Buddha or by other Enlightened Beings or followers of the Buddha who were sanctioned by the Buddha to proclaim his teachings. Therefore, Sutras can be called the Sacred Texts or Scriptures in Buddhism.

2. This chapter was lectured during a six-week summer study and practice session at the Buddhist Lecture Hall in San Francisco in 1969.

edition of eighty-one rolls is not the complete text, yet it still contains an introduction, a text-proper, and a conclusion.

After Shakyamuni Buddha spoke the *Flower Adornment Sutra*, it was not kept in this world, not even in India. Who took care of it? The Dragon King stored it in his palace, where he venerated and made offerings to it. Every day the Dragon King would bow in obeisance to the Sutra. Six hundred years after Shakyamuni Buddha's Final Nirvana, there was a monk, a Bodhisattva, in the world named Nagarjuna. Nagarjuna Bodhisattva had exceptional intelligence. No one was as smart as him. After he read and studied all the literature of the world, including all the essays, discourses, and classics, he resolved to go to the Dragon's Palace to read the Treasury of Buddhist Sutras. When he got there, he discovered that there were three versions of the *Flower Adornment Sutra*, including a long version, a medium version, and a short version. The long version contained verses as numerous as the smallest atomic particles in ten three thousand great-thousand world systems.[3] The smallest atomic particles in a single world system are measureless and infinite. The number of smallest atomic particles in a great-thousand world system is much greater. What is a great-thousand world system? One world system consists of one Mount Sumeru, one sun, one moon, and one set of Four Continents. A collection of 1,000 Mount Sumerus, 1,000 suns and 1,000 moons is called a small-thousand world system.[4] A group of 1,000 small-thousand world systems is a middle-thousand world system. And a group of 1,000 middle-thousand world systems is one great-thousand world system. Think about this. If you counted all the smallest atomic particles in a great-thousand world system, how many would there be? That number is

---

3. A three thousand great-thousand world system is also called a great-thousand world system for short. Some translators also came up with the term "trichiliocosm" for this.

4. This is also called a "chiliocosm."

certainly uncountable. Now we are saying the verses in this long version of the text are so numerous they are equal to the atomic particles in ten three thousand great-thousand world systems.

How many chapters did this long version contain? They were as numerous as the smallest atomic particles in a "world with its four continents." The four continents include southern Jambudvīpa, eastern Purvavideha, western Aparagodaniya, and northern Uttarakuru. These four continents, as well as Mount Sumeru, are called a "world with its four continents." The number of chapters in this large version was as many as the smallest atomic particles in a world with its four continents. If you calculated this, how many chapters would you say there were? I also could not count them.

The medium version of this Sutra had 498,800 verses and 1,200 chapters. The short version had 100,000 verses and forty-eight chapters. 100,000 verses are a great many, and forty-eight chapters are also not few in number. Nagarjuna Bodhisattva had an exceptional memory, so he was able to retain the entire text of the short version in his mind. When he returned to India, he wrote down all that he had memorized. Later this text was transmitted to China from India. At that time only eighty rolls and thirty-nine chapters were transmitted. Nine of the original forty-eight chapters were not transmitted to China.

The *Flower Adornment Sutra* was spoken in seven locations and in nine Dharma[5] assemblies. Within Buddhism, if you are able to understand the *Flower Adornment Sutra*, then you have comprehended the Buddha's

---

5. The word "dharma" has several meanings. In Buddhism it refers specifically to the teachings and practices taught by the Buddha. Another meaning of dharma is a "thing", which, using Western philosophical terminology, includes both phenomena and noumena. Here it means a gathering in which the Buddha's teachings are expounded and practiced.

Complete Body. By understanding the *Shurangama Sutra*, one understands the Buddha's Summit.[6] By understanding the *Dharma Flower Sutra*, one understands the Buddha's Body, but not his Complete Body. If you understand the truths within the *Flower Adornment Sutra*, then you have fathomed the Buddha's Complete Body, the wisdom-life of the Buddha. The *Flower Adornment Sutra* is analogous to the great ocean, and all of the other Sutras are like the small rivers and streams that flow into it. These small rivers and streams cannot compare to the great ocean.

At the present time, in the entire world the number of people who can explain the *Flower Adornment Sutra* are very few indeed. You might say there isn't anyone at all who can explain it, but then aren't we explaining it now? There are even those who study Buddhism for their entire lives, who have never heard of the name of the *Flower Adornment Sutra*. Wouldn't you say this is pitiful?

Let's not mention the ability to explain this *Flower Adornment Sutra*; there are very few people who have merely read the Sutra even once. If you read this Sutra as quickly as you can, it will take about twenty-one days to read it through once. Therefore, this Sutra is very difficult to encounter.

As mentioned above, the Sutra was spoken in seven locations and in nine assemblies as described in the following verse:

> The Bodhi-field was first, the ninth the Jeta Grove,
> The third and fourth, the Trayastrimsha and Suyama.
> The Universal Light Palace, the second, seventh and eighth,
> The Tushita and Others' Transformations were the fifth and sixth.

---

6. "Buddha's Summit" is found in the title of Shurangama Sutra, thus its designation here. The complete title of the Shurangama Sutra is The Sutra of the Foremost Shurangama at the Great Buddha's Summit Concerning the Tathagata's Secret Cause of Cultivation, His Certification to the Complete Meaning and all Bodhisattvas' Myriad Practices.

The Buddha first perfected the spiritual path in the Bodhi-field beneath the Bodhi Tree. There he spoke the first six chapters of the *Flower Adornment Sutra*, which consisted of eleven rolls. The second assembly was in the Universal Light Palace. There he also spoke six chapters that made up four rolls. The third assembly was in the Trayastrimsha Heaven where he proclaimed another six chapters in three rolls. The Suyama Heaven was the location of the fourth assembly, where four chapters in three rolls were expounded. The fifth place was the Tushita Heaven, where he discoursed on three chapters in twelve rolls. The Transformation of Others' Bliss Heaven was the venue of the sixth assembly with one chapter in six rolls being explained. The seventh location was once again at the Universal Light Palace. Eleven chapters in thirteen rolls were spoken there. The Universal Light Palace was also the place for the eighth assembly, where one chapter in seven rolls was proclaimed. The ninth assembly was in the Jeta Grove, where one chapter and twenty-one rolls were explained. The literal translation of the Chinese characters for the Jeta Grove is a charnel ground. This is a place where the bones of the deceased are buried. Presently such a place is called a graveyard. These are the seven locations and the nine assemblies where the *Flower Adornment Sutra* was spoken.[7]

In the short version of the Sutra, 45,000 verses were transmitted to China from India. The remaining 55,000 verses, comprising nine chapters in this

---

7. Nine Assemblies and Seven Locations

1) Under the Bodhi Tree	6 chapters	11 rolls
2) Universal Light Palace	6 chapters	4 rolls
3) Trayastrimsha Heaven	6 chapters	3 rolls
4) Suyama Heaven	4 chapters	3 rolls
5) Tushita Heaven	3 chapters	12 rolls
6) Transformation of Others' Bliss Heaven	1 chapter	6 rolls
7) Universal Light Palace	11 chapters	13 rolls
8) Universal Light Palace	1 chapter	7 rolls
9) Jeta Grove	1 chapter	21 rolls

version, were not brought to China. Although China did not obtain the complete text of this short version of the Sutra, the portion they received contained an introduction, a text-proper, and a conclusion. For this reason, the Tang Dynasty National Master Qingliang (清涼國師), promulgator of the *Flower Adornment Sutra*, felt that the portion of the text transmitted to China could by itself be considered to be a complete Sutra. This Master was a "transformation-body" of Flower Adornment Bodhisattva. Why do I say this? It's because he only lectured on the *Flower Adornment Sutra* and did not explain any other Buddhist Sutras.

National Master Qingliang was named Chengguan (澄觀)[8] and his Dharma name was Daxiu (大休) . He was from the city of Kueiji. His surname was Xiahou (夏侯) . He was born in the fifth year of the Kaiyuan period (718 C.E.) during the reign of Emperor Xuanzong (685–762 C.E.) . He was nine feet and four inches tall.[9] His arms were extremely long and reached down below his knees. He had forty teeth, compared to the normal person's thirty-two. People rarely have this many teeth. It is a sign of nobility. The Buddha had forty-two teeth. At night if you looked at his eyes they dazzled with light. Yet during the day his eyes were the same as those of an ordinary person. Furthermore, his eyes were very focused with an unmoving gaze.

During the fourth year of the Jianzhong period (783 C.E.), he wrote the *Flower Adornment Sutra Commentary and Sub-commentary*. In China this

---

8. The Master's original monastic name was Chengguan. The additional name Qingliang was given to him by the Emperor Dezong (742–805 C.E.) in 799 after the emperor had a profound religious experience upon hearing one of the Master's lectures on the *Flower Adornment Sutra*. The Emperor Dezong, whose reign was 785-805, was the second emperor to take the Master as his teacher.

9. It is hard to translate these Chinese terms into English to determine his actual height. But it would be safe to say he was probably close to seven feet in height.

work is the most celebrated text for those who study this Sutra. Before he wrote this commentary, he beseeched the ocean-wide assembly of Bodhisattvas of the *Flower Adornment Sutra* to assist him. Then, one night he had a dream in which the peaks of all the mountains turned the color of gold. Upon waking, he realized that his dream symbolized "light shining everywhere." After that dream he wrote the *Flower Adornment Sutra Commentary* without deliberation. The words just flowed from his pen. Normally when a person composes a literary work they have to repeatedly stop and think about what they're going to write. However, he wrote this commentary so quickly it was as if he were merely transcribing it. He completed this explanation of the *Flower Adornment Sutra* in four years, and then had another dream. It's not for sure this was a dream. It was a state that seemed to be real, yet was also like a dream. In this dream-like state he transformed into a dragon. This single dragon in turn became limitless and measureless millions upon millions of dragons, and each dragon flew off to other worlds throughout the universe. This is the profound state of the Flower Adornment. His transforming into many dragons symbolized the extensive dissemination of the Dharma.

During his life, National Master Qingliang passed through the reigns of nine emperors during the Tang Dynasty, and seven of these emperors bowed to him as their teacher. Therefore, it is said,

> *"Passing through nine reigns,*
> *The teacher of seven kings."*

After National Master Qingliang entered Parinirvana, his body was buried. At that time a monk was going to China from India. On the way he encountered two youths clad in dark-colored garments, who were flying overhead. The monk, who was an Arhat,[10] used his spiritual powers to detain them in space. He asked, "Where are you going?" They responded, "We're going to China to obtain a molar from Flower Adornment Bodhisattva, and then bring it back to Manjushri Hall in India to make offerings to it." When the Arhat arrived in China he told the emperor that he had seen two youths wearing dark-colored garments who were going to obtain a molar from Flower Adornment Bodhisattva. Thinking that they were probably referring to National Master Qingliang, the emperor had his body exhumed, and just as expected, one molar was missing. Therefore, all of these kinds of events are wondrous beyond words. Flower Adornment Bodhisattva came to China as the National Master Qingliang. This explains why he had such exceptional physical features.

National Master Qingliang classified the first five rolls of the *Flower Adornment Sutra* as the introduction, the middle fifty-five and one-half rolls to be the text-proper, and the final nineteen and one-half rolls to be the conclusion. Although the entire Sutra was not brought to China from India, the portion that was translated in China contains the three main sections of a complete text. Therefore, those who propagated the *Flower Adornment Sutra* in China were all great Bodhisattvas. If they were not Bodhisattvas, they would not have been able to expound on the states of the Flower Adornment. This state is absolutely the most amazing and wondrous. It's "the wonder of wonders and the mystery of mysteries."

Although there are not a lot of people attending this year's summer session, I've observed that all of you have a good foundation in learning Buddhism. Therefore, while you are here you should pay special attention

---

10. Arhat literally means "one worthy of offerings." In Buddhism this term refers to a person who has attained a level of enlightenment and is thus replete with profound wisdom and advanced spiritual abilities.

to your study and practice of the Buddha-dharma. Why is this? Time is precious. This year's session is only six weeks long. If you are not attentive, then you will have wasted your time. I also will have spent a lot of time and energy explaining the Sutra, yet you will not have understood what I have taught. People become Buddhas one at a time, not one group at a time. Although only a few people have come here to learn the Buddha-dharma, if they are successful, they will become Buddhas or Patriarchs. We should be most happy about this. Regardless of whether people are many or few, we still should do things in the prescribed way according to the rules. Every day don't allow a single minute or even a single second to pass by in vain. During these six weeks, we want to obtain some genuine good and lasting benefit, and truly savor the flavor of the Buddha-dharma. Therefore, as the Sutra is being lectured every day, each person should take notes and submit them to me each day. There will be a weekly test and a final exam at the end of the six-week period. No matter what, you should study hard during this time, and not be careless or negligent. Be especially attentive to your study and practice of the Buddha's teachings, and then it will be of some value. This is my hope for each of you.

SUTRA:

Translated on Imperial Command by the Tang Dynasty Tripitaka Master Prajna of Kubha.

COMMENTARY:

When listening to or explaining a Sutra you must first have some understanding of the Sutra. For example, is this a Sutra of the Great

Vehicle or the Small Vehicle?[11] Speaking about the Great Vehicle and Small Vehicle, I will tell you a case history concerning these two. In ancient India, (fourth or fifth century C.E.), there were two Bodhisattvas named Vasubandhu and Asanga. These two Bodhisattvas were brothers. However, because Vasubandhu Bodhisattva had some unwholesome causes and conditions from the past, he became a Buddhist of the Small Vehicle, and studied its teachings and principles. Asanga Bodhisattva, on the other hand, studied and practiced the Great Vehicle. Vasubandhu Bodhisattva was exceptionally intelligent. His intelligence was not the same as that of ordinary people. Although Asanga Bodhisattva tried to influence him to believe in the Dharma of the Great Vehicle, he lacked the ability to bring about this change in his brother. Vasubandhu Bodhisattva exclusively praised the Small Vehicle and criticized the Great Vehicle as being wrong.

Then Asanga Bodhisattva thought of an expedient method to convert his brother. What was this expedient? He pretended to be ill. He then requested his brother to come and pay him a visit, telling him, "I'm going to die soon. I'm so old now, and if you do not come and visit me, we will not have the opportunity to see each other again." Then Vasubandhu Bodhisattva came to visit him. When Asanga Bodhisattva saw him, he said, "Now that I'm about to die, you are welcome to read my Great Vehicle Sutras. If you read them, I will be able to pass away in peace." Vasubandhu Bodhisattva complied with his brother's request and began to read his Great Vehicle Sutras. Which Great Vehicle Sutra did he read? The *Flower Adornment Sutra*. The more he read, the more he saw how inconceivable it was. He thought, "Wow! The state of the Flower Adornment is wonderful beyond words. It's like the sun in the

---

11. Great Vehicle in Sanskrit is "Mahayana." Although Small Vehicle in Sanskrit is "Hinayana," the more common and less pejorative term is the "Theravada" School. Theravada literally translates as "doctrine of the elders."

sky shining upon the myriad things of the world. It is also like the net-like banner of the king of the Great Brahma Heaven. In each hole of the net is a pearl. Each of these pearls receives and reflects the light of all the other pearls."

Realizing that he had been mistaken about the Great Vehicle, he cried out, "Quick, give me a sword!"

> "Why do you want a sword?" his brother asked.
>
> "I'm going to cut out my tongue!" he responded.
>
> "Why do you want to cut out your tongue?" his brother questioned him.
>
> "In the past I used my tongue to praise the Dharma of the Small Vehicle and slandered the Sutras of the Great Vehicle. That's a grave offense, so I should cut out my tongue."
>
> "You don't need to do that," his brother said.
>
> "Why not? My transgressions are so serious; I want to cut out my tongue!"

His brother said, "Suppose you are standing up and then you fall down to the ground. Wouldn't you use your hands to push against the ground and raise yourself back up? Would you just lie there on the ground and not get up at all? In the past you had used your tongue to malign the Great Vehicle and praise the Small Vehicle. Now you can use your tongue to praise the Great Vehicle."

After hearing this Vasubandhu Bodhisattva thought, "That makes a lot of sense!"

He then decided not to cut out his tongue, but instead he withdrew into the mountains to study and cultivate according to the Sutras of the Great Vehicle, particularly the *Flower Adornment Sutra*. Then he composed the *Shastra on the Ten Grounds*.[12] On the day he completed his Shastra the earth shook and trembled. In addition to this, light was emitted from his mouth. Having heard about these auspicious portents, the king came to visit him and asked, "Have you become an Arhat?" Vasubandhu Bodhisattva said, "No, I haven't become an Arhat." "Then, why did the earth shake and tremble here? And why did light issue forth from your mouth?" the king questioned. Vasubandhu Bodhisattva responded, "In the past, when I was young, I studied and practiced the Small Vehicle and maligned the Great Vehicle. Now I've corrected my mistake. I have been studying and practicing the *Flower Adornment Sutra*, and I've composed a Shastra on the Ten Grounds. Only after I finished writing this Shastra, did the earth quake and light radiate from my mouth. It's not that I became an Arhat." The king said, "Oh! The *Flower Adornment Sutra* is so subtle and wondrous!"

The translator of the first 80 rolls of the *Flower Adornment Sutra* was Tripitaka Master Shikshananda, whose name literally means, "delight in learning." After Tripitaka Master Shikshananda translated the *Flower Adornment Sutra* from Sanskrit into Chinese, he gave a series of lectures on the entire Sutra. When he lectured to the point in the Sutra that describes the ocean of kshetra-lands as numerous as the smallest atomic particles in world systems, there was an earthquake in the lecture hall and the surrounding area.

Also, when he first began the translation of the *Flower Adornment Sutra*, Empress Wu Zetian (625-705 C.E.), also known as the Celestial Empress, had a dream. In her dream, sweet dew rained down from the sky. The next day it actually did rain, and the rain had a sweet taste. This signified that the translation of the *Flower Adornment Sutra* was extremely important.

---

12. The Ten Grounds (Sanskrit: Dasha-bhumika) Chapter is one of the most important chapters in the *Flower Adornment Sutra*.

After Tripitaka Master Shikshananda completed his translation, he lectured on the Sutra. When he expounded on this Sutra the great earth quaked in six ways.[13] Then Empress Wu Zetian issued an imperial decree that praised Tripitaka Master Shikshananda. There are numerous inconceivable states and experiences connected with the *Flower Adornment Sutra*. There are so many it is difficult to explain them all.

During the **Tang Dynasty** there was a state named **Kubha** (current day Kabul, Afghanistan). **Tripitaka** refers to the Three Treasuries or Baskets of the Buddhist Canon. These are the Treasury of Sutras, the Treasury of the Vinaya, and the Treasury of the Shastras.[14] A **Dharma Master** is someone who takes the Dharma as his master. That is, the Buddha-dharma is one's teacher. Or he is one who gives the Dharma to others. Who is the Tripitaka Dharma Master? It is **Tripitaka Master Prajna**. Prajna is a Sanskrit word that means wisdom. Why wasn't Prajna translated as wisdom, rather than being left in Sanskrit? It is one of the five types of terms that are not translated. In this case it is not translated out of veneration for the term.[15] **Translated on Imperial Command** means that the emperor decreed that the Sutra be translated from its Indic language into Chinese.

---

13. The six types of quaking are: shaking, rising, and surging, which are connected with movement, and reverberating, roaring, and striking, which are also connected with sound.

14. Vinaya refers to the all the texts spoken or sanctioned by the Buddha dealing with the rules and regulations for monastic training and moral discipline. Shastras refer to commentarial works composed after the Buddha's time.

15. The other four reasons a term is not translated are: it has many meanings, it is an esoteric word, it refers to something not existing in the language of the translator's country, or it is the tradition or custom not to translate the term.

SUTRA:

Entering the Inconceivable State of Liberation by means of the Practices and Vows of Samantabhadra Bodhisattva.

COMMENTARY:

Entering means, "to reach" the **Inconceivable State of Liberation**. Inconceivable means there is no way one can imagine it. Basically, the state of liberation is not a state. If it were a "state" it would not be liberation. Then why does it say, "**inconceivable state of liberation**"? "State" here is merely used as an analogy, because when one attains freedom there is nothing whatsoever that can be grasped.

Samantabhadra[16] **Bodhisattva**'s name means "Universally Worthy One." Universally means his spiritual integrity[17] pervades the entire universe. What is meant by worthy? Worthy means his virtue is akin to that of the foremost sages.

Practices and Vows Chapter. Practices refer to the great practices that he cultivates. Vows are the great vows made by him. The vows made by him during his spiritual cultivation are the greatest. Therefore, he is called Samantabhadra Bodhisattva of great practice.

There are four great Bodhisattvas. Among all Bodhisattvas, Manjushri Bodhisattva is foremost in wisdom. Guanshiyin (Avalokiteshvara)

---

16. Samantabhadra translated in Chinese is 普賢 Pu Xian. Pu is literally "universal, everywhere, or all" and Xian includes the meanings of "worthy, sage, holy, or sacred."

17. The Chinese character "道dao" has many meanings depending on the context. Its most common meaning is "path" or "way." Here its meaning is closely related to the idea of virtue. However, this is a special virtue acquired from cultivation of the spiritual or Buddhist Path. That's why it is referred to as spiritual integrity.

Bodhisattva is foremost in kindness and compassion. Earth Store (Kṣhitigarbha) Bodhisattva is foremost in strength of vows. Samantabhadra Bodhisattva is foremost in practice.

In the Flower Treasury Ocean of Worlds, mentioned in the *Flower Adornment Sutra*, Samantabhadra Bodhisattva is the Dharma-requesting host. Before the Buddha speaks Dharma, one of his disciples must first request that he speak the Dharma. In the *Lotus Flower of the Wonderful Dharma Sutra*, Venerable Shariputra was the Dharma-requesting host, and in the Shurangama Sutra, Venerable Ananda requested the Dharma on behalf of the assembly who were receptive to the teachings.

SUTRA:

At that time, after Samantabhadra Bodhisattva, Mahasattva finished praising the Tathagata's supreme merit and virtue...

COMMENTARY:

At that time refers to the time right after the previous chapter had been spoken. **Samantabhadra Bodhisattva** is the Bodhisattva whose spiritual integrity fills up the entire world and whose virtue is akin to that of the foremost sages. What does Bodhisattva mean? Those who have already heard lectures on the Sutras understand what this term means. However, I'm afraid that those who are listening to the Sutra for the first time might not understand what this means. Bodhisattva is a Sanskrit word. "Bodhi" literally means "enlightenment" and "sattva" literally means "sentience." The two together mean to enlighten those with sentience. "Those with sentience" refers to all living beings.

Today someone had asked why a flower is called an insentient thing when it does possess life. That's a good question. I will briefly explain this for you. Plants and trees are insentient. Although they are insentient, they have a "nature." What nature do they have? The life-nature. What is the life-nature? The life-nature is what is called "humaneness"[18] in Confucius' teachings. Humaneness is the nature. It is the Dao[19] or it can be said to be the mother of the myriad things of the universe; that is, the mother of all things. Do human beings have this humaneness? Of course they do, otherwise they would not be called human beings. What would they be called then? You can call them anything you wish. As it is said, "Human beings are those who are humane."[20] When these two, human beings and humaneness unite, it is called the Dao or Way of Nature.

Confucius brought humaneness to light. All the plants and trees have this humaneness. Why do I say this? This is because they all have vitality. In the spring their branches and leaves grow, their flowers blossom, and they bear fruit. This is because they have the nature of humaneness. Not only do they have this nature, but flowers, plants, and trees also have their own very dull awareness. Someone said that if you cut a flower, it actually makes a sound in fear that cannot be heard by people. However, it can be detected with scientific instruments. This is quite ordinary. Why does it make a sound? It is because it has this nature. But this nature is not fully developed. It has a tiny amount of this nature. Let me explain this with the following analogy. For example, if humans had 100 pounds of this nature, flowers, plants, and trees by comparison would not even

---

18. The Chinese character "仁ren" translated as "humaneness," has the quality of kindness or benevolence. It is best expressed by the biblical injunction "love thy neighbor as thyself." However, in this context it is referring to a quality found within nature.

19. Here the same Chinese character "道dao" (see footnote 6) is referring to the origin of all things in the world, as opposed to a quality possessed by an individual. The Dao is the unconditional and unknowable source and guiding principle of all reality. It is also the process of nature by which all things change, and which is to be followed for a life of harmony.

20. Doctrine of the Mean XX, 5, words of the Great Teacher Confucius, compiled by his grandson Zi-se.

have an ounce of this nature. They have a very slight amount of this nature—equal to a hairsbreadth. This is just an analogy. Do not take it literally and say, "That Dharma Master said that humans have 100 pounds of the nature." Don't be so attached. Flowers, plants, and trees after a period of time develop a type of awareness.

In China, a camphor tree and a gingko tree wanted to do the ritual for receiving the moral precepts. Someone may ask, "You said that they don't have sentience, yet how could they appear in human form and take the moral precepts? Isn't this a big contradiction?"

This is not the least bit contradictory. Since you do not understand this state, you think it is contradictory. However, once you understand this, you realize that it is quite ordinary. These trees were very old and they had a lot of experiences while living among people in the world. They gradually acquired a human-like nature as well as increasing their humaneness and therefore, after obtaining more humaneness, they developed feelings. Having these feelings enabled them to want to receive the moral precepts. Before they received the moral precepts, it's not known how many evil things they had done. Later they realized that what they had done was wrong, and they wanted to receive the moral precepts. They even wanted to enter the monastic order. We all should understand this point.

Samantabhadra Bodhisattva teaches and transforms all living beings. He does not only rescue those with sentience, he also rescues those without sentience. "Those with and without sentience perfect the wisdom of all modes and realize the Buddha's Path together." The Bodhisattva also wishes to rescue all the plants, flowers, and trees. Just think how great his practice is. We ordinary people only wish to rescue other people or those with sentience, but he also rescues those that don't even have sentience. Therefore, he is called Samantabhadra Bodhisattva. Bodhisattva can also be translated as a "living being with a great resolve for the path." He is also a living being, but his resolve for the spiritual path is great. It can also be translated as "one who is forthright and honest." "Forthright and honest" means that everything he does is done openly. That is, he is not selfish, not concerned about personal gain, not jealous, and not obstructive to others.

After the word Bodhisattva, is the word "**Mahasattva**," which means a "great Bodhisattva." Samantabhadra Bodhisattva is a great Bodhisattva among Bodhisattvas. He is not a minor Bodhisattva. Who is a minor Bodhisattva? You who have just made the resolve for Bodhi (literally "brought forth the Bodhi-mind") are a minor Bodhisattva. After you have maintained the resolve for Bodhi for a long time, then you are a great Bodhisattva. Upon receiving the Bodhisattva Precepts, you are a neophyte Bodhisattva. After you've held the Bodhisattva Precepts for a long time and have cultivated accordingly, then you become a great Bodhisattva. After 300 or 500 years then you are considered to be an elder Bodhisattva. During last year's summer session two disciples received the Bodhisattva Precepts. They are now one-year old Bodhisattvas. When they have held the Bodhisattva Precepts for two years, they will be two-year old Bodhisattvas. Then they can be called minor Bodhisattvas. But now we're referring to a great Bodhisattva—a great Bodhisattva among Bodhisattvas. Who is he? Samantabhadra Bodhisattva.

Finished praising the Tathagata's supreme merit and virtue. What does praising mean? Praising means to laud and commend. Who is being lauded? The Buddha, the World Honored One. Exalt[21] means to glorify. The Tathagata's merit and virtue is being exalted as most supreme.

---

21. "Praising" actually consists of two characters in Chinese: 稱歎, which literally means "to praise and exalt."

Who is the Tathagata? Tathagata or "Thus Come One" is one of the ten titles of the Buddha. In the past, all the Buddhas had many names. Since it was difficult to remember the many names that all Buddhas had, they were reduced to 10,000 names. Yet it was still difficult for people to remember all of these 10,000 names, so they were again reduced to 1,000 names. Though every Buddha had these 1,000 names, it was still too many to remember. So they were reduced again to 100 names. Because living beings' ability to remember is very poor, they could not remember all of these names, either. Finally, they were reduced to ten names. Tathagata is one of these ten titles of the Buddha. "Tatha" or "thus" means "without movement" or "stillness." "Agata" or "come" represents "movement." This means that within stillness there is movement and within movement there is stillness. Tathagata means "one who has ascended the true path." This refers to stillness. And he is "one who has come to realize Proper Enlightenment." This refers to movement. Although his name has the meaning of movement and stillness, yet the Buddha's fundamental nature has neither movement nor stillness. That is, movement and stillness are non-dual. Movement is stillness and stillness is movement. How can we say this? Movement is generated from stillness, and stillness is only apparent when there is movement. Therefore, this non-duality of movement and stillness is called the Tathagata.

In the previous chapter of the Flower Adornment Sutra, Samantabhadra Bodhisattva had praised the Tathagata's supreme merit and virtue. This merit and virtue is the most supreme among all other kinds of merit. None can compare to the Tathagata's merit and virtue. One could never finish speaking of or describing the merit and virtue of the Tathagata. Although one could never finish describing it, Samantabhadra Bodhisattva relied on his great practices and vows to praise the Tathagata's most supreme merit and virtue.

What is "merit"? Merit is what we create, and virtue comes from what we do. How is merit created? For example, a teacher in a school does all in his power to teach, doing more than his salary requires. If you are able to go beyond the call of duty, expending your energy to do additional work, that's how to create merit. Virtue is the result of doing beneficial things for all people. You help other people, yet do not seek any reward. You don't want to get something in return. For example, you lend $50,000 to a certain person without the hope of some personal gain, such as wanting him to give you $500,000 when he repays you. If that's your intention in giving, then there is no virtue in that. Virtue is being able to do favors for others without seeking a reward and benefiting all people without wanting them to do something beneficial for you in return.

There is great and small virtue. Not only should we do acts that show great virtue, we also should not overlook small virtuous deeds. What are small virtuous deeds? These are deeds that give only a little bit of benefit to another. If you do many of these small acts of virtue, then your virtuous nature will naturally become great. However, if you do not do any virtuous deeds, then you will never have a virtuous nature. Therefore, it is said, "The path is to be practiced." The path is to be cultivated, not merely talked about. You can't just recite the words "cultivate the path" over and over again from morning to night without actually putting it into practice. That's merely paying lip service. It's useless. The saying continues, "Virtue comes from what is done." If you do not actually practice it, then you will lack virtue. It is also said, "The path is to be followed. If it is not followed, what use is the path? Virtue comes from what we do. If it is not done, how could one have virtue?"

One could never finish praising the Tathagata's merit and virtue. After Samantabhadra Bodhisattva finished praising the Tathagata's merit and virtue, he then spoke as follows:

SUTRA:

He told all the Bodhisattvas and Sudhana.

COMMENTARY:

"**He told all the** measureless and boundless number of **Bodhisattvas** in the Flower Adornment Dharma-assembly…" The word "all" can refer to very many Bodhisattvas or very few Bodhisattvas, depending on who is present. However, in this context it means very many. In the Flower Adornment Dharma-assembly it would be inappropriate to say only one, because there are so many Bodhisattvas there that they are beyond calculation.

Sudhana is a child. Although he is a child, his spiritual powers are tremendous. The wonderful uses of his spiritual powers are most inconceivable. The youth Sudhana has 53 spiritual teachers, but having so many teachers has had a bad influence on Buddhism in China. It has caused a lot of confusion within Buddhism. How is this? Buddhist disciples wanting to emulate him say, "The youth Sudhana has 53 teachers, so I should have at least 10 or 20, or even 30 would not be too many." This kind of behavior by Buddhist disciples in China is very superstitious and improper. I have always opposed this, not because I fear that my disciples will bow to someone else as their teacher, but because it's the most despicable custom in Buddhism. Someone asks, "Why is it not despicable for the youth Sudhana to have 53 teachers, yet it is despicable for Chinese disciples to have 30 or 40 teachers?"

Every situation has its own underlying truth. It is true that the youth Sudhana had 53 teachers, but his first teacher told him to bow to and follow the second one as his teacher. Each teacher instructed him to do this. He did not sneak off on his own to do this. It's not that he thought,

"Oh, I've heard that such and such a person has virtue. He's an adept cultivator of the path!" and then go off on his own and bow to and follow that person as his teacher without telling his first teacher. To do that is called bowing to and following someone as your new teacher, while turning your back on your original teacher. You're betraying your first teacher. If you treat your first teacher well, why would you bow to another person as your teacher?

It's like we are, as human beings. Having one father is enough. You can consider Shakyamuni Buddha to be your second father, but you can't have three, four, five, six, seven, or even eight fathers. Your teacher is the father of your world-transcending Dharma-body,[22] why would you want to have so many teachers?

After the youth Sudhana had finished learning all of his first teacher's virtue, knowledge, and the miraculous uses of his spiritual powers, there was nothing left for his teacher to teach him. Then that teacher told him, "Go south and bow to and follow a certain person as your next teacher." After he mastered all the skills of his second teacher, that teacher instructed him saying, "Go further south, and bow to a certain Venerable One, Bodhisattva, or Bhikshu as your next teacher. That person's accomplishment is greater than mine." Each teacher recommended Sudhana to the next teacher. He didn't sneak off on his own to find other teachers. So each teacher recommended the youth Sudhana to the next teacher, until he had studied with a total of 53 teachers. He embodied all the miraculous functions of the spiritual powers of all of these 53 teachers. Therefore, his spiritual abilities are incredibly great. Even though he is a mere child, he has tremendous talent.

---

22. Dharma-kaya literally translates as "Dharma-body." It refers to the enlightened state of the Buddha that all beings have the potential to realize.

However, because of his influence, some Chinese people developed the custom of recklessly bowing to and following one teacher after another. These people are the dregs within Buddhism.

When I was in China and Hong Kong, I would not allow people who had already taken refuge in the Three Jewels to again take refuge under me. Why is this? It is because I regarded them as being the dregs within Buddhism. They were the very worst Buddhist disciples because they were sneaking off on their own to take me as their teacher without the approval of their teacher. This is turning one's back on one's good teacher. You can only take refuge in the Three Jewels one time, not over and over again. In the case of formally receiving the moral precepts, for example receiving the three, four, five, or eight precepts for laity, or the ten major and forty-eight minor Bodhisattva Precepts, they can be taken more than once. However, taking refuge in the Three Jewels can only be done once, and when you do so you are taking one person as your teacher. You cannot have a teacher for each of the four directions. In the future, when you die, whose disciple will you be? You'll have no place of refuge. If you take refuge with more than one teacher like this, it's as if you did not take refuge at all because you've done it too many times.

In Buddhism we must speak the truth. In Chinese Buddhism there are several elder disciples, who from the time they were young, ran around taking refuge over and over again. In the end, they had taken refuge with tens or even hundreds of teachers during their lifetime. If you ask them, "What is the meaning of taking refuge?" They just stare at you, unable to utter a word. They don't know. Although they've taken refuge tens or hundreds of times, they don't know what it means. Isn't that pathetic? They say, "All monastics are my teachers. I can take refuge with all of them." However, I believe they do not even have a single teacher. Why is this? This is because they do not really have faith in their teachers. If you have faith, then you can be liberated. Without faith, you can't be liberated. In China especially, there's a lot of animosity among Bhikshus. Why is this? It is because of this disciple issue. For example, let's say that this Dharma Master's disciples go and become disciples of another Dharma Master. That would seem to infer that the first Dharma Master lacked virtue. If he had virtue, why would his disciples leave him to follow another teacher? This causes disputes to arise between Dharma Masters. One tells the other, "You snatched my disciples!" Then they fight with each other, and once they fight, their true colors are exposed. What is their true color? The fire of ignorance. For example, in China, Dharma Master Taixu and Dharma Master Yuanying fought over disciples. Because of this they were as incompatible as fire and water. "You have treated me badly, so I'm going to treat you likewise." This was due to the fact that some disciples of one of them surreptitiously went to the other Dharma Master to become his disciple. These Dharma Masters thought: "You're afraid that I'm going to steal your disciples, and I'm afraid that you're going to steal my disciples." In this way, they ended up in this mess.

Therefore, although the youth Sudhana has an extremely important position in the *Flower Adornment Sutra*, he inadvertently had a bad influence on Buddhism in China. Why would a monk do this, when he knows that it is wrong to accept someone else's disciple as his own? They know this is not in accord with Dharma, so why do they still do it? Now I will tell you what's really going on behind such actions. It is to take advantage of the situation. When you accept a disciple, you obtain a red envelope containing money. If you don't accept disciples, then you won't receive as much money. Once someone becomes your disciple they think, "Oh! He's my teacher, and I should do my best to make offerings to him." Then they take out their money to make an offering. Money confuses the minds of these monks, so that even though they clearly know it is wrong, they still take others' disciples as their own disciples. Isn't this a big mess?

Who's responsible for this situation? First, it's due to the youth. Second, we can say it's caused by "good wealth,"[23] that sways the monks to think, "This wealth is good!" This youth is a little child with a lot of money. So people think having money is very colorful and alluring. This causes cultivators of the spiritual path to be so terribly influenced, that they do things they know are clearly wrong. This is one of the worst customs in Buddhism. I hope this kind of situation will not occur in America.

Taking refuge in the Three Jewels should only be done once. If you want to take refuge, you should find a good teacher. Do not turn your back on your teacher after you have taken refuge under his auspices. That would be to betray him.

The youth Sudhana's practice of having 53 teachers influenced Buddhism in China to have improper and superstitious customs. Before Buddhism has become widespread in America, we should not allow this practice to be disseminated to the people here. For example, in Christianity people become baptized only once. They don't say "The first time I was baptized, I wasn't completely purified. Therefore, I should be baptized again." Then after that they want to be baptized again. After their second baptism they're still not purified completely, so they want to be baptized again. No matter how many times one is baptized, one is still the same. In Buddhism we also should not be this way. We should not take refuge over and over again, thinking, "Probably the first time I took refuge the Buddha didn't know it. So I should take refuge a second time." If the Buddha didn't know it the first time, then if you take refuge a second, third, a thousand or even ten thousand times, the Buddha still would not know. Why is this? It's not that the Buddha was sleeping, and therefore didn't see you taking refuge.

---

23. The youth Sudhana's name translates literally as "good wealth," thus the play on words here.

The Buddha is one who is greatly awakened. If you have the sincere intent to take refuge in Buddhism, the Buddha already knows it. Therefore, it is said, "The path of the response that is invoked is inconceivable." If you say that the Buddha was not aware of your taking refuge, then fundamentally you lack faith in the Buddha, and have not really taken refuge. Even if you take refuge in that way several million times it would still be of no use. When you take refuge, you must honor your teacher and the spiritual path. You should be very respectful towards your teacher. My intention in telling you this principle is not because I want the disciples who have taken refuge with me to revere and honor me. My disciples are already very respectful towards me. I do not need to tell them to be even more respectful towards me.

How then should one be? After taking refuge, be sure to remember to never oppose your teacher or be disrespectful towards him. Those who are disrespectful to their teacher will fall into the hells. Which hell? Doesn't the *Sutra of the Past Vows of Earth Store Bodhisattva* mention the Thousand Blades Hell? Disciples who are disrespectful and disobedient towards their teachers fall into this Thousand Blades Hell. These kinds of living beings do not obey or follow their teacher's instructions. They want to do things in their own newfangled way. They want to do as they please, rather than follow their teacher's instructions. Not only do they not obey their teacher, they malign or scold their teacher. They hit or even murder their teacher. Don't laugh. These things really do happen sometimes.

This world has every type of living being that you can imagine. There are those who have murdered their teachers by poisoning them. They used all kinds of methods to harm their teachers. For example, to sit in your teacher's chair or to casually play with his alms bowl is a moral transgression. There are many subtle ways that one can make mistakes like this. With the exception of those things that your teacher tells you to do, anything you recklessly do on your own is a moral transgression. This matter is of critical importance. You cannot do whatever you please. When with your teacher, you as a disciple, are not free to do as you wish. Therefore, at all times and places, you cannot malign your teacher or talk about him behind his back. These things are karmic transgressions of the mouth.

SUTRA:

Good men! If all of the Buddhas of the ten directions continuously spoke of the merit and virtue of the Tathagata for kalpas²⁴ as numerous as the smallest atomic particles in ineffably ineffable numbers of Buddha kshetra-lands,²⁵ they would not be able to finish.

COMMENTARY:

This section of the Sutra says that one could never finish describing the Buddha's merit and virtue. It says, **Good men!** That is all of you good people who have taken refuge in the Three Jewels, received the Five Moral Precepts, and cultivate the Ten Good Karmas. Now I will tell you about the merit and virtue of the Tathagata, the Buddha. **If all of the Buddhas of the ten directions** within all of their Buddha-lands **continuously spoke of the merit and virtue of the Tathagata for kalpas as numerous as the smallest atomic particles in ineffably ineffable numbers of Buddha kshetra-lands.** Ineffably ineffable means that one could not use any words or language whatsoever to fully describe them. Smallest atomic particles mean the most infinitesimal particles. Ultimately what

---

24. Kalpa is a period of time in Buddhist cosmology equal to about 16 million human years.

25. Kshetra literally means "field." In Buddhism it refers to the field of influence of a Buddha. It refers to a system that includes billions of worlds.

are these smallest particles? They are "particles that border on becoming empty space." These particles cannot be seen with the human eye. For example, you can see the particles that float in the air when the sun shines through a window. If you were to divide these visible particles into seven parts, you would not be able to see them anymore. These are the smallest atomic particles. They **continuously spoke**, means to speak without pause for kalpas as numerous as these smallest particles. If they spoke like this unceasingly for such a long time, they would not be able to finish. One could never finish speaking about the merit and virtue of the Tathagata.

SUTRA:

If one aspires to perfect the gateway to this merit and virtue, one must cultivate ten kinds of great practices and vows.

COMMENTARY:

The Buddha has measureless and boundless merit and virtue that could never be fully described. Is it the case that only the Buddha can have this kind of merit and virtue and other living beings do not have a share in it? No. Buddhism is most egalitarian. It absolutely does not have any tyrannical or dictatorial principles within it. Buddhism teaches that every person can become a Buddha. Not only can all people become Buddhas, all living beings, including those that fly in the sky, swim in the water, move on the earth, and even plants can become Buddhas. That is, all living creatures and all plants, including flowers, grasses and trees, as well as those creatures born from wombs, from eggs, from moisture or those born by transformation—all of the 12 species of living creatures[26] can become Buddhas. The Buddha didn't say, "Only I can become a Buddha, and you cannot." Nor is it like certain religions that teach, "I'm the only one, true God, and all others are false." In Buddhism it is only to be feared that you won't become a Buddha. Once you do, then you are a true Buddha. There are no false Buddhas. All Buddhas are true Buddhas and all living beings can become true Buddhas. The Buddha does not teach, "I alone am allowed to become a Buddha, and you are not. I will not permit you to become a Buddha." To have that kind of a teaching is too narrow-minded. It's meaningless to say, "I am the only true God." One would be a very solitary and lonely God. Because all living beings can become Buddhas, there are many Buddhas. The path of all Buddhas is the same. There is no difference among them. If all of us wish **to perfect the gateway to this merit and virtue**, that is, achieve this gateway to the Buddha's merit and virtue, each **one must cultivate ten kinds of great practices and vows.** If you successfully cultivate to perfection these ten types of great practices and vows, then you can realize the Buddha's merit and virtue.

SUTRA:

What are the ten? The first is to worship all Buddhas. The second is to praise the Tathagatas. The third is to extensively cultivate making offerings. The fourth is to repent of karmic obstacles and reform. The fifth is to follow and rejoice in merit and virtue. The sixth is to request the turning of the wheel of Dharma. The seventh is to beseech the Buddhas to remain in the world. The eighth is to always follow and learn from the Buddhas. The ninth is to constantly conform with living beings. The tenth is to transfer all merit and virtue.

---

26. This includes those born from wombs, eggs, moisture, and by transformation, as well as those with form, without form, not totally with form, not totally without form, with thought, without thought, not totally with thought, and not totally without thought.

Good Wealth said, "Great Sage, what is the meaning of 'to worship all Buddhas' up to and including 'to transfer all merit and virtue'?"

COMMENTARY:

What are the ten? What are these ten kinds of great practices? This is just asking, "What are the names of these ten kinds of practices and vows?" **The first is to worship all Buddhas.** What is to worship? It means to have good manners and propriety. It's a way people show respect for one another. If you have good manners to others, then they will reciprocate. Why should we have good manners towards others? It's a way of showing respect to them. Propriety is one of the five eternal virtues which are: humaneness, righteousness, propriety, knowledge, and trustworthiness. The reason that humans are different from animals is because they have propriety. Without it they'd be no different from animals. One must have propriety when showing one's respect towards another person. It is even more necessary to have respect towards the Buddha. We should have propriety and revere him.

In the past the Chinese people did not want to bow to the Buddha. They were just like Americans of today. When I first came to America many people told me, "Bowing to the Buddha is the one thing Americans dislike the most." And I responded, "That's the best! They don't want to bow, but I will absolutely require them to bow. If they don't bow, I will not teach them any Buddha-dharma." There's no courtesy involved here. If you bow, then I will teach you. If you don't, then even though you want me to teach you Buddhism, I will not teach you. Why is this? If you do not have proper decorum towards the Buddha, what use would it be to teach you? Chinese people were also like this in the past. Although they believed in the Buddha, they didn't want to bow to him. They were being just like a monkey. Monkeys also don't have the sense to know to bow to the Buddha. If you try to teach them, they don't want to bow either. Horses and cows are unable to bow to the Buddha. Although they may revere the Buddha in their hearts, they do not bow to him. Chinese people were the same way. They revered the Buddha, but did not worship him. They believed in the Buddha, but would not bow to him.

At that time there was a Bodhisattva named Ratnamati.[27] He saw this situation, and thought, "This is really pathetic. What use is it to believe in the Buddha, yet not bow to him?" At that time he went to China and established seven types of worship to the Buddha. In this way he taught the Chinese people to bow to the Buddha. Wherever Buddhism has spread, the situation is pretty much the same. Therefore, when Buddhism first came to China, the Chinese people did not want to bow to the Buddha. And now that Buddhism has just come to America, Americans also do not want to bow to the Buddha. Why don't they want to bow to the Buddha? This is because they have never bowed to the Buddha before. Thus they are rather egotistical and conceited. I often say that their "ego" is bigger than Mount Sumeru. If one is greater than Mount Sumeru, then how could one bow to the Buddha? There are those who, when they see people bowing to the Buddha, just stand there like a block of wood. Others just sit there like a rock. They have all kinds of individual styles like this.

Those of us who have faith in the Buddha should bow to the Buddha. If you do not bow, then how can we talk about having faith? Therefore, you must bow to the images of the Buddha. One may think, "These images are carved out of wood, so what use is there in bowing to them?" It is definitely not the case that the wooden image itself is actually the Buddha. Don't misunderstand this! The Buddha pervades all places. There is not a single place where the Buddha's Dharma-body is not located. The wooden image is only a symbol for the Buddha. It is just a representation

---

27. circa 500 C.E.

of him. It's analogous to the flag that each country possesses. Each citizen pays his or her respect to the country's flag. The flag is merely a piece of cloth or plastic, so what benefit is there in showing respect towards it? It is also a symbol. The country's flag represents the life of the country. Therefore, we pay homage to the country's flag in order to show our respect for our country.

The image of the Buddha is the same way. It's just a symbol for the Buddha. It's not to say that the image is the Buddha. Why do we bow to the image of the Buddha? The Buddha pervades all places. Does this mean that we should bow to the four cardinal directions and the four intermediate directions as well? No. We must have a point to focus upon. At this focal point there needs to be an object that symbolizes it. It's just like a country. If you wish to venerate your country by paying homage in every province and county in the country, how could you ever have enough time to do this? Therefore, it will suffice for you to pay homage to the country's flag. The meaning behind bowing to the image of the Buddha is the same.

In bowing to the Buddha there are seven types of worship. The first is "worshipping with conceit." What does this mean? Although one is bowing to the Buddha, one still has not renounced one's ego. You feel that bowing to the Buddha is unnatural. You think, "Why should I bow to him?" You always feel very unhappy as you make your prostrations to the Buddha. You force yourself to do it, or you see others bow and think, "I should bow, too. If they bow to the Buddha and I do not bow, it will make me stand out and that will be embarrassing. Therefore, I'll bow to the Buddha." Although one bows to the Buddha, one hangs onto one's ego and feels conceited. This is the first type of worship, "worshipping with conceit."

The second type of worship is "worshipping to seek fame." What does this mean? You hear people praising someone saying, "So-and-so bows to the Buddha a lot. He really works hard in his cultivation of the spiritual path. He bows to the Buddha, he bows to the Sutras, and he even bows in repentance ceremonies! He truly works hard in his spiritual cultivation!" When he who is 'worshipping to seek fame' hears people praise that person, he also wants to attain the same recognition and fame as that cultivator. Then he also bows to the Buddha and bows in repentance ceremonies, thereby following and rejoicing in the merit of others. Although he follows and rejoices in others' merit, he doesn't really bow to the Buddha; rather he is bowing to recognition and fame. He seeks fame as a "cultivator." This is called "worshipping to seek fame."

In addition to what was stated above, one who worships with conceit, also harbors this thought, "This is really superstitious. What use is it to bow like this? This is too superstitious!" And the person who worships to seek fame may worship without having faith in the Buddha, yet he may also not lack faith. Rather he sees that when a person bows to the Buddha, people make offerings to him. There are people who honor him too, and there are also people who praise him as a genuine cultivator of the spiritual path. Therefore, because he seeks to get offerings, honor, and praise, he also bows to the Buddha.

The third type of worship is "worshipping with body and mind in conformity with others." What does this mean? Seeing others bow, I also bow. One's body and mind just follow along with others. "Whatever they do, I will do." One doesn't pay attention to whether or not there are any benefits in bowing to the Buddha. One doesn't care whether one bows with sincerity or whether one feels bowing is superstitious. One does not seek for fame; rather one merely follows what other people are doing. This is called, "worshipping with body and mind in conformity with others." Worshipping like this has neither merit nor demerit. It's merely an ordinary, routine practice.

The fourth type of worship is "worshipping with wisdom and purity." One uses one's true wisdom and purity of body and mind to bow. This is the way a wise person bows to the Buddha. One has purified the three karmas of body, mouth, and mind. When you bow to the Buddha you do not commit any moral transgressions with your physical body. That is, while bowing you do not take the life of other creatures, you do not steal others' possessions, nor do you commit any sexual misconduct. Therefore, your karma in body is pure. When you bow to the Buddha, you do not have thoughts of greed, hatred, or delusion. On the contrary, with wisdom you reverently bow to the Buddha. In this way your karma in thought is also pure. When you bow to the Buddha you are mindful of the Buddha. You may recite the Buddha's name or chant Sutras or mantras. In this way your karma of speech is also pure. In speech you do not indulge in frivolous talk, lying, harsh speech, or divisive speech. When your three karmas of body, speech, and thought are pure like this, then that's called "worshipping with wisdom and purity." You are bowing to the Buddha with true wisdom.

The fifth type of worship is "worship that pervades the Dharma-realm." What does this mean? You contemplate like this: "Although I have not yet become a Buddha, my mind and nature fill up the entire Dharma-realm. While I am here bowing before this one Buddha, I am also bowing to all the Buddhas throughout the Dharma-realm. I am not only bowing to one Buddha, rather I have transformation bodies that bow in worship before each Buddha. All of these bodies simultaneously make offerings to all of the Buddhas and Bodhisattvas." Take a look at this state. Everything is a creation of the mind alone. Your mind pervades the Dharma-realm. This kind of worship and practice also pervades everywhere throughout the Dharma-realm. Someone asks, "What is the Dharma-realm? I've been listening to the Sutra lectures for several days, but I still don't know what is meant by the Dharma-realm." The Dharma-realm contains all the three-thousand great-thousand world systems. None of them are not included within it. There's nothing outside the Dharma-realm. In this way your body exhausts the reaches of space and pervades the Dharma-realm, and your reverential worship is the same way. The merit and virtue you gain also exhausts the reaches of space and pervades throughout the Dharma-realm. This is the fifth type of worship called, "worship that pervades the Dharma-realm."

The sixth type of worship is, "worship having proper contemplation and practice with utmost sincerity." What is meant by "proper contemplation?" It means we focus our minds on a single point and contemplate while bowing to the Buddha. While bowing to this one single Buddha, we are bowing to all the Buddhas in the Dharma-realm. Bowing to all the Buddhas in the Dharma-realm is the same as bowing to one Buddha. Because it is said, "All the Buddhas of the ten directions and the three periods of time share the same Dharma-body." All Buddhas share the same path. Therefore, we bow with concentrated mind while contemplating the Buddhas. When we practice like this, we do not have false thinking.

It should not be the case that when we are bowing to the Buddhas our mind wanders off to the movie theater or goes to the horse-racing track. Or perhaps it runs off to the hunting grounds or to the dancing hall. Maybe while you're bowing your mind jets off to a bar or to a restaurant. Without having to purchase any tickets, you're able to travel anywhere, and you're able to dash off to all locations. Suddenly you're in the heavens, and suddenly you're back on earth. Sometimes you scoot off to New York and then unbeknownst to yourself you've returned back here in San Francisco. You think, "Wow! Originally I was here bowing to the Buddha, and then I was in New York and now I've returned to San Francisco. I've really got spiritual powers!" But actually this isn't even "ghostly powers." This is just fantasizing, and is improper contemplation, not proper contemplation. When one practices with proper contemplation, one does not have this kind of false thinking.

When you bow to the Buddha single-mindedly, your mind is not doing two different things at the same time. Don't think about other things while bowing to the Buddha. This is called, "worship having proper contemplation and practice with utmost sincerity." When you bow like this, it is billions of times better than bowing while having false thinking. Therefore, in cultivation you want to select a method and then become immersed in it. That is, you want to understand the Dharma-method you are practicing. If you don't understand your Dharma, then even though you are bowing just like everyone else, it is different. When they bow that is all that they are doing, whereas when you are bowing, you're false thinking. You think to yourself, "Wait a while. After I'm finished bowing, I'll get some coffee to drink, or perhaps some wine." For example, I believe a certain person had this kind of false thought when he was bowing to the Buddha. When he finished bowing, he forgot everything else and just ran outside. Where did he run off? He went drinking. Now it wouldn't matter if he wanted to go alone. However, he wanted to take all the other people who were bowing with him to go drinking as well. This was extremely pathetic. This is not, "worship having proper contemplation and practice with utmost sincerity." Rather this is improper contemplation. If you don't bow properly, but instead have false thoughts while you're bowing, then your worship is devoid of merit and virtue.

The seventh type of worship is "impartial worship based on reality." Worship based on reality means worshipping, yet not worshipping; and not worshipping, yet worshipping. Someone might say, "If you say it is worship without worshipping and not worshipping yet worshipping, then I don't need to bow to the Buddha and that's just the same as bowing to the Buddha." No, that is not what is meant here. It means that although you are bowing to the Buddha, you are not attached to the attribute or characteristic of bowing. If you think that when you're not bowing to the Buddha, that's the same as bowing to the Buddha, you are wrong. That's being a megalomaniac. Just like the person that came here the other day, who told me he had already reached the "void." Isn't this extremely foolish? People like this are hopeless. There is no way to rescue them. Why is this? This kind of attachment is really ludicrous.

Impartial worship based on reality means that while bowing to the Buddha, "I'm impartially bowing to the Three Jewels." One reveres the Buddha, the Dharma, and the Sangha—worshipping them without discrimination. "Not a single thought is generated, and not a single thought is extinguished." This is the unborn, everlasting worship that is impartial worship based on reality. "When not a single thought arises, the entire substance is revealed." If one can truly bow to the point that not a single thought arises, then "all the worlds of the ten directions reveal the Perfect Body." Although your body is here, yet it is just as big as the entire Dharma-realm. This is the "attribute of reality," which has no attributes. You bow and yet you are without the characteristic or attribute of self, others, living beings, or a life span. You merge with the Dharma-realm. Your body is the Dharma-realm and the Dharma-realm is your body. Isn't that amazing?

In the past your body was just as tiny as Mount Sumeru. In terms of the entire Dharma-realm, Mount Sumeru is just like a speck of dust in the Dharma-realm. You shouldn't think that it is really huge. Now, in this state, Mount Sumeru is within your Dharma-body. Your body contains Mount Sumeru. Take a look at this. Isn't this wonderful? All the myriad things in the entire cosmos are contained within your nature. There is nothing that you do not understand. This is impartial worship based on reality. It's an inconceivable state. If you can reach this state while bowing to the Buddha, could you ever fully describe the wonders of this experience? You could never finish describing them.

This is a very simple explanation of the seven types of worship of the Three Jewels. To discuss this in greater detail, there are "300 kinds of decorum and 3,000 kinds of awe-inspiring deportments." There are many types of etiquette. Therefore, in China there is an ancient classic entitled the *Book of Rites*. It is solely a record of all the various forms of etiquette and propriety. In this book it says that wherever a person goes, there is an appropriate place for him to sit. There's a place for adults to sit and a proper place for children to sit. Also, men and women each have their own appropriate place to sit. Elders have their own seats as well. No one can sit at random. I'll give you an example of this. Where should children sit? The Book of Rites says, "Children should sit in the corners." Children should not sit at the front. They are supposed to sit in the corners.

Speaking about propriety, I recall that when I was a young child, I liked to talk a lot about proper etiquette. What kind of etiquette did I teach? I wanted other people to venerate me. How did I want them to do this? In those days in China, people talked about the emperor, so as a child I liked to pretend I was the emperor. All of the children in the village, perhaps thirty, fifty, or even a hundred of them, all had to obey my commands. I told all of these children to build a mound. Then I sat on the mound and ordered them to bow to me. This was before I was even twelve years old. It was really strange that all of these children listened to me. They did not object to bowing to me. This is how I wanted people to bow to me when I was a child.

When I was twelve years old, I saw a child who had died. Only then did I realize that everyone must die. Thereafter, I changed this crude behavior of mine, and no longer told people to bow to me. On the contrary, I wanted to bow to others. How did I begin this practice of bowing? I began by bowing to my father and mother. In the morning I made a full prostration to my father and mother, and then again in the evening I bowed to them. I bowed to each of them three times. Therefore, I bowed six times in the morning and six times in the evening. Then I thought to myself, "My father and mother are not the only ones in the world. There is also heaven and earth, the emperor and my teacher." Thereafter, I also bowed to heaven and earth, to the emperor and my teacher. At that time, I did not know who my teacher was because I had not yet met him. I thought to myself, "In the future I will definitely have a teacher. Although I have not yet met him, I will bow to him beforehand anyway." Then I bowed to heaven and earth, to the emperor, my close relations, and my teacher. From the point of view of common people, this practice was really superstitious.

Later, I thought, "There are also sages in the world. I should bow to them. There are also saints. I must also bow to them." After that I learned that there was a Buddha in the world. So I bowed to the Buddha. I also bowed to the Bodhisattvas, Shravakas, and Those Enlightened to Conditions. Then I thought, "In the world there must be a person who is the best of the best. I should bow to that person as well. There's also a person who is the most good. I must bow to him. Because he does so much good, I should represent all people in the world and show how grateful we all are by bowing to him. He does good and helps the poor. I should show my gratitude to him on behalf of the poor by bowing to him. I eventually ended up bowing quite a lot.

Then I thought, "Evil people are very pathetic. I should bow to the Buddha on behalf of these evil people. I beseech the Buddha to forgive them and reduce their karmic offenses and enable them to turn away from evil and go towards the good." In this way, I bowed on behalf of evil people. I bowed to the Buddha on behalf of people in the world who have moral transgressions. I also bowed in repentance before the Buddha on behalf of those individuals who are not reverent and obedient to their fathers and mothers. Because I felt that of all the bad people, I was the worst, I wanted to bow to the Buddha on behalf of them all.

Each time I bowed I made over 830 full prostrations. What time did I bow like this? I'll tell you. My way of practicing was really weird. In the morning before anybody was awake, I'd get up. After I got dressed and washed my face, I went outside and commenced bowing. After lighting incense, I'd always go outside to bow. Regardless of how windy it was, whether it was raining or even snowing, I would keep my practice of bowing outside. When it snowed, I'd just go ahead and bow in the snow, not paying attention to how freezing cold it was. I'd bow and get up over and over again until I made over 830 prostrations. This took more than one and a half hours each time. In the evening I waited until everyone went to sleep, and then I again went outside and did my bowing. I bowed in this way, every morning and evening, for many years. Later, when I began my three-year vigil of mourning at my mother's gravesite,[28] I decreased this to just nine bows each time. I was not able to bow so many times then, because it took up too much time. This is the way I practiced bowing in my youth. I believe many of you wanted to know about my

---

28. Upon his mother's death, the Venerable Master did the traditional Confucian practice of showing his reverence and gratitude to his mother by mourning at her gravesite for three years. He actually dwelt there in a small make-shift hut.

practice of bowing when I was young, so that is why I have mentioned this to you now.

The first is to worship all Buddhas. Worship also means "to revere"[29] which is explained as to observe all of the rules. That is, you follow the rules of etiquette. Everything you do should be in harmony with the principle of propriety. If you do not maintain propriety, then you are not being reverent or respectful. For example, when you are respectful towards another person, then you practice propriety when you are in their presence. If you do not respect someone, then you will be very lax and negligent, with impropriety, and just do as you please.

Now we are talking about worship and reverence to all Buddhas. All Buddhas refers to all of the Buddhas of the ten directions and the three periods of time. The Buddha is one who is greatly enlightened. He is a person who is greatly awakened. Common worldly people are born as if in a drunken stupor and die as if in a dream. They do not realize that the three realms of existence are suffering. Therefore, they do not wish to get out of the three realms. This is to be unenlightened. Those of the Two Vehicles are enlightened ones among common worldly people. What have they become enlightened to? They have enlightened to the fact that the impermanence of the realm of birth and death, Samsara, is extremely dangerous. Therefore, they have cultivated and attained the truth of emptiness, but it is a lop-sided emptiness. They've enlightened to the Dharma of the 12 Links of Conditioned Origination, and they've enlightened to the Dharma of the Four Noble Truths. These individuals are known as Arhats and Those Enlightened to Conditions. When compared to common worldly people, these individuals are considered to be enlightened. Although they enlighten themselves, they are not able to

---

29. This vow actually consists of two Chinese characters meaning literally to worship and to revere i.e. 禮 li and 敬 jing.

enlighten others. They only benefit themselves and do not benefit others. They are only able to enlighten themselves.

The Bodhisattva is different from the Arhats. Not only does he enlighten himself, he is also able to enlighten others. He benefits others, as well as himself. The Buddha is different from the Bodhisattva. Although the Bodhisattva is able to enlighten himself and enlighten others as well, yet his enlightenment is not perfect. The Buddha is perfect in enlightenment and perfect in practice. He is perfectly awakened and his cultivation is also perfect. His own enlightenment is perfect and his enlightenment of others is also perfect. Therefore, the Buddha is called one who is greatly enlightened because he has perfected the three types of enlightenment: enlightenment of himself, enlightenment of others, and enlightenment and practice. He is replete with myriad merit and virtue; thus he has become a Buddha.

It is not the case that there is only one Buddha. In the teachings of the Theravada they acknowledge the existence of only one Buddha, our Shakyamuni Buddha. They do not realize or acknowledge that there are Buddhas in other regions of the cosmos. The Dharma of the Theravada was first taught to the five Bhikshus at the Deer Park. Those of the Theravada are only aware of our Buddha, Shakyamuni, and are not aware of all of the other measureless number of Buddhas. There are actually measureless numbers of Buddhas in the worlds in the other regions of the cosmos. Because the Theravadins do not know about these other Buddhas, they claim that the Buddhas of the ten directions of space do not exist.

Is it the case that because they say that the Buddhas of the ten directions do not exist, they actually do not exist? Whether or not they acknowledge that there are Buddhas throughout the ten directions of space, they do exist. The Buddhas of the ten directions and our Shakyamuni Buddha are one. Therefore, it is said, "The Buddhas of the ten directions and the three periods of time share the same Dharma-body."

Samantabhadra Bodhisattva has made these vast vows and practices. Ultimately how great are they? The state of these vows is inconceivable. There is no way one can know their magnitude. Therefore, Samantabhadra Bodhisattva is called the "king of vows."

The first is to worship all Buddhas. This does not mean to worship and bow to only one Buddha, for example Shakyamuni Buddha or Amitabha Buddha. "Worshipping one is worshipping all. One Buddha is all Buddhas." Worshipping one Buddha is worshipping all Buddhas, and worshipping all Buddhas is worshipping one Buddha. This means that one worships all Buddhas without being attached to them, and one worships a single Buddha without being attached to him. You should practice the "impartial worship based on reality." When bowing to all Buddhas or one Buddha, you need not attach to attributes or appearances. For example, you don't say, "This time my merit and virtue is enormous! I've bowed to so many Buddhas; no one else has such spiritual cultivation like me!" You shouldn't be attached to appearances like this. This is the first, to worship all Buddhas.

In speaking of worshipping all Buddhas, is it the case that Buddhas want us to worship them? If you worship the Buddha, he is the Buddha. And if you don't, he's still the Buddha. It's not the case that when we worship the Buddha, he gains some advantage from it or it makes him greater. Nor does it mean that when we do not worship him, the Buddha misses out on getting some benefit or is thereby diminished. When we worship the Buddha, we are fulfilling our obligation as living beings to show our reverence for him. Yet on the part of the Buddha, he is neither enlarged nor diminished by it. Therefore, when we worship the Buddha we should not be attached to the worship.

The second is to praise the Tathagatas. Why do we praise the Tathagata? He doesn't really need our praise. He's not like common people who become so overjoyed when you praise them, even their noses and eyes beam with delight. And if you don't praise them, their noses and eyes get upset and angry. If the Buddha were like that, he'd be no different from an ordinary person, and then we wouldn't want to bow to him or praise him. Why? If he were a common person, what need would there be to bow to or praise him?

If the Buddha does not really want us to praise him, then why should we? Isn't that contradictory? No, it is not. When we praise the Buddha, it generates merit and virtue for our own inherent nature. What merit and virtue will we have? Every person's inherent nature has light. When you praise the Buddha, your light will be revealed, and its illumination will obliterate your darkness. The merit and virtue from praising the Buddha will invisibly prevent you from creating moral transgressions or having false thoughts. The fewer false thoughts you have, the more your wisdom-light will be uncovered. Why are people who cultivate the spiritual path afraid of having false thoughts? It's just for this reason. Once you have a single false thought, a layer of black grime defiles your inherent nature. If you don't have false thoughts, then the light of your inherent nature will be revealed. When you laud the Buddha, your heart is joyful, and by taking delight in the Buddha, you unite with the light of the Buddha's wisdom because the light of your own inherent nature is unveiled.

What's an example of praising the Tathagatas?

> *Above and below heaven, there is nothing like the Buddha.*
> *In the worlds of the ten directions, he is beyond compare.*
> *I have seen all that there is throughout the entire world,*
> *And of all things none is like the Buddha.*

This verse begins with, *above and below heaven*, and below heaven means on the earth, where there is *nothing like the Buddha*. No spirits, Arhats, Pratyeka-Buddhas, or Bodhisattvas can be compared to the Buddha. *In the worlds of the ten directions, he is beyond compare*. Not only is there nothing that can compare with the Buddha above in heaven and on the earth below, even if you went to the worlds of the ten directions it would still be the same. Take a look at our world. We have five great continents of Africa, the Americas, Europe, Asia, and Australia. Yet this only makes up one world. However, this verse is referring to all the measureless and boundless worlds of the ten directions of space. Now we are developing a spaceship that will be able to transport people to the moon.[30] We can say that the moon is another world. However, it is a small world. There are many, many humans and other things in all the worlds of the ten directions, yet none can be compared to the Buddha. *I have seen all that there is throughout the entire world*. In the entire world, I have seen everything. *And of all things none is like the Buddha*. Again, there is absolutely nothing that can be likened to the Buddha.

Another praise goes like this:

> Amitabha Buddha's body is the color of gold.
> His hallmarks, attributes, and radiance have no equal.
> The white hair curl (urna) is like five Sumeru Mountains.
> His violet eyes are clear, pure, and as vast as the four great seas.
> The transformation Buddhas within his light are innumerable.
> The multitude of transformation Bodhisattvas are also boundless.
> His forty-eight vows take living beings across.
> With lotuses of nine grades he causes them all to reach the Other Shore.

---

30. This series of lectures was given in June-July 1969, right before the first moon landing of July 20, 1969.

Amitabha Buddha's body is the color of gold. The teaching-host of the Land of Ultimate Bliss in the West, Amitabha Buddha, has a body that is golden. *His hallmarks, attributes, and radiance have no equal.* His 32 Hallmarks, 80 Subsidiary Attributes, and his all-pervasive radiance are beyond compare. *The white hair curl (urna) is like five Sumeru Mountains.* How big is the white hair curl between Amitabha Buddha's eyebrows, which emits light? It is as big as five Sumeru Mountains. How big are Amitabha Buddha's eyes? *His violet eyes are clear, pure, and as vast as the four great seas.* His immaculate violet colored eyes are as large as the four great seas. If his eyes are so tremendous, just think how magnificent the Buddha's body must be!

The transformation Buddhas within his light are innumerable. Within Amitabha Buddha's light he has created by transformation so many Buddhas that they are measureless and boundless in number. *The multitude of transformation Bodhisattvas are also boundless.* He has also created by transformation many Bodhisattvas. He not only creates many transformation Buddhas, but also many Bodhisattvas. Not only Bodhisattvas, but Shravakas have also been created. He has not only created Shravakas, but he has also created Those Enlightened to Conditions and measureless and boundless living beings within the six paths of existence.

His forty-eight vows take living beings across. Amitabha Buddha has forty-eight vows with which he liberates all living beings. *With lotuses of nine grades he causes them all to reach the Other Shore.* The lotus flowers are divided up into nine grades. And each of these nine are further divided into nine grades as well. Therefore, nine times nine makes eighty-one grades in all. Each of these eighty-one grades of lotus flowers is able to lead living beings to the Other Shore of Nirvana. That is, they are reborn in the Land of Ultimate Bliss.

This is just a small example of praising the Tathagatas, which is the second practice of merit and virtue that one should cultivate.

In the Vajra Sutra it says, "The Tathagata: there is no place that he comes from, and also no place that he goes, therefore he is called Tathagata (literally: one who comes thus)." Tatha means "thus" or "suchness" and represents stillness. Gata means "to come" or "to return" and represents movement. One can say that the Tathagata seems to have come, yet his basic substance is unmoving. He is said to come, yet he has not come from anywhere. He is said to go, yet he doesn't go anywhere. "Thus" refers to noumenon and "Come" refers to phenomena. This is also the state of the non-obstruction of phenomena and noumenon mentioned in the Sutra.

This Sutra mentions four Dharma-realms: the Dharma-realm of phenomena, the Dharma-realm of noumenon, the Dharma-realm of the non-obstruction of noumenon and phenomena, and the Dharma-realm of the non-obstruction of phenomena and phenomena.

Tathagata represents the Dharma-realm of the non-obstruction of noumenon and phenomena, and it is also one of the ten titles of a Buddha.

The third is to extensively cultivate making offerings. "Extensively" literally means vastly and greatly. "Cultivate" means to put into practice. That is to extensively cultivate making offerings. There are many types of offerings of Dharma. One can use one's body to make offerings, or one may use one's mind to make offerings, or one may use both body and mind to make offerings.

What's meant by using one's own body to make offerings? An example of this is the two assemblies of followers who renounce the householder's life and become Bhikshus or Bhikshunis. In this way they use their own bodies to make an offering to the Buddhas. These people utilize their bodies to do Buddhist activities and cultivate the Buddha-dharma. Not only can one use one's own body to make offerings, one can also use one's mind. You use a sincere heart to cultivate the Buddha-dharma by bowing to the Buddhas and reciting the Sutras every day without ever forgetting. Further, one always likes to do things for Buddhism; one delights in practicing the Buddha-dharma. This is called offering with one's body and mind.

Another way in which one can offer with one's body and mind is as a householder. Although unable to become a monastic, one takes the time in one's busy daily life to bow to the Buddhas. One goes to the temple, lights incense, and bows in worship to the Buddha. If one doesn't have time to go to the temple, then in one's home, with utmost earnestness, one can light incense and bow to an image of the Buddha or visualize that one is worshipping the Buddha. Perhaps one must do this in one's home because the temple is far away or because of some other circumstances.

One can make offerings of incense, flowers, fruit, or new clothes, or one can light oil lamps or candles. Although there are many ways to make offerings, there are basically ten types of offerings. These in turn can expand into a hundred kinds, a thousand kinds, or even ten thousand kinds. When making offerings before one Buddha, we visualize that we are making offerings to all of the measureless and boundless numbers of Buddhas throughout the entire Dharma-realm. You might contemplate, "Before each Buddha, I manifest a body that makes offerings to every single one." Visualizing in this way is called making offerings in the entire Dharma-realm, which in turn creates merit and virtue that is equal to the entire Dharma-realm. One thus attains wisdom identical to the Dharma-realm. Then one has achieved the fruition and stature that is the same as the Dharma-realm. To extensively cultivate making offerings means that one expends all of one's energy to make offerings. One uses as much strength as one possesses to make offerings to the Three Jewels of the

Buddha, Dharma, and the Sangha. Samantabhadra Bodhisattva cultivates this, the third practice.

The fourth is to repent of karmic obstacles and reform. To repent is to feel remorse for past mistakes, that is the offenses one created in the past. To reform means to refrain from making transgressions in the future. To repent is to change one's past mistakes and to reform means to create no moral transgressions in the future. The process is to cut off evil that has already arisen and to prevent future evil from arising. Reform also means to further increase good that has already arisen and to cause good that has not yet arisen to be produced. One can also say that this is to cause good that has already arisen to continue unabated and to enable good that has not yet arisen to increase without cease. This is what to repent and reform means.

When we talk about karmic obstacles, there are three types of obstacles: karmic obstacles, retribution obstacles, and affliction obstacles. Repenting of karmic obstacles and reforming also includes repenting of and reforming retribution obstacles and affliction obstacles. There are many types of karma, but in general, there are three types, which are body, mouth, and mind. The karma created by the body includes killing, stealing, and sexual misconduct. Killing or taking life on a coarse level is murdering a large life-form. On a fine level it is exterminating a very subtle form of life like an ant, mosquito, or a fly. This is coarse and subtle killing. There is also killing in one's thoughts, which means that in your mind you have the thought of killing. Even though you have not actually committed the act of killing, yet you have already transgressed the moral precepts in your nature and that is considered a violation of the Bodhisattva Precepts. Following the criteria of the Bodhisattva precepts, the causes of killing, the supporting conditions of killing, the dharmas of killing, and the karma of killing are all violations of the moral precepts.

Stealing is the same way. For example, in large terms this would be to steal another person's country. In smaller terms it would be to steal one's citizens. In even more subtle terms this would be to steal a needle, a thread, a blade of grass or a piece of wood belonging to someone else. In general, to take someone else's property when it has not been given to you is stealing.

Sexual misconduct also has gross and subtle variations. The subtle violation extends to even having a thought of lust, thus making your own nature impure. The three karmas of killing, stealing, and sexual misconduct are like this.

There are three evils in thought. They are greed, hatred, and delusion. One creates bad karma with thoughts of greed, hatred, and delusion. There are four evils of the mouth. They are frivolous speech, false speech, harsh speech, and divisive speech. Therefore, there are various ways in which one creates karmic transgressions. Now we should resolve to repent and reform. We should vow not to make the same mistakes again, nor should we create new transgressions. This is called, "to repent of karmic obstacles and reform."

How do we repent and reform? Before the Buddha, one should be deeply sorry and distressed, feeling that in the past one has really made mistakes. One should shed tears in bitter sorrow before the Buddha, and while weeping, repent and vow to reform. If you sincerely repent and reform, your karmic obstacles will naturally be extinguished.

The fifth is to follow and rejoice in merit and virtue. To follow means to comply or go along with. To rejoice in means to take delight in. Merit is the merit that is created, and virtue is the virtue that one does. To follow and rejoice in can mean to have others follow and rejoice in the merit and virtue that you create, or you follow and rejoice in the merit and virtue of others. If you wish to repent of karmic obstacles and reform, then you must follow and rejoice in merit and virtue. That is, you should create various types of virtue. When you repent of karmic obstacles and reform, you may not be able to totally extinguish your karmic obstacles. Thus, you should create all kinds of merit and virtue. By doing this you are also repenting of karmic obstacles and reforming. Repenting of karmic obstacles is the same as following merit, and vice versa.

If they are the same, why have a separate fifth vow? The fourth vow is to solely practice repenting of karmic obstacles and reforming. Once you do that, you should also sincerely cultivate the fifth vow of following and rejoicing in merit and virtue. This includes doing good deeds. That is to say you follow goodness and refrain from creating offenses.

How does one follow and rejoice in good merit and virtue? It means you wish to do beneficial things for others. What does creating merit mean? It means to do more things for the public good. The Chinese character for merit (功) consists of the radical for work (工) with the character for effort (力) added to it. This means that you must exert some effort to create merit, to do things for the public good. At the present time, most of these activities that are done for the public good are undertaken by the government. In the past, governments were not involved in projects like repairing bridges and roads. One creates merit by doing things for the community at large. These deeds have lasting benefit and are visible to everybody. Each person can see who is responsible for doing these good things.

For example, let's say you have several buildings constructed for a school, and on the main entrance of each building there is a plaque with your name on it. This is creating merit. Virtue is that which is acquired in one's heart through practice. Doing good things that delight your heart is virtue. Unlike merit-making actions, these kinds of virtuous deeds may not be known by others.

There is apparent virtue and hidden virtue. When you create apparent virtue, it causes ordinary people to be very happy. It's very evident to them. Hidden virtue is doing things that benefit everyone, yet people are unaware of it. For example, last night I mentioned that if you had spiritual powers you could invisibly help all living beings, yet none of them would know about it.

This vow is to follow and rejoice in merit and virtue. You do good deeds that you want others to emulate. In this case, others follow and rejoice in your merit and virtue. When you are aware of other's good deeds, you should expend your effort to assist them in doing these deeds. This is to follow and rejoice in merit and virtue.

Ultimately this vow refers to following and rejoicing in the merit and virtue of all living beings in the Dharma-realm. You help them do all the good things that they like to do. This includes following and rejoicing in the merit and virtue of the Buddhas, the Bodhisattvas, the Shravakas, Those Enlightened to Conditions, and all living beings. What is following the Buddha's merit and virtue? For example, you lecture on the Sutras and speak the Dharma to teach and transform living beings. If you teach and promote the practice of the Six Perfections and myriad practices, that is following and rejoicing in the merit and virtue of the Bodhisattvas. If you teach people to cultivate the 12 Links of Conditioned Origination, that is to follow and rejoice in the merit and virtue of Those Enlightened to Conditions. If you enable everyone to know about the Dharma of the Four Noble Truths, then that is to follow and rejoice in the merit and virtue of the Shravakas. If any living being in the six paths of existence follows and rejoices in the merit and virtue of gods and humans, he will cultivate the five moral precepts and the ten good karmas. Therefore, in elucidating to follow and rejoice in merit and virtue there are infinite kinds. This is just a general explanation.

The sixth is to request the turning of the Wheel of Dharma. What is the "Wheel of Dharma"? Wheel, literally a circular wheel, is able to vanquish demons of the heavens and those of heterodox paths, and thereby enable the Proper Dharma to remain in the world for a long time.

After the Buddha became a Buddha, he made three turnings of the Dharma Wheel of the Four Noble Truths in order to rescue the first five Bhikshus. Turning the Wheel of Dharma means to speak the Dharma. If you request the Buddhas, Bodhisattvas, Shravakas, Those Enlightened to Conditions, Arhats or Dharma-masters to speak the Dharma, that is to request the turning of the Wheel of Dharma.

For example, every day before we lecture on the Sutras, two Dharma-masters or two lay-people come up and formally request the Dharma. This is to request the turning of the Wheel of Dharma, which is one of the practices of Samantabhadra Bodhisattva. What good comes from requesting the turning of the Wheel of Dharma? If there is a person who turns the Wheel of Dharma in our world, then the demon-kings will not dare to manifest in our world. If no one turns the Wheel of Dharma, then the demon-kings will openly appear in the world.

When the Wheel of Dharma is turned because of your request, you have generated merit and virtue. This also includes to follow and rejoice in merit and virtue. By your requesting Dharma, you will enable your wisdom to unfold. This is due to the fact that by requesting a Dharma-master to speak the Dharma for the people, you are benefiting everyone. Therefore, these ten great vows are interrelated. For example, if one wishes to repent of karmic obstructions and reform, then one should follow and rejoice in merit and virtue. If you follow and rejoice in merit and virtue, you should request the turning of the Wheel of Dharma.

Turning the Wheel of Dharma is not only lecturing the Dharma and Sutras, it includes all the activities that you do for Buddhism. For example, now in this lecture hall, you see people printing the lectures. That is turning the Wheel of Dharma. Transcribing the lectures is also turning the Wheel of Dharma. Now you are tape recording the lectures, translating them, and taking notes as well. Each of these activities is turning the Wheel of Dharma. By taking notes you will remember them more clearly. Then in the future, you will be able to explain them for others. By doing this you are preparing to turn the Wheel of Dharma. When we read the Sutras, recite the Sutras, or bow to the Sutras, we are turning the Wheel of Dharma. Therefore, turning the Wheel of Dharma does not merely refer to one type of activity.

Again, turning the Wheel of Dharma includes anything that you do in Buddhism that benefits others. Even the written Chinese verses in front of us are turning the Great Wheel of Dharma. Whether it is lecturing the Sutras every evening or our daily meditation sits, everything we do here is turning the Wheel of Dharma. If you understand this, then it is requesting that the Wheel of Dharma be turned. What if you don't realize this? Then when you do this work you feel it's too wearisome, strenuous, and difficult. This is being afraid to turn the Wheel of Dharma.

The seventh is to beseech the Buddhas to remain in the world. The Buddha comes into the world, dwells in the world, and then wishes to enter Parinirvana. When the Buddha is in the world it is just like having the sun whose light shines upon the entire earth. But when the Buddha enters Parinirvana, the world becomes enveloped in darkness. Therefore, Samantabhadra Bodhisattva makes a great vow to "beseech the Buddhas to remain in the world." This means you request the Buddha to not enter

Parinirvana, but to always dwell in the world. Because the Buddha fulfills the wishes of living beings, if all living beings beseech the Buddha to remain in the world, then he will not enter Parinirvana. What will happen if you don't beseech him to remain in the world? When he is finished teaching and transforming all the beings that should be taught by him, he will enter Parinirvana. Therefore, we should beseech the Buddhas to remain in the world.

The eighth is to always follow and learn from the Buddhas. This is to emulate and follow the Buddha and learn the Buddha-dharmas at all times. We should not fear learning Buddha-dharmas, even though they are numerous. The more you learn, the more wisdom you will have. For example, why did the Venerable Ananda have such an exceptional memory? It is said, "Buddha-dharmas as great as the waters of the ocean flowed into Ananda's mind." Buddha-dharmas are analogous to the waters of the vast ocean. All were able to enter into the mind of Ananda. Venerable Ananda in life after life had focused on erudition, and consequently, his memory-power was superb. Within "to always follow and learn from the Buddhas" is the implication that you do not become negligent, lax, or muddled. Rather you "diligently cultivate moral precepts, samadhi-concentration, and wisdom and extinguish greed, hatred and delusion." You energetically cultivate morality, concentration, and wisdom. And you eliminate the three poisons, which are thoughts of greed, hatred, and delusion. If you are able to do this, then you are always following and learning from the Buddhas.

The ninth is to constantly conform with living beings. "Constantly" means constant and unchanging. "Conform" means to follow or accord with. That is to conform to the conditions and states of living beings. Living beings are totally confused and topsy-turvy. Does this mean that you should always conform with living beings' confusion? Living beings are basically quite ignorant. Should you go down the same road of delusion? To always conform with living beings means that you follow the same mannerisms as them in order to rescue them while "going against the flow." What does this mean? Living beings are totally confused. Their confusion is analogous to water flowing to the east, and you steer your ship so it's going west. That is called "going against the flow."

If you merely go along with living beings, you cannot become a Buddha. If you wish to become a Buddha, you cannot follow living beings. So why does Samantabhadra Bodhisattva want to "constantly conform with living beings?" As was just explained above, he wants to go against the flow to bring living beings into conformity. That is to go against the flow to rescue them. This is to say, "Going against the flow of the six-sense objects of worldly people and entering the flow of the Dharma-nature of the sages." This is to always conform with living beings. On the other hand, if you go along with living beings in an improper way, then when they want to create bad karma, you will go along with them and create bad karma too. If you, as a Bodhisattva, constantly conform with living beings in an improper way, then when they create bad karma, you go along and create transgressions. Living beings give rise to delusion and then create bad karma. They create bad karma and then have to undergo the retribution. So does this mean that you also generate delusion, create bad karma, and undergo the retribution? Wouldn't this be the same as a living being? If you do this, you will have changed to become a common living being.

To make it clear, to constantly conform with living beings means that you never become weary or annoyed with conforming with living beings in order to teach and transform them. You wish to cause living beings to "turn away from ignorance and return to enlightenment." Thus they can leave the path of delusion and become enlightened. To always conform with living beings is the paramita of vigor. The paramita of vigor means that you never become fed up with living beings who create offenses, regardless of how great their offenses are. You do not say, "Oh! You living beings have created so many karmic offenses! I'm not going to rescue you! Just go ahead and fall into the hells!" The Bodhisattva never has this kind of thought. Even though living beings create karmic offenses, Bodhisattvas have a heart of loving-kindness, compassion, rejoicing, and equanimity. With these they rescue living beings. This is the paramita of true vigor.

When Shakyamuni Buddha was on the stage of creating the causes for becoming a Buddha, he was practicing the paramitas of giving and vigor. Once while cultivating the spiritual path in the mountains, it snowed for many days, so the entire mountain was blanketed in snow. A mother tiger with cubs went searching for something to eat, but was unable to find anything. Both the mother and her cubs were on the verge of starvation. They were so weak that they were unable to walk. Then Shakyamuni Buddha thought, "I'll give my body to the tigers. After they eat my flesh, I vow that they will bring forth the Bodhi-mind and realize the unsurpassed path." Then he covered his head with his clothes and threw himself off the mountain so he landed right next to the tigers. Thus he sacrificed his body for the tigers. This is an example of the way Shakyamuni Buddha complied with living beings and practiced the paramitas of giving and vigor.

Constantly conforming with living beings requires that we rescue them. We shouldn't think, "Samantabhadra Bodhisattva says we must constantly conform with living beings. Some of them ingest disorienting drugs. I should join them and take some of these confusing drugs. Some drink alcohol. I should conform with them and have some wine. Others engage in befuddled conduct. I will go along and engage in the same behavior." This is not what is meant by conforming with living beings. Rather it means to pull them out of the mud, thereby enabling them to conform with you in practicing the spiritual path. Don't misconstrue that conforming with living beings means that you run off and do what they do. Otherwise, running hither and thither, you will lose your own home and no longer recognize your own hometown.

In Chinese this vow is literally to constantly conform with living beings, but when translating it into English you should change it to always or constantly have living beings conform with you. This is changing the order of the Chinese words. My way of explaining this as "living beings conforming with you" is most consonant with the Dharma.

The tenth is to transfer all merit and virtue. "All"[31] means that one transfers the merit and virtue from every activity that one does. Who do you transfer it to? To all Buddhas. All the merit and virtue that I create during the day is transferred to all Buddhas. Therefore, there's a verse that says,

> *I wish that this merit and virtue will beautify the Buddhas' Pure Lands*
> *Repaying four types of kindness from above,*
> *and rescuing those in the three paths of suffering below.*
> *May those who see or hear this*
> *immediately bring forth the Bodhi-mind.*
> *When this body born of retribution passes on,*
> *We will be born together in the Land of Ultimate Bliss.*

---

31. "All" is actually a translation of the two Chinese characters, 普皆. The Venerable Master literally said the following in his commentary: "The character '普 pu' in Chinese means to pervade everywhere. '皆 Jie' means completely or thoroughly. This means that one transfers the merit from every activity that one does."

This verse is an example of transferring one's merit. Transference[32] has two aspects. One is to return, and the other means to go out. You must return back before you can go out. Where do you return to? You transfer all of your merit. I want to take everything that I have done and transfer the merit from being a common person to becoming an Enlightened Sage. That is, as a living being we transfer to all Buddhas. This is transference. Therefore, a common person transfers to become a Sage and living beings transfer to the Buddhas. One transfers from phenomena to noumenon. And one transfers from the Small Vehicle to the Great Vehicle. All of these are forms of transferring merit.

One transfers from oneself to others. What does this mean? Let's say I have a friend. I transfer all of the merit and virtue that I have created to him and enable him to bring forth the Bodhi-mind, so that he realizes the unsurpassed path. One transfers from phenomena to the noumenon. Although the things I do are visible, the noumenon of transference is invisible. I wish to take the visible merit and virtue I create and transfer it to the infinite, inexhaustible Dharma-realm. From the small, one transfers to the great. Now I follow the Theravada, the Small Vehicle. However, instead of practicing the Dharmas of the Theravada, I cultivate the Dharmas of the Mahayana, the Great Vehicle.

Previously I recited several lines of a verse of transference, which I will now explain. For example, today I've finished lecturing the Sutra. Lecturing Sutras is a way of giving Dharma. Indeed, it is the most supreme form of giving. It is even greater than the merit and virtue from giving the seven precious things to all the living beings in a three-thousand great-thousand world system. Although the merit from lecturing Sutras is so tremendous, I do not want it for myself. Why? *I wish that this merit*

---

32. In Chinese transference is "hui xiang 迴向." "Hui 迴" means to return. "Xiang 向" means to go towards.

and virtue, from lecturing the Sutras and Dharma, turning the wheel of the magnificent Dharma, *will beautify the Buddhas' Pure Lands.* I use this merit to adorn and beautify all the Pure Lands of the Buddhas of the ten directions of space. *Repaying four types of kindness from above...* I repay the various types of kindness bestowed upon me by heaven, the earth, the ruler of the country, and my father and mother, as well as that of my teachers and elders. *And rescuing those in the three paths of suffering below.* I rescue those undergoing suffering and torment in the three paths of the hells, the hungry ghosts, and animals. *May those who see or hear this...* If anyone sees me lecturing the Sutras or hears this Dharma, may they immediately *bring forth the Bodhi-mind.* May everyone quickly bring forth the Bodhi-mind and follow the path of enlightenment. *When this body born of retribution passes on...* The body that we have now is a body born from retribution. After we no longer have these bodies, *we will be born together in the Land of Ultimate Bliss.* Together we will all be reborn in the Land of Ultimate Bliss.

Sudhana said, "Great Sage! What is the meaning of 'to worship all Buddhas' up to and including 'to transfer all merit and virtue?'" The youth Sudhana heard Samantabhadra Bodhisattva make these ten great vows. Although he already understood them, he was afraid that all of us living beings would still not comprehend these ten magnificent vows. Therefore, the youth Sudhana intentionally asked, "What do you mean by worshipping all Buddhas? What do you mean by praising the Tathagatas? What is it to extensively cultivate making offerings? How does one repent of karmic obstacles and reform? How does one follow and rejoice in merit and virtue? How does one request the turning of the Wheel of Dharma? What does one do to beseech the Buddhas to remain in the world? What does one do to always follow and learn from the Buddhas? How does one constantly conform with living beings? What does it mean to transfer all merit and virtue?"

To Worship All Buddhas

SUTRA:

Samantabhadra told Sudhana, "Good man, to worship all Buddhas is explained like this. There are Buddhas, World Honored Ones, in the ten directions and the three periods of time, to the exhaustion of the dharma-realm and the reaches of space, that are as numerous as the smallest atomic particles in all Buddha kshetra-lands. Because of the power of Samantabhadra's practices and vows, I have a profound mind of faith in and understanding of them as if they were right before my eyes. With pure karma in body, speech, and thought, I always worship them."

COMMENTARY:

Samantabhadra Bodhisattva said to the youth Sudhana, **Good man**. You are a good man who cultivates the spiritual path. "You have asked, "What is the meaning of to worship all Buddhas?"" " Now I'll explain this for you." **To worship all Buddhas is explained like this. There are Buddhas, World Honored Ones, in the ten directions and the three periods of time, to the exhaustion of the dharma-realm.** "To the exhaustion" literally means to reach the point that it no longer exists. However, the dharma-realm can never not exist. **And the reaches of space.** Space also can never not exist. This means exhausting the reaches of space and pervading throughout the dharma-realm. The ten directions include north, south, east and west, northeast, northwest, southeast and southwest, and above and below. The three periods of time are the past, present and future. **Are as numerous as the smallest atomic particles.** Smallest atomic particles are literally the "most minute particles." **In all Buddha kshetra-lands** refers to all of the worlds or lands of the Buddhas. There are so many Buddhas, World Honored Ones, in the ten directions and the three periods of time, throughout the dharma-realm and the reaches of space that they are as numerous as atomic particles.

Because of the power of Samantabhadra's practices and vows. I practice the conduct of Samantabhadra Bodhisattva. His practice is so great that it exhausts the dharma-realm and the reaches of space. Because I rely on the practices and vows cultivated by Samantabhadra Bodhisattva, **I have a profound mind of faith in and understanding of** all Buddhas, **as if they were right before my eyes.** When bowing in worship to the Buddhas, you should make the following contemplation in your mind: "I am in front of the Buddha. The Buddha is right before my eyes."

There is a verse that you should know when you are bowing to the Buddha. This verse is normally used as a reflection when one is performing the Great Compassion Repentance. It says,

> *The worshipper and worshipped are by nature empty and still.*
> *The path of the response invoked is difficult to conceive.*
> *This Bodhimanda[33] is like the pearl of the Heavenly Lord.*
> *Shakyamuni Tathagata's image appears within it.*
> *My body appears right before Shakyamuni Buddha.*
> *I bow my head at his feet and submit my life in worship.*

The worshipper and worshipped are by nature empty and still. The person who is bowing to the Buddha is the "worshipper." The Buddha that we are bowing to is the "worshipped." Whether we are referring to our self or to the one that we are bowing to, both are empty and still in their basic nature. Within this emptiness there is a kind of force or power that can respond when invoked. Therefore, the verse continues, *The path of*

---

33. Literally means a "place of Enlightenment," which usually refers to a Buddhist monastery or temple. It can also refer to the place in the vicinity of the Bodhi Tree where the Buddha first became a fully Enlightened Buddha.

the response invoked is difficult to conceive. This path is inconceivable. Although ultimately the Buddha and you are empty, when you bow to the Buddha a response is invoked in the path between the two of you. This kind of situation cannot even be imagined. It's difficult to conceive of. "The path of words is severed." You wish to speak about it, but you're at a loss for words. "The activities of the mind are extinguished." Your mind wishes to think about what this experience is all about, but it cannot do so. *This Bodhimanda is like the pearl of the Heavenly Lord.* This Bodhimanda is like the pearl that sits before the Heavenly Lord. What is the function of this pearl? All images of the world appear within this pearl. *Shakyamuni Tathagata's image appears within it.* Shakyamuni Buddha's body appears within the reflected light of the pearl. *My body appears right before Shakyamuni Buddha.* My body manifests an image that appears before Shakyamuni Buddha. *I bow my head at his feet and submit my life in worship.* Before the Buddha, I make a five-point prostration (head, two arms and two legs) and wholeheartedly bow to the Buddha. You should have this kind of intention when you bow. This is what is meant by the Sutra's words, "I have a profound mind of faith in and understanding of them as if they were right before my eyes." When you bow, you imagine that the Buddha is before you and that you are in front of him. You appear before each other.

Confucius said, "Sacrifice as if they are present. Sacrifice to the spirits as if the spirits are present."[34] This means when I sacrifice on behalf of the dead, it's as if they are actually present. You perform the sacrificial rites on behalf of the deceased ones as if they are present. So Confucius also said, "As if they are above you."[35] When you worship and sacrifice on behalf of the spirits, they are right above you. He also said, "As if they

---

34. *Analects, Book III,* Chapter 12, Section 1
35. *Doctrine of the Mean,* Chapter 16, Section 3

are on the left and right."[36] It's also as if they are to your left and right. "As if" implies that you imagine that they are right above you and to your left and right. When you bow to the Buddha, it is the same way. It's as if he is above you or to the left and right. If the Buddha is right in front of you, you will certainly be extremely reverent when you worship him and won't be too casual. For example, when you see a person, you make a gesture of respect. If the person is not present, you will be more casual.

With pure karma in body, speech, and thought. This means to be completely pure. You cannot commit any of the ten evil karmas, and then bow to the Buddha. You must have pure karma in body, speech, and thought when you do this. Previously I explained that there are three evil karmas performed by the body. They are killing, stealing, and sexual misconduct. You can't take the life of a living creature, and then say "Oh! I've done something wrong by killing. I'll just bow to the Buddha to repent of my offense." However, you don't bow to the Buddha when you haven't killed. You only bow to the Buddha when both of your hands are completely smeared with blood. That's having impure karma of the body. Nor can you go someplace where a person has something of great value and steal it, and then afterwards think, "Oh! My stealing is a violation of the moral precepts. I must quickly go before the Buddha and bow in repentance." This, also, is not having pure karma. Whether you are a man or a woman, if you engage in all sorts of improper sexual behavior, and then think, "Oh! I've done so many bad things. I should quickly bow and seek repentance before the Buddha." This is having impure karma when bowing to the Buddha. If you want to have an efficacious response from your bowing, you must refrain from killing, stealing, and sexual misconduct.

---

36. *Doctrine of the Mean*, Chapter 16, Section 3

There are three evil karmas in the mind. They are greed, anger, and delusion. I frequently talk about greed. Why are people always busy and in a hurry, never resting from morning until night? It's just because of greed. Greedy intentions control you, so that you never have a single moment of respite. When you are unable to attain what you want, then you get upset and afflicted. Why are you so afflicted? It's an indication of your own foolishness. You're so deluded, that you get all upset. People with wisdom never get afflicted, regardless of what situation they encounter.

How deluded and foolish do people become? It's quite laughable and pathetic. It's like a person who has never studied. He's never attended elementary school, high school, or college. He sees that a person who has acquired a Ph.D. has much honor and glory. People address him with the title "doctor." Then the person, who has never studied, also wants a Ph.D. Who would award a Ph.D. to someone who has never studied in school at all? It's impossible. It is also like a person who has never learned the Buddha-dharma or listened to lectures on the Sutras. He hears that becoming a Buddha is the most exalted state, and thus expects to become a Buddha. Isn't this foolish? Or one does not have any accumulated wealth, yet wants to make money by doing business. If you don't have any capital, how can you have a business and make money? Another situation is the most laughable. A person has not bought a lottery ticket, yet he expects to win the grand prize. This is ridiculous and impossible!

Still another foolish way of looking at things is expressed in the following verse:

> *May the flowers ever be beautiful each day.*
> *And why can't the radiant moon be full each night.*
> *May the waters of the earth become wine,*
> *And money grow on all the trees of the forests.*

A person loves flowers the most. He wishes that flowers remain beautiful forever, and never wilt. Isn't that just wishful thinking? Another person thinks, "It's best when the moon is full. Why must the moon wane? It should be bright and shining every night." A person who likes to drink wine wishes that wherever there is water it will change and become wine. Whenever he wants a drink, he can conveniently drink some wine. He thinks that would be the greatest. However, this is something that can never come about. Another one who is greedy for wealth thinks, "Oh! All the trees in the forest should transform into money-trees. Then whenever I need some cash, I can go and pick some money from the trees. That would be terrific!" Again, this is impossible.

May the flowers ever be beautiful each day. The first person who wishes the flowers to ever remain beautiful, wants beautiful things to stay the same forever. The others want wine and money to be freely available everywhere. *And why can't the radiant moon be full each night.* Amongst the four vices of wine, lust, avarice, and temper, this belongs to "temper." Although he wants the moon to be full each night, this is not possible. Therefore, he becomes displeased. Being displeased is related to the vice of temper. Thus these lines of the verse represent the desires for sex, alcoholic drink, wealth, and anger. If one were not so foolish and deluded, one would not have so many afflictions.

We can create many types of bad karma with our mouth. There is frivolous speech, which means we say improper things. For example, men talk about women and women talk about men. They say things that haven't the least bit of usefulness or goodness. This is speaking in a debased manner. There is false speech in which one tells lies. An example of a major lie would be when you murder a person, and then when asked, "Did you murder this person?" You say, "I didn't murder him. It wasn't me." There are also average lies and minor lies. There is harsh speech, which refers to cruel and evil speech. People don't want to even hear such talk. The last one is divisive speech, wherein someone uses double-tongued speech to create conflict between people.

All of the above are karmic obstructions. If you have any of these faults, then your karma in body, speech, and thought is impure. When bowing to the Buddhas, you want your karma in body, speech, and thought to be pure.

I always worship them. Always means that you constantly cultivate pure body, speech, and thought karma while worshipping the Buddha. Just now I explained how killing, stealing, and sexual misconduct are impure. Although these are impure, if you bow to the Buddha with the wish to change these faults and start anew, it is much better than not bowing at all. However, this cannot be called bowing to the Buddha with pure karma in body, speech, and thought. When you worship the Buddha, you want the three karmas of body, speech, and thought to always be pure.

SUTRA:

In each and every place where there are Buddhas, I manifest ineffably ineffable number of bodies as numerous as the smallest atomic particles in a Buddha kshetra-land.

COMMENTARY:

One worships and reveres the Buddha, **in each and every place where there are Buddhas.** The Buddhas are measureless and boundless, and in our minds we imagine manifesting our own measureless and boundless number of bodies to worship them everywhere. **I manifest ineffably ineffable number of bodies as numerous as the smallest atomic particles in a Buddha kshetra-land.** The bodies we manifest are so numerous one could never finish describing them. "As numerous as the smallest atomic particles in a Buddha kshetra-land." The number of bodies is like the smallest atomic particles in a Buddha land. The Buddha-dharma has inconceivable states like this. If you produce a mind that totally fills up the dharma-realm, then you will have so much merit and virtue it will also pervade the dharma-realm.

Take Sudhana's experience with Maitreya Bodhisattva as an example. When he started his quest he first bowed to Manjushri Bodhisattva as his teacher. Then Manjushri Bodhisattva told him to go south to pay respect in over 100 locations and he encountered 53 good teachers in succession. When he found Maitreya Bodhisattva, he saw his dwelling with its towers adorned with the seven precious things. These towers were infinitely multi-layered. That is, each tower had towers inside it, and each of these towers in turn had towers within each one of them. The towers went on in this way ad infinitum, so that it was not known how many towers there were altogether. In each of these many towers was a Maitreya Bodhisattva proclaiming the Dharma. The youth Sudhana saw numberless Maitreya Bodhisattvas, but he also saw that there were just as many manifestations of himself bowing to the Maitreya Bodhisattvas in each of these places. Like the towers, there was layer upon layer without end, so it could not be known how many there were.

Therefore, as I now explain The *Flower Adornment Sutra*, you should also cultivate this kind of "contemplation of the dharma-realm." For example, even though you are practicing bowing to the *Dharma Flower Sutra*, here in the Buddhist Lecture Hall, you should contemplate that you are in front of all the Buddhas of the ten directions as numerous as smallest atomic particles, so that before each Buddha, you are bowing to the *Dharma Flower Sutra*. You should produce this kind of infinite and inexhaustible mind. Because "everything is only made from the mind," if the scope of your mind fills up the entire dharma-realm, and you manifest bodies to bow to that many Buddhas, then all of these Buddhas will accept your bows.

SUTRA:

Every single body worships all Buddhas everywhere, who are as numerous as the smallest atomic particles in ineffably ineffable numbers of Buddha kshetra-lands.

COMMENTARY:

Each of your bodies everywhere worships Buddhas like particles in ineffably ineffable Buddha-lands. Although you have not yet become a Buddha, you imagine that you are able to manifest a body like this before each Buddha to worship all Buddhas everywhere.

There are not a lot of people attending our Summer Study Session,[37] but some of you are quite sincere and sit in meditation very well. In cultivating the path, if we have a lot of people this is good and if we have few people it is even better. One person is not too few, and ten thousand people are not too many. Why? Cultivating the spiritual path means that one cultivates one's own path. No one can represent you in cultivation, nor can you cultivate on behalf of someone else. Therefore, there is a saying, "I eat my fill myself. I end my own birth and death as well."

Ananda felt that because the Buddha was his older cousin, he did not need to cultivate the spiritual path, and thus he did not develop samadhi-power. What was the consequence of this? All the other Arhats cultivated and became enlightened sages, whereas Ananda was stuck at the position of a sage of the first fruition or level of enlightenment (Stream-Enterer).

---

37. This chapter was lectured during the first six-week session of the 1969 summer session at the Buddhist Lecture Hall in San Francisco.

Today some people told me that their hands or legs sometimes shake involuntarily. They asked, "What's the reason behind this?" This is a stage that one ought to go through when sitting in meditation. Someone else asked, "Why haven't I had this experience?" It's because your skill is still not adequate, or you have already gone through this state in the past. Your hands or legs can move by themselves and sometimes your eyes involuntarily open and close over and over again, and you don't understand why. You don't want to open and shut them, yet they do so on their own. This might seem very unusual to you. When this happens some people might ask, "Am I possessed by a demon? Has the demon-king come to make my body shake like this?" Others might ask, "Am I sick?" Or some people might be so frightened that they think they are on the verge of insanity.

You need not react in this way. This is merely the workings of your *qi* (energy) and your blood. Because in the past you had not worked hard at cultivation, so your blood and *qi* did not flow freely. However, now you are making an effort to practice, so your blood and *qi* are trying to penetrate through the areas that were previously blocked. When they reach these blockages, you may shake or twitch. Normally your arm or leg will twitch 36 times in accord with the body's 36 joints. This is also analogous to the six kinds quaking. If your house (your body) shakes, don't be afraid, because this is just the way the blood and qi function.

SUTRA:

When the reaches of space come to an end, my worship will also come to an end. However, the reaches of space can never come to an end, therefore my worship has no end. In the same way, when the realms of living beings come to an end, when the karma of living beings comes to an end, and when the afflictions of living beings come to an end, my worship will also end. Since the realms of living beings up to and

including their afflictions have no end, my worship has no end. It continues in thought after thought without cease. I never tire of this karma in body, speech, and thought.

COMMENTARY:

When the reaches of space come to an end, my worship will also come to an end. What is empty space?[38] Empty means unreal. Space means non-existent. When does space exist? You don't know. Is there any time that it ends? No. Space has no beginning or end—it is beginningless and infinite. When did space begin? Never. When will it no longer exist? Never. The Sutra says that when the reaches of space no longer exist, my worship will also come to an end. My worship of the Buddhas of the ten directions will no longer exist when space is exhausted. However, it is impossible for space to not exist, therefore my worship will never end. I continuously worship all Buddhas. Therefore, the Sutra says, **However, the reaches of space can never come to an end, therefore my worship has no end.** This worship is infinite and inexhaustible. Exhausting the boundaries of future time, I will worship all Buddhas.

In the same way, when the realms of living beings come to an end. I worship all Buddhas in the same way until the realms of living beings no longer exist. **When the karma of living beings comes to an end,** that is, when the karma of living beings ceases, **and when the afflictions of living beings come to an end, my worship will also end.** When these three things, the realms of living beings as well as their karma and afflictions come to an end, my worship will end.

Since the realms of living beings up to and including their afflictions have no end. There is no time when the realm of living beings can end.

---

38. Space actually consists of the two Chinese characters, 虛空, which literally mean "empty space."

This is also the case for the karma of living beings and their afflictions. **Up to and including their afflictions have no end.** The afflictions of living beings are generated by ignorance. Their karma is created by afflictions. And living beings themselves are created by the force of karma. The realm of living beings, their karma, and their afflictions can never cease; they can never come to an end. **My worship has no end.** Therefore, the power of my vow to worship all Buddhas also is without end.

It continues in thought after thought without cease. My sincere thought to worship and revere all Buddhas is continuous. Each thought connects with the next in succession, one after another. They are continuous and unceasing. **I never tire of this karma in body, speech, and thought.** My body, mouth, and mind never become weary. My body and mind will never become tired. With pure karma in body, speech, and thought, I worship the Buddhas forever without end.

To Praise the Tathagatas

SUTRA:

Moreover, good man, to praise the Tathagatas is explained like this. In each of the smallest atomic particles in all the kshetra-lands in the ten directions and three periods of time, to the exhaustion of the dharma-realm and the reaches of space, there are Buddhas as numerous as the smallest atomic particles in all worlds. In each and every place where there are Buddhas, a vast ocean-wide assembly of Bodhisattvas surrounds them. Using a profound and supreme understanding, I should manifest knowledge and vision.

Each body has an eloquence that surpasses the subtle and wondrous tongue of Sarasvatī, the Goddess of Eloquence. Each tongue puts forth an inexhaustible ocean of sounds. From each sound comes an ocean of all words, which praise and exalt the ocean of all the merit and virtue of all the Tathagatas. To the ends of the boundaries of the future, these praises are continuous and unceasing. To the ends of the dharma-realm, there is no place they do not pervade.

In this way, when the reaches of space, the realms of living beings, the karma of living beings, and the afflictions of living beings come to an end, my praise will also end. However, because the reaches of space up to and including afflictions have no end, therefore this praise of mine is without end. It continues in thought after thought without cease. I never tire of this karma in body, speech, and thought.

COMMENTARY:

Moreover means "let me repeat this." He said, **Good man**. The Bodhisattva, Samantabhadra said, "You are a good man who cultivates the five moral precepts and the ten good karmas, as well as the esoteric practices of the Bodhisattvas." He spoke like this because although the youth Sudhana did appear in the body of a virgin youth, in reality he was a great Bodhisattva. Therefore, the Bodhisattva, Samantabhadra said, "Good man." **To praise the Tathagatas is explained like this.** In speaking about this vow, what does it mean 'to praise the Tathagatas'? I will now explain this for you. **In each of the smallest atomic particles in all the kshetra-lands in the ten directions and three periods of time, to the exhaustion of the dharma-realm and the reaches of space.** The dharma-realm includes the dharma-realm of all Buddhas, the dharma-realm of Bodhisattvas, the dharma-realm of Shravakas, the dharma-realm of Those Enlightened to Conditions, the dharma-realm of gods, the dharma-realm of asuras, the dharma-realm of humans, the dharma-realm of animals, the dharma-realm of hungry ghosts, and the dharma-realm of hell-beings. These make up the ten dharma-realms. And the ten dharma-realms do not go beyond the single thought of the human mind that appears right now. A single thought is replete with the ten dharma-realms, and the ten dharma-realms in turn include measureless dharma-realms. Therefore, there are measureless and boundless dharma-realms.

"And the reaches of space." This includes the reaches of space. "In all the kshetra lands" means in in all Buddha-lands. **There are Buddhas as numerous as the smallest atomic particles in all worlds**. That is, in each atomic particle in all Buddha-lands, there are Buddhas as numerous as the smallest atomic particles. **In each and every place where there are Buddhas, a vast ocean-wide assembly of Bodhisattvas surrounds them**. There are measureless, uncountable, and boundlessly many great Bodhisattvas in that place. The text says "ocean-wide assembly" to represent the fact that the Bodhisattvas are so numerous that they resemble the vast ocean. They come together and surround each Buddha. **Using a profound and supreme understanding, I should manifest**

knowledge and vision. Samantabhadra Bodhisattva says, "I should, by means of this most profound and most supreme understanding that I have cultivated, manifest knowledge and vision." Knowledge refers to wisdom and vision refers to the "seeing nature."

Each body has an eloquence that surpasses the subtle and wondrous tongue of Sarasvatī, the Goddess of Eloquence. Before each one I speak with an eloquence that surpasses all people as well as the subtle and wonderful tongue of the Goddess of Eloquence. This goddess has the most exceptional ability to speak, debate, and make subtle distinctions. Yet Samantabhadra Bodhisattva exceeds the unobstructed eloquence of this goddess, Sarasvatī.

There are four kinds of unobstructed eloquence. The first is the unobstructed eloquence in phrasing. This means that one's words and speech are without any limitation or impediment and that one is skilled in debating. The second is the unobstructed eloquence in the Dharma. When one lectures the Dharma:

> From one Dharma measureless numbers of Dharmas are produced,
> And measureless numbers of Dharmas return to one Dharma.

The third is the unobstructed eloquence of meaning. The meanings or principles expressed are such that within a single meaning one explains measureless meanings. And then these measureless meanings return to a single meaning. The fourth is the unobstructed eloquence in delight in speaking. One delights in speaking the Dharma. One never grows weary of speaking, but always delights in speaking the Buddha-dharma. "A subtle and wonderful tongue" refers to a person who is a most capable speaker. Everyone believes and enjoys hearing whatever he or she says. If your tongue is not skilled, then no one will believe or want to listen to you when you speak.

Each tongue puts forth an inexhaustible ocean of sounds. With these subtle and wonderful tongues one speaks an ocean of measureless, boundless, and inexhaustible subtle and wonderful sounds. **From each sound** comes praises of the Tathagatas. **Comes an ocean of all words** means that there is profusion of speech, which is nonetheless delightful to hear. **Which praise and exalt...** From the midst of these numerous sounds and words, they all praise and exalt the Tathagatas. **The ocean of all the merit and virtue of all the Tathagatas** refers to the Tathagatas of the ten directions and the three periods of time. They praise the Buddhas with their ocean of various kinds of merit and virtue. **To the ends of the boundaries of future** means that at the time when one reaches the end of the boundaries of the future, **these praises are continuous and unceasing.** Their praise of the Tathagatas is never cut off. **To the ends of the dharma-realm, there is no place they do not pervade.** There is no place in the entire dharma-realm where these sounds do not pervade. Within everyplace in the dharma-realm, there are these kinds of sounds that praise the Tathagatas.

In this way, when the reaches of space... In this way one praises the Tathagatas even if the reaches of space come to an end. If **the realms of living beings, the karma of living beings, and the afflictions of living beings come to an end, my praise will also end.** My praising will come to an end. However, if it is the case that the reaches of space never come to an end, the dharma-realm never ends, the realms of living beings never end, the karma of living beings cannot end, the afflictions of living beings cannot end, therefore my sounds of praise for the Tathagatas will never end. **However, because the reaches of space up to and including the afflictions have no end,** because none of these come to an end, **therefore, this praise of mine is without end.** There is no time in which my praising will be finished. **It continues in thought after thought without cease.** In the midst of each and every thought, it continues in succession without ever being cut off. **I never tire of this karma in body, speech, and thought**. With body, mouth, and thought, I always praise the Tathagatas without ever becoming tired.

To Extensively Cultivate
Making Offerings

▼

SUTRA:

Moreover, Good Man, to extensively cultivate making offerings is explained like this. In each of the smallest atomic particles in all the Buddha kshetra-lands in the ten directions and three periods of time, to the exhaustion of the dharma-realm and the reaches of space, there are Buddhas as numerous as the smallest atomic particles in all worlds. In each and every place where there are Buddhas, an ocean-wide assembly of various kinds of Bodhisattvas surrounds them. Due to the power of Samantabhadra's practice and vows, I give rise to deep faith and understanding and manifest knowledge and vision. I make offerings of superb and wonderful gifts to all of them. That is to say, I make offerings of clouds of flowers, clouds of garlands, clouds of celestial music, clouds of heavenly canopies, clouds of heavenly clothing as well as all varieties of heavenly incense, including incense paste, burning incense, powdered incense, and other clouds of gifts such as these. Each offering is the size of Mount Sumeru, the king of mountains.

COMMENTARY:

Moreover... Why does the Bodhisattva say, moreover? He has discussed the first two vows, to worship all Buddhas, and to praise the Tathagatas, and now he will explain another vow to extensively cultivate making offerings. "Moreover" indicates the beginning of the next vow, setting it apart from the previous sections.

Good Man. Samantabhadra Bodhisattva again calls out, "Good Man." This refers to the youth Sudhana. **To extensively cultivate making offerings is explained like this.**

Now we will explain the Dharma-door of making offerings. What does it mean to extensively make offerings? You should now listen attentively, and I will explain this for you.

In each of the smallest atomic particles in all the Buddha kshetra-lands in the ten directions and three periods of time, to the exhaustion of the dharma-realm and the reaches of space. "In all" includes everything; it includes the dharma-realm and the reaches of space. "To the exhaustion of the dharma-realm" means reaching to the end of the dharma-realm, totally pervading the dharma-realm, and filling up the dharma-realm. "And the reaches of space" refers to totally pervading the reaches of space and filling up all of space.

The ten directions are north, south, east, and west—the four basic directions—and, northeast, northwest, southeast, and southwest—the four intermediate directions—above and below. The ten directions refer to locations in space. The three periods of time refers to all the Buddhas of the past, all Buddhas of the present, and all Buddhas of the future.

"In each of the smallest atomic particles in these Buddha-lands." Each of the atomic particles can be further divided up into seven parts. Each of these parts is called "a particle bordering on nothingness." In each of these atomic particles, there is a world. And in each of these worlds there is a Buddha who is turning the wheel of Dharma. This is called "the large appearing within the small." Although atomic particles are so small, each can contain an entire world. And although a world is so large, it does not go beyond a single atomic particle. This is an example of the large appearing within the small. The small can also appear within what is large. It is also said,

> On the tip of a single hair there appears the kshetra-land of the Precious King,
> And sitting within an atomic particle he turns the wheel of Dharma.

A Buddha land can appear on the tip of a hair, and a Buddha land can appear in an atomic particle. Therefore, what is large can appear in what is small, yet the large does not obstruct the small. And what is small can appear in the large, yet the small does not obstruct the large. The large and small are in harmony with one another and are totally fused without obstruction. In fact, the small is the large, and the large is the small. This state is multi-layered and infinite. It is like lights that shine upon and reflect one another.

There are Buddhas as numerous as the smallest atomic particles in all worlds. Within each of the atomic particles, there are numerous and measureless worlds. How can one understand or fathom the Buddha-dharma? Within a single atomic particle there are measureless and limitless numbers of worlds, and within each world there are Buddhas as numerous as atomic particles. **In each and every place where there are Buddhas, there is an ocean-wide assembly of various kinds of Bodhisattvas surrounding them.** There are various different kinds of assemblies. There are Dharma assemblies where the *Diamond (Vajra) Sutra* was spoken. There are assemblies where the *Dharma Flower Lotus Sutra* was spoken with the Dharma Flower Lotus assembly of Bodhisattvas surrounding the Buddha. There were assemblies where the *Prajna-wisdom Sutras* were spoken with the Prajna-wisdom assembly of Bodhisattvas surrounding him. There were assemblies where the *Agama Sutras* were spoken with the Agama assembly of Bodhisattvas surrounding him. There were assemblies where the *Vaipulya Sutras* were spoken with the Vaipulya assembly of Bodhisattvas surrounding him. There were assemblies where the *Flower Adornment (Avatamsaka) Sutra* was spoken with the Flower Adornment assembly of Bodhisattvas surrounding him. There were assemblies where the *Shurangama Sutra* was spoken with the Shurangama assembly of Bodhisattvas surrounding him. Thus, various different ocean-wide assemblies of Bodhisattvas surround the Buddha.

Due to the power of Samantabhadra's practice and vows... By means of the power of these vows that are cultivated everywhere, **I give rise to deep faith and understanding.** I produce a mind of profound faith and understanding. The Buddha-dharma is like a vast ocean. If you have faith, then you can enter this ocean. If you lack faith, then you will not be able to enter this ocean. Therefore, it is said, "The immense ocean of the Buddha-dharma can only be entered by means of faith."

And manifest knowledge and vision... I make appear a single thought of knowledge and vision. That is, a single thought of wisdom. **I make offerings of superb and wonderful gifts to all of them**. I only use these most supreme, incomparable, and wonderful gifts. All of these things are used to make offering to the Buddhas and Bodhisattvas. What are these superb and wonderful offerings? **That is to say**, measureless and boundless numbers of **flowers**, which are in profusion, like clouds. And there are also **clouds of garlands**, which are flowers strung together to make the most beautiful garlands, streamers, and pennants. There are also **clouds of celestial music**. The gods in the heavens above make music and this music can be used as an offering. They use this to make offerings to the Buddhas. The Jade Emperor has gandharvas and kinnaras who play music for him. This music can be used as offerings to the Buddhas.

Clouds of heavenly canopies... When you light incense, the vapors condense to form a cloud canopy of incense. It is shaped like an umbrella, which covers living beings. In the *Shurangama Mantra* there is the Great

White Canopy, which appears in the sky when you recite the mantra. There are never any disasters or difficulties in any place covered by this canopy. No earthquakes or natural disasters will occur. There will be no disasters or difficulties whatsoever.

Clouds of heavenly clothing... The clothing of the gods is very light, like nylon. You can say that clothing made of nylon is like that of the gods. It is extremely light, and yet very beautiful.

As well as all varieties of heavenly incense... In the heavens there are many kinds of incense. If you recite the Great Compassion Mantra with a sincere heart, there will be a fragrant smell. This fragrance is not like sandalwood or any of the other scents that humans create when burning incense. This fragrance is not like anything we know in the human realm. If you are sincere, then this fragrance may manifest. If you are not sincere, it will not occur. This happens because when you recite the mantra, the ghosts and spirits use this fragrance to make an offering to you.

Including incense paste... These are fragrant pastes that can be applied on your body. You might say, "Isn't this just perfume or cologne?" These are not things that you actually put on your body; rather they are placed before the Buddhas as an offering.

Burning incense, powdered incense, and clouds of gifts such as these... Just like the clouds of incense discussed previously. **Each offering is the size of Mount Sumeru, the king of mountains.** How many of these offerings are there? Their number is so large they are as great as Mount Sumeru. Wouldn't you say these offerings are great?

SUTRA:

I burn all kinds of lamps. This includes butter lamps, oil lamps, and lamps of many fragrant oils. The wick of each lamp is as great as

Mount Sumeru. The quantity of oil in each lamp is like the waters of the great ocean. With all manner of gifts such as these, I constantly make offerings.

Good Man, of all offerings, the offering of Dharma is supreme. That is to say, it is the offering of cultivating according to the teachings, the offering of benefiting living beings, the offering that gathers in living beings, the offering of undergoing suffering on behalf of living beings, the offering of diligently cultivating the roots of goodness, the offering of never forsaking the karma of the Bodhisattvas, and the offering of never being apart from the Bodhi-mind.

COMMENTARY:

The offerings made by Samantabhadra Bodhisattva are described by saying that they are as numerous as Mount Sumeru. How big is Mount Sumeru? *Sumeru* is Sanskrit and means "wonderfully high." Therefore, it is called Wonderfully High Mountain. "Wonderfully" here means "inconceivably high." This mountain is surrounded by seven rings of fragrant oceans. And then outside these seven rings of fragrant oceans are the Four Great Continents, which are Purvavideha in the east, Jambudvipa in the south, Aparagodaniya in the west, and Uttarakuru in the north. How high is Mount Sumeru? It is 84,000 yojanas high. The sun and moon are located half way up its slope, as are the Heaven of the Four Kings. Therefore, Mount Sumeru is taller than the Heaven of the Four Kings. Since your offerings are as great as Mount Sumeru, then their measure is inconceivably great.

I burn all kinds of lamps. To "burn" means to "light." What benefit is there in burning all kinds of lamps? If you light lamps before the Buddha, keen eyesight is the reward you will obtain from giving this offering. If you do not have keen eyesight, it is because you did not offer lamps to the Buddha. If you cause the space before the Buddha to be bright, then your eyes will be bright.

There are many kinds of lamps, not just one type. **This includes butter lamps**, which burn butter made from cows' milk, and **oil lamps**, which burn common oil. In the Secret School, there is a Dharma called *Homa* in which the Vajra Master lights a fire in front of himself and recites mantras. He may burn butter in the fire, common oil, clothing, or other articles as offerings to the Buddha. The more valuable the offerings that you burn are, the more merit and virtue you will have. If one burns gold in the fire as an offering, the merit will be especially great.

In actuality, it is not the value of the items burned that determines the amount of merit and virtue derived. For example, if you burn gold, it does not necessarily mean that your merit and virtue is great, or if you burn dirt, that your merit and virtue is small. What matters is your sincerity. If you can offer the most valuable objects with a mind of extreme sincerity, this shows that your mind is true. If you have an earnest mind, then there is merit and virtue, but you do not have to burn gold to gain it.

On the other hand, you might think, "What benefit is derived from burning these things, since in the end they are destroyed?" This shows you do not have a sincere mind, and the merit and virtue derived is considerably less. If your mind is true, you can give up anything to the fire. The merit and virtue derived depends upon the sincerity of your renunciation. This is the *Homa* Dharma and several lamps like this are used in the practice of the Secret School.

In addition to these oil lamps, there are **lamps of many fragrant oils** including sesame oil lamps. **The wick of each lamp is as great as Mount Sumeru. The quantity of oil in each lamp is like the waters of the great ocean.** You might ask, "Who could possibly make offerings like this? Who can make offerings of items that are as great as Mount Sumeru and light lamps that are like the waters of the great ocean?" The *Flower Adornment Sutra*, talks about the measure of the dharma-realm and a nature like the dharma-realm. If you have a true and sincere mind when you give offerings, then the measure of your offerings will be like Mount Sumeru and the quantity will be like the waters in the great ocean. You don't need to make offerings that are actually that great in size. If your heart is sincere, then the quantity will be great. It will be as vast as worlds equal to the number of the grains of sand in the Ganges River.

With all manner of gifts such as these, I constantly make offerings. Using many different kinds of offerings as previously mentioned and in such vast quantities, I will constantly make offerings.

In the past in China, there was a very poor person who bought a catty of oil to offer to the Three Jewels. He prepared to go to Gold Mountain Monastery the next day to light lamps before the Buddha as an offering. At that time the Abbot of Gold Mountain who was a "bright eyed one," one who has opened the Five Spiritual Eyes, told the guest prefect of the monastery, "Tomorrow, open the main gate. A great Dharma protector will arrive around ten in the morning to make offerings to the Buddha. After he has made his offerings to the Buddha, don't let him depart. Invite him to eat in the Abbot's quarters. You should be very polite to this Dharma-protector."

The next day the guest prefect had the grounds swept clean and the main gate opened for the great Dharma protector. The Abbot put on his long ceremonial robe and went out to greet the great Dharma protector.

What was this Dharma protector like? He was extremely poor and was only able to bring one catty of oil to offer to the Buddha. When he came to bow to the Buddha, the Abbot personally welcomed him, and invited him to eat in the Abbot's quarters. Why did the Abbot treat a person who made such a small offering so well? This man throughout his life had only made enough money to purchase this one catty of oil. This one catty of oil represented his whole life savings.

A rich person who had arrived at the monastery at the same time watched these proceedings and thought, "This person has given just a single catty of oil, and the Abbot is treating him so nice." The next day the rich man bought 1,000 catties of oil and brought them to the monastery as an offering to the Buddhas. He thought that if an offering of just one catty of oil could occasion such good treatment, certainly with an offering of 1,000 catties, one would be treated even better.

Who would have guessed that before the rich man sent his offerings, the Abbot had told the guest prefect, "Tomorrow, open the side gate. A Dharma protector is sending oil to burn in the lamps before the Buddha. You can invite him to eat in the guest hall. He doesn't need to come to the Abbot's quarters."

The guest prefect did as he was told, but did not understand what was going on at all. After the rich man had paid his visit, he asked the Abbot, "Why did you open the main gate for the poor person who gave only one catty of oil and personally invite him to eat in the Abbot's quarter, whereas, you didn't open the main gate or even greet the person who was so rich that he could afford offering 1,000 catties of oil? And further, why did you have him eat in the guest hall?"

The Abbot replied, "You should know that the person who gave one catty of oil, used all his money to buy the oil as an offering to the Buddha. Whereas, the one who gave 1,000 catties is very rich, and he could have easily given 100,000,000 catties of oil and it would not have been a big deal to him. Thus, there was no need for me to greet him." Then the guest prefect understood.

Therefore, when you make offerings to the Buddha it does not matter how much you give. However, you must have a sincere mind. If your mind is extremely sincere and earnest, you will obtain merit and virtue. If your mind is not sincere, then even if you give a lot, you will not have much merit and virtue.

Offerings the size of Sumeru, King of Mountains, are not really as large as Mount Sumeru. If the resolve you make in your mind is as large as Mount Sumeru, then your offerings will be just as great. If the resolve you make in your mind is small, the merit and virtue from your offerings will also be slight.

Samantabhadra again said, **"Good Man, of all offerings, the offering of the Dharma is supreme."** Of all offerings one can make, the offering of the Dharma is best. The greatest offering is lecturing the Sutras and explaining the Dharma for others. The *Brahma Net Sutra says*, "For every day you lecture the Sutras and speak the Dharma, you can eat three ounces of gold." You will not feel that it's excessive. Your offering of speaking the Dharma entitles you to eat food worth three ounces of gold. However, you do not want to think that because you can receive offerings worth three ounces of gold each day, that you can just eat that food without a mind of repentance. Even though the Sutra says this, you can't be conceited and tell others, "Since I'm explaining the Sutras and speaking the Dharma, I am deserving of you buying food for me worth three ounces of gold every day." You should not be so conceited.

In the *Diamond* (Vajra) *Sutra* it says that if you made an offering of the seven jewels to everyone in a three-thousand, great-thousand world-system, this offering is not equal to explaining a four-line verse from the Sutra. The merit from a single four-line verse is greater. Therefore, amongst all the kinds of offerings, the offering of the Dharma is supreme. The offering of the Dharma is the greatest.

Now every day I teach you the Dharma so that you can hear the Sutras. This is giving the Dharma. One can use the Dharma as an offering to the Buddha. Here we turn the wheel of the Dharma by lecturing the Sutras. This is making an offering of the Dharma.

That is to say, it is the offering of cultivating according to the teachings. For example, one teaches the paramita of giving, and then others practice giving. One teaches the paramita of upholding the moral precepts and some people practice this by eating only one meal a day. Someone might explain the paramita of patience. They say that one should cultivate patience and not get angry. People who truly understand the Buddha-dharma practice patience. They cultivate to the point that there are no people, no self, no living beings, and no life span.

When some hear of the paramita of vigor, they become constantly vigorous throughout the day and night. They constantly cultivate according to the Dharma. Some hear about the paramita of dhyana-samadhi. They learn how practicing the four dhyanas and the eight samadhis can produce measureless merit and attain all kinds of states of liberation. These people base their cultivations on the paramita of dhyana-samadhi. When some hear of the prajna paramita, they cultivate wisdom and do not give rise to foolish thoughts.

Others hear about the Four Noble Truths of Suffering, the Origination of Suffering, the Cessation of Suffering, and the Path to the Cessation of Suffering. They learn that one is to understand suffering, cut off origination, strive for cessation, and cultivate the path. Then, they rely on the Dharma of the Four Noble Truths to cultivate. When some hear about the Twelve Links of Conditioned Origination, they rely on this Dharma to cultivate. Others hear an explanation of the Four Measureless Minds of loving-kindness, compassion, rejoicing, and equanimity, and they cultivate in accordance with the Four Measureless Minds.

To sum it all up, you actually put into practice whatever Dharma you learn. This what is meant by the "offering of cultivating," according to the teachings. In explaining how the offering of the Dharma is most supreme, Shakyamuni Buddha gave up his life for half a verse in a past life when he was on the stage of planting causes for Enlightenment. In his quest for the Dharma he sacrificed his life for two lines of verse. A verse or gāthā is a poem of four lines. He gave up his life for half a verse. One day he heard a rakshasa ghost say,

> All activities are impermanent.
> This is the Dharma of production and extinction.

When Shakyamuni Buddha heard this he said, "What you've spoken is the Buddha-dharma. However, you've only spoken half of it. Will you speak the second half for me?"

The rakshasa ghost replied, "That's right. What I spoke was the Buddha-dharma. However, I'm famished. I've got to find a person to eat. After I've eaten a human, then I can explain this Dharma. I'm so hungry that I have no energy to speak this Dharma."

Shakyamuni Buddha said, "How about if you speak first, and then eat me?"

The rakshasa ghost said, "You'll let me eat you?"

Shakyamuni Buddha replied, "Yes, but you must give me this Dharma first. After I understand it, then I'll gladly let you eat me."

The rakshasa ghost said, "Okay." Then he recited the rest of the verse. He said,

> *After production and extinction are extinguished,*
> *Then this state of quiescent cessation is happiness.*

Then he said, "Now I can eat you. I've already finished speaking this Dharma. "

Shakyamuni Buddha said, "Wait a bit, and then I'll let you eat me."

The rakshasa said, "Are you having regrets about this? Now you don't want to pay your debt? We made an agreement and now you feel that it doesn't count?"

Shakyamuni Buddha replied, "No, that's not the case. Since you have spoken these four verses of Buddha-dharma, and most people have not heard the Buddha-dharma, I want to use a knife to carve these lines into a tree. Afterwards, you may eat me. Would this be okay with you?"

The rakshasa ghost thought a while and said, "Okay. Go ahead and carve it into a tree." Then Shakyamuni Buddha used a knife to carve the four-line verse into the base of a tree.

Then he thought, "Trees are not that durable." Now the rakshasa ghost was eager to eat him. Then the Buddha made a new request, "Wait a bit more! Since I want everyone to know about the Buddha-dharma, I want to chisel this four-line verse into a rock. After I do that, you can eat me. I'm not doing this for myself, but I wish all living beings will understand the Buddha-dharma."

The rakshasa ghost thought it over and said, "Okay. Get to work and don't dilly dally and waste time." At that time Shakyamuni Buddha carved this four-line verse into a rock. When he had finished, he invited the rakshasa ghost to eat him.

Then the rakshasa said, "Oh, you are really going to let me eat you!"

Shakyamuni Buddha replied, "Of course. I don't lie. What do you mean, 'Really let me eat you?' Please go ahead."

The rakshasa ghost then said, "You really are a cultivator of the path. You are a true cultivator. Now that I know you are truly cultivating, I'll see you later." After saying this, the rakshasa ghost flew up into space, appearing in the body of the Bodhisattva Guan Shi Yin (Avalokiteshvara or the Bodhisattva Who Observes the Sounds of the World), who had manifested to test him.

Therefore, in cultivating the path, you must have a sincere mind. Do not do things just for yourself. If a ghost wants to eat you, forget yourself for the sake of the Dharma. You should be able to give up your life for the sake of the Dharma. Therefore, the sutra text above says, "Of all offerings, the offering of Dharma is supreme."

The offering of benefiting living beings. Those who cultivate the path of the Bodhisattva speak the Dharma for others in order to benefit living beings. This is "the offering of benefiting living beings."

The offering that gathers in living beings. "To gather in" means that you look upon all living beings as being the same as your own sons and daughters. You compassionately gather in all living beings without discrimination. This is the offering that gathers in living beings.

The offering of undergoing suffering on behalf of living beings. Those who cultivate the path of the Bodhisattva make vows to undergo suffering on behalf of living beings. They constantly make vows before the Buddha, saying, "May all living beings avoid the many different kinds of disasters including those of knives, sickness, floods, fire, epidemics and so forth. I wish that I myself might undergo the suffering that all living beings should undergo. And furthermore, no living being should undergo the suffering that I should undergo." This is the resolve made in the mind of a Bodhisattva.

The offering of diligently cultivating the roots of goodness. The Bodhisattva diligently cultivates his own roots of goodness and he exhorts and influences all living beings to diligently cultivate roots of goodness as well. This is also a kind of offering.

The offering of never forsaking the karma of the Bodhisattvas. What is "the karma of a Bodhisattva?" It is the Six Perfections and myriad practices. To constantly cultivate the Six Perfections and myriad practices, which means to practice the path of the Bodhisattva, is called "the offering of not forsaking the karma of the Bodhisattva."

And the offering of never being apart from the Bodhi-mind. One always brings forth the Bodhi-mind. One never ever separates from the Bodhi-mind. One only does those things that benefit living beings. Not only is one never apart from the Bodhi-mind, one also exhorts and influences all living beings to never separate from the Bodhi-mind. One exhorts them to always bring forth the Bodhi-mind and to always give rise to the true enlightened mind.

SUTRA:

Good Man, the measureless merit and virtue created from making the previous offerings, when compared to the merit and virtue from a single thought of the offering of the Dharma, does not equal one one-hundredth, one one-thousandth, one part in a hundred thousand

kotis of nayutas, one part in a kala, one part by reckoning, one part by calculation, one part that can be demonstrated by comparison, or one part in an Upanishad. Why is this? Because all Tathagatas venerate the Dharma. Because cultivating according to the teachings gives birth to all Buddhas. If a Bodhisattva makes the offering of Dharma, he will have made an offering to the Tathagatas. Cultivating in this way is a true offering. It is a vast and most supreme offering.

In this way, when the reaches of space, the realm of living beings, the karma of living beings, and the afflictions of living beings come to an end, my making offerings will also end. However, because the reaches of space up to and including the afflictions of living beings can never end, therefore my making offerings is also without end. It continues in thought after thought without cease. I never tire of this karma in body, speech, and thought.

COMMENTARY:

Therefore, Samantabhadra Bodhisattva again said, **Good man, the measureless merit and virtue created from making the previous offerings** is so great that it is measureless and boundless, but **when compared to the merit and virtue from a single thought of the offering of the Dharma it does not equal one one-hundredth.** The Sutra spoke previously of a vast amount of merit and virtue, yet when using the Dharma as an offering, one merely needs the merit and virtue of a single thought. An ordinary offering does not equal one one-hundredth part of the merit derived from giving the Dharma, nor does it equal **one one-thousandth,** up to the point that it does not equal **one part in a hundred thousand *kotis of nayutas*** of the merit and virtue derived from the giving of Dharma. *Koti* is a Sanskrit word which means "10,000,000." It means "hundreds of thousands of millions of Nayutas." *Nayuta* is also a large number.

One part in a kala... A *Kala* is an inconceivable number. **One part by reckoning,** or **one part by calculation.** You may use any means of reckoning or calculation, or **one part that can be demonstrated by comparison.** Also, it does not equal **one part in an *Upanishad*.** *Upanishad* is the name of one who is mentioned in the *Shurangama Sutra* where it says, "With Upanishad as their leader." Translated, the word means "the essence of a particle" and "atomic particle," and so it is a number as great as the number of atomic particles. They cannot equal one part of the merit and virtue derived from the offering of the Dharma.

Why is this? Why is it that the merit and virtue from the offering of the Dharma is so great? **Because all Tathagatas,** because all Buddhas, the Tathagatas, **venerate the Dharma.** Not only should all common ordinary people venerate the Dharma, but even the Buddhas themselves honor and venerate the Buddha-dharma. This is because if there were no Buddha-dharma, no one could become a Buddha.

If you wish to become a Buddha, you must learn the Buddha-dharma. If you wish to learn the Buddha-dharma, the Dharma must be transmitted by the Sangha. Monastics are entrusted with the Buddha-dharma. Therefore, you should learn the Buddha-dharma from monastics. The merit and virtue derived from giving the Dharma as an offering to all Buddhas, Tathagatas, and to all living beings, is inconceivable. There is no way one can say just how much it is. This is because all Buddhas, the Tathagatas, venerate the Buddha-dharma.

Because cultivating according to the teachings gives birth to all Buddhas. Because one relies on what the Buddha-dharma teaches to cultivate, one can become a Buddha. If you proclaim the Buddha-dharma and people cultivate according to it, they can become Buddhas. This is what is mean by "gives birth to all Buddhas."

If a Bodhisattva makes the offering of Dharma, if a Bodhisattva practices the giving of the Dharma, **he will have made an offering to the Tathagatas.** On the one hand, the Bodhisattva makes offerings to the Tathagatas, and on the other hand, they themselves can become Tathagatas. **Cultivating in this way is a true offering.** This is truly making offerings. The offering of the Dharma is a true offering. **It is a vast and most supreme offering.** The offering of the Dharma is the most extensive and supreme offering.

In this way, when the reaches of space, when there is no more space, **the realm of living beings,** when there are no more living beings, **when the karma of living beings,** when the karmic obstructions of living beings are no more, **and the afflictions of living beings come to an end, my making offerings will also end.** When these four things, the reaches of space, living beings, the karma of living beings, and the afflictions of living beings no longer exist, then my giving of offerings will also not exist. I need give no more. **However, because the reaches of space,** the realms of living beings, the karma of living beings, and **the afflictions of living beings can never end**—there is no way they can ever be exhausted and no way they can ever be finished—**therefore, my making offerings is also without end.** Therefore, my resolve to extensively make offerings is also inexhaustible and never-ending.

It continues in thought after thought without cease. The power of this vow to make offerings continues in thought after thought and is never cut off. **I never tire of this karma in body, speech, and thought.** When I make offerings with my body, I never grow weary. When I make offerings with my mind, I never grow weary. And even when I make offerings with my mouth, I never become tired.

There is a saying about the karma of body, mouth, and mind:

When no anger appears on one's face, that itself is a complete offering.
When the mouth is without anger, one emits a wonderful fragrance.
When the mind is without anger, that itself is a precious treasure.
To be without confusion and greed is the offering of incense.

When one is without a hateful or angry facial expression, then one has made a complete offering. When you do not engage in harsh speech, your breath is fragrant. When you have no thoughts of anger in your mind, it is like making an offering of a precious treasure. And the perfect offering is to be without confusion and greed. This is a true offering.

To Repent of Karmic Obstacles and Reform

SUTRA:

Moreover, Good Man, to repent of karmic obstacles and reform is explained like this. The Bodhisattva reflects to himself, 'I, from beginningless kalpas in the past, because of greed, hatred, and delusion, have created measureless and boundless evil karma with my body, mouth, and mind. If this evil karma had a substance and form, it could not be contained within the reaches of space.

COMMENTARY:

After explaining the previous vow, to extensively make offerings, the Bodhisattva says, **Moreover, Good Man**. Now we want to repent of our karmic obstacles and reform. There is no such thing as practicing making offerings yet failing to repent of and reform your karmic obstacles. So Samantabhadra Bodhisattva says, **to repent of karmic obstacles and reform is explained like this.** "Repentance" has been explained as repenting of previous mistakes. One is penitent for the karmic offenses that one has created in the past. "Reform" means that one reforms one's previous transgressions and does not commit these offenses again in the future.

In Buddhism we learn to "bow repentances." This means that we earnestly bow before the Buddhas while repenting of our mistakes. In doing this, you must be extremely sincere and not be careless or sloppy. Then your repentance will be efficacious. Take a look at the example of the Great Master Zhi Zhe. At the time he was alive (6th century) the *Shurangama Sutra* had not yet come from India to China. He just went ahead and bowed to the name of the *Shurangama Sutra* while facing west. He bowed for eighteen years yet still did not get to see or read the *Shurangama Sutra*. If a person at the present time bowed for eighteen months, not to speak of eighteen years, and did not get any attainment from it, he would think, "What use is there in bowing like this? I'm not going to bow anymore!"

For his entire life the Great Master Zhi Zhe also bowed to the *Dharma Flower Sutra*. Not only that, he wrote out the Sutras, and he even wrote out the entire Tripitaka (Buddhist Canon) time and time again. The Buddha images he painted and made from wood totaled over 80,000. And from morning to night he bowed repentances.

When the Great Master Zhi Zhe was born, his mother saw an auspicious five-colored light in their home, and so he was named Zhi Zhe, "the Wise One." When he was in his early teens, he heard a Dharma Master lecture on and recite the Universal Door Chapter of the *Dharma Flower Sutra*. After hearing it but once he had it memorized. It was just as if he had read it in a previous life. Later when he went to see the Great Master Nan Yao, the Great Master said, "Oh, you've come. In the past we were part of the Vulture Peak Assembly and we heard the *Dharma Flower Sutra*. Do you remember that? Now our conditions have ripened, and we have come together again here." The Great Master Nan Yao then taught him the Peaceful and Happy Conduct Chapter, and told him to recite and bow to the *Dharma Flower Sutra*.

Master Zhi Zhe bowed until he reached the Chapter on the Events in the Past Lives of Medicine King Bodhisattva. Then he immediately became enlightened.

After his enlightenment, he told the Great Master Nan Yao about his experience: "I bowed to the Sutra and recited it until I got to the lines, 'This is called true vigor; this is a true offering of the Dharma.' Then I saw Shakyamuni Buddha at Vulture Peak still speaking the *Dharma Flower Sutra*. What does this mean?"

The Great Master Nan Yao acknowledged and approved his experience. He said, "Only you could have this subtle and wonderful experience, and only I could recognize it. Therefore, it had to be you to attain this state, and it had to be me to understand it and confirm it for you. So now you have attained the initial expedient of the Dharma Flower Samadhi, the *I-xuan* Dharani, 'the single-turning' Dharani."

After the Great Master gave him the seal of approval, Master Zhi Zhe had genuine unobstructed wisdom and eloquence. The Great Master Nan Yao said to him, "With your wisdom you can defeat thousands upon tens of thousands of common Dharma Masters in debate. None of them can equal you." After this the Great Master Zhi Zhe's wisdom greatly blossomed. He then applied himself even more vigorously in cultivating the *Dharma Flower Sutra*.

When it was time for him "to perfect the stillness," he had an attendant recite the *Dharma Flower Sutra* for him while he listened. After he finished reciting, Great Master Zhi Zhe told the attendant to bring him some mouthwash. After he had rinsed his mouth, he spoke some verses, sat down, and "perfected the stillness."

When the Great Master was at Tian Tai Mountain, there were many fishermen in the area, and so he bought up all the land there for one hundred miles. Then, within this area, no one fished or killed animals.

Further, all the local people took refuge with him. The Great Master Zhi Zhe was inconceivable, and he specialized in bowing repentances.

The Bodhisattva reflects to himself. Most people who bring forth thoughts of repentance and reform are Bodhisattvas. Ordinary people without the roots of goodness basically do not repent, how much the less reform. This is like those who take refuge with the Three Jewels. Some like to recite Sutras and bow to the Buddhas, and some do not. Some start out with the idea that everyone should recite Sutras, and so everyone begins reciting, and after a while, they themselves stop reciting. This just shows that they have not gotten rid of their karmic obstacles. "**I, from beginningless kalpas in the past**. In past lives, during kalpas that have no beginning in time, **because of greed, hatred, and delusion, have created measureless and boundless evil karma with my body, mouth, and mind**. Due to a mind of greed, hatred, and delusion, I have created all kinds of evil karma with my body, mouth, and thought. This karma is beyond measure and is without limit. **If this evil karma had a substance and form**, if it had a shape, a substance, or an appearance, **it could not be contained within the reaches of space**. My karma would fill up all of space until it was overflowing. If these karmic obstacles had an actual shape and appearance, they would fill up all of space so that it would be bursting at the seams. Space itself would become obliterated. There would no longer be any space. Take a look at just how great our karmic obstacles are! They cannot even be contained within all of space.

SUTRA:

With my three karmas purified, before the assemblies of all Buddhas and Bodhisattvas in kshetra-lands throughout the dharma-realm that are as numerous as the smallest atomic particles, I now sincerely repent of and reform my offenses and will never create them again. I will always dwell in all the merit and virtue of the pure moral precepts.

In this way, when the reaches of space, the realms of living beings, the karma of living beings, and the afflictions of living beings come to an end, my repentance will also end. However, the reaches of space up to and including the afflictions of living beings can never end.

Therefore, my repenting and reforming is without end. It continues in thought after thought without cease. I never tire of this karma in body, speech, and thought.

COMMENTARY:

With my three karmas purified, before the assemblies of all Buddhas and Bodhisattvas in kshetra-lands throughout the dharma-realm that are as numerous as the smallest atomic particles, I now sincerely repent of and reform my offenses and will never create them again. The Bodhisattva considers that his own karmic obstacles are extremely numerous. Therefore, he says with his "three karmas purified" which means he does not create any more bad karma with his body, mouth, or mind. His three karmas of body, mouth, and mind are pure. Then in kshetra-lands that are as numerous as the smallest atomic particles, before all the Buddhas and great Bodhisattvas, he brings forth his sincerest and most earnest mind to repent and reform and never create these kinds of karmic offenses again.

I will always dwell in all the merit and virtue of the pure moral precepts. At all times I dwell and maintain the pure moral precepts and all the merit and virtue derived from my practice of upholding them.

In this way, when the reaches of space, when there is no more space, when there are no longer any living beings, even up to the point that **the karma of living beings, and the afflictions of living beings come to an end, my repentance will also end.** At that time my vow to repent and reform will be finished and then will no longer exist. **However, the reaches of space up to and including the afflictions of living beings can never end.** It is not possible for the reaches of space, the realm of living beings, the karma of living beings, or the afflictions of living beings to no longer exist. **Therefore, my repenting and reforming is without**

end. The power of my vow to repent and reform can also never end. **It continues in thought after thought without cease.**

It never ceases for a moment. **I never tire of this karma in body, speech, and thought without weariness.** One never becomes tired. The more one bows repentances, the better. One would never say, "This bowing is a lot of difficulty and suffering. I'm really tired of it." One never grows weary. The more one bows, the more energetic one becomes. The more one repents, the happier one becomes. This is true repentance and reform.

To Follow and Rejoice in Merit and Virtue

SUTRA:

Moreover, Good Man, to follow and rejoice in merit and virtue is explained like this. All the Buddhas, the Tathagatas, are as numerous as the smallest atomic particles in all the Buddha kshetra-lands of the ten directions and the three periods of time, throughout the dharma-realm and the reaches of space. From the time they first brought forth the Bodhi-mind for the sake of All-wisdom, they diligently cultivated and amassed blessings without regard for their bodies and lives.

They did this throughout kalpas as many as the smallest atomic particles in ineffably ineffable numbers of Buddha kshetra-lands. During each kalpa they gave up their heads, eyes, hands, and feet, as many times as there are the smallest atomic particles in ineffably ineffable Buddha kshetra-lands.

In this way, they cultivated all the difficult ascetic practices, perfected the various paramitas, entered and realized each of the Bodhisattva grounds of wisdom, and accomplished the unsurpassed Bodhi of all Buddhas. Upon their Parinirvana, their sharira were divided and distributed. I follow and rejoice in all of their roots of goodness.

Moreover, I follow and rejoice in the merit and virtue of all the different types of beings in the six paths of existence and the four kinds of birth in all the worlds of the ten directions, even if it is as small as a single particle.

I follow and rejoice in all the merit and virtue of all the Shravakas, Pratyeka-Buddhas, Learners, and Those Beyond Learning in the ten directions and the three periods of time.

I follow and rejoice in the vast, great merit and virtue of all the Bodhisattvas, who in their quest for Unsurpassed, Right and Equal Bodhi, cultivate measureless difficult ascetic practices.

So it is that even if the reaches of space, the realms of living beings, the karma of living beings, and the afflictions of living beings come to an end, still my following and rejoicing in merit and virtue are without end. It continues in thought after thought without cease. I never tire of this karma in body, speech, and thought.

COMMENTARY:

This is the fifth of Samantabhadra Bodhisattva's vows, which is to follow and rejoice in merit and virtue. When talking about "following and rejoicing in," there are those who follow, but not rejoice in. There are those that rejoice in, but do not follow. There are also those that both follow and rejoice in. And finally, there are those that neither follow nor rejoice in. To follow but not rejoice in means that they reluctantly do acts of merit and virtue. To rejoice in but not follow means they take delight in merit, but they do not do acts of merit and virtue. So there are those who do acts of merit and virtue reluctantly and those who don't do anything at all, even though they rejoice in other's merit and virtue.

Although a deed may be good, they don't do it themselves. However, they tell or encourage others to do it. They say, "Oh, do more meritorious deeds. That would be the best." So this is rejoicing but not following. Further, there are some people who both follow and rejoice in, which means that they do acts of merit and virtue, and they also rejoice in it. This is to both follow and rejoice in merit and virtue. Still others do not follow nor rejoice in merit and virtue, which means they do no acts of merit and virtue nor rejoice in it at all. These are the four ways to follow and rejoice in merit and virtue.

"Merit" can be created and is quite visible for all to see. Virtue refers to virtuous conduct. It is hidden and not always visible to others.

Moreover, Samantabhadra said to the Youth Sudhana, "I will again explain this for you, **Good Man**." The vow **to follow and rejoice in merit and virtue is explained like this**. Now I will tell you. **All the Buddhas, Tathagatas, are as numerous as the smallest atomic particles in all the Buddha kshetra-lands of the ten directions and the three periods of time**: all the Buddhas, Tathagatas, are as numerous as atomic particles, **throughout the dharma-realm and the reaches of space**, to the exhaustion of space.

From the time they first brought forth the Bodhi-mind for the sake of All-wisdom, from the very first time they brought forth the Bodhi-mind wishing to cultivate All-wisdom, **they diligently cultivated and amassed blessings**. They were very diligent and never lazy in their cultivation of blessings and wisdom. How does one accumulate blessings? It is done from a various number of aspects, and not just one. There is a saying, "Don't skip doing a good deed just because it is small, and don't do a bad deed just because you think it is insignificant." Do not decline to do something just because you think the merit of the action is small, because great merit and virtue is made up of an accumulation of small acts of merit and virtue.

Moreover, you should not think that an evil deed is too small to matter. For example, you should not think that a little lie is of no major importance. If you tell a lot of little lies, they become a big lie. In the same way, you should not think that killing an ant is a small and unimportant matter, because if one day you kill a person, it will have begun with your killing this ant. You should pay attention to little things and not follow your whims and wishes.

To "diligently cultivate and accumulate blessings" is something that you should pay attention to. You ought to do even small acts of merit and virtue. They will accumulate bit by bit and become great merit and virtue. Mount Tai is made up of individual particles of dirt. Even though these particles are small, many of them gathered together make up a mountain. Creating blessings is the same.

Without regard for their bodies and lives. All Buddhas, Tathagatas, sacrificed their most precious lives to teach, transform, and rescue living beings. For example, Shakyamuni Buddha, during one of his past lives, cut off his flesh to feed an eagle.

At that time the eagle was preying on a small bird. The bird knew that a certain old cultivator was compassionate, so it flew under the cultivator's arm to escape from the eagle. The eagle tried to snatch the bird to eat it, but Shakyamuni, who was cultivating during the stage in which he was planting causes in past lives, wished to protect it.

However, the eagle said, "You can protect the bird, but if it lives, then I will die. If I don't have something to eat, I will starve to death. If you save the bird but don't save me, you are being unfair and without compassion. If you can't save me, you shouldn't save the bird either."

Shakyamuni Buddha said, "Since you eat meat, it will suffice if I give you some meat to eat."

The eagle replied, "Yes. Go find some meat to eat."

The Buddha then said, "I'll give you my own flesh to eat," and he cut a piece from his body and gave it to the eagle.

After eating it, the eagle said, "I'm still not full. Give me another piece." And again, Shakyamuni Buddha cut some flesh from his body and gave it to the eagle to eat. After the eagle had eaten all his flesh, he still wasn't full.

Shakyamuni Buddha said, "If you aren't satisfied after eating all my flesh, then you can eat my bones. You can eat whatever you find left to eat."

The eagle replied, "You really are a cultivator of the Way. In the future you will certainly become a Buddha." After he said this he flew up into the sky. Originally, he was a god who had come to test Shakyamuni Buddha.

It is not known how many times Shakyamuni Buddha gave up his life to teach and transform living beings. Therefore, it is said that there is no place in the entire world, even one as small as an atomic particle, where all the Buddhas of the ten directions and the three periods of time have not given up their bodies and lives. In the past Shakyamuni Buddha made vows to give away 1,000 bodies to rescue living beings. Are we of the present time capable of making vows of this magnitude? Can we give up our bodies and lives to teach and transform living beings? If you can, then you are one who follows and rejoices in the merit and virtue of the Buddhas.

If you cannot, then even though you may feel that Buddhas of the past are very special and even though you may respect them, because you cannot give up your body and life, you only rejoice but do not follow. On the other hand, if you can think, "The Buddha was a living being, and he renounced his body; I too am a living being, so I too can make a vow to give up my body for the sake of rescuing living beings." If you renounce your body, you need to do it in a way that really solves the problem of birth and death for living beings or saves the wisdom life of living beings' Dharma-body. You do not want to give up your life in a stupid senseless way. When you renounce your life, there should be some value in it. This is to follow and rejoice.

When we hear about renouncing our body and life, we say, "It's too difficult! I can't do that! I won't accept this kind of dharma. How can one disregard their body and life by giving it up? I won't practice this kind of ascetic practice." A person who thinks like this is called one who neither follows nor rejoices. If originally you were not going to sacrifice your life, but you do it because of special circumstances, or you do it for fame or to gain profit, or other various reasons, then you are following without rejoicing. For example, in a certain country there were monks who burned their bodies for political reasons. They renounced their bodies, but they were not happy about it. They were angry and wished to fight. This is called following without rejoicing.

They did this throughout kalpas as many as the smallest atomic particles in ineffably ineffable numbers of Buddha kshetra-lands. In life after life they gave up their bodies and lives, passing through great eons the number of which cannot be known, including through eons as numerous as the smallest atomic particles in Buddha-lands. **During each kalpa they gave up their heads, eyes, hands, and feet, as many times as there are smallest atomic particles in ineffably ineffable numbers of Buddha kshetra-lands.** And they did this throughout eons in numbers that cannot be expressed or explained which are as numerous as there are atomic particles that are just barely bigger than nothingness. They gave that many heads and eyes; they renounced their hands, feet, brains, and marrow that many times. They gave their heads, hands, feet, brains, marrow, their bodies, and their lives.

In this way, they cultivated all the difficult ascetic practices. They cultivated ascetic practices that people find impossible to cultivate. For example, at present there are those who wish to give their eyes to the world after they die to be used in eye transplants so that others may see. Some people donate their hearts, and others donate their lungs, kidneys, livers, and stomachs. They give away their organs to others. We look at these people and on the surface they appear as people, but in actuality they are Buddhas and Bodhisattvas who have vowed to become people to do these things. So even now in this world you can see all these Buddhas who practice giving like this. They have this kind of magnanimous spirit of giving which is especially great. The kind of ascetic practice discussed here is not just vowing to limit one's food intake. Here we are talking about the ascetic practices involved in giving one's body and life to all living beings in order to rescue and aid them. These are ascetic practices that are really difficult to practice.

Perfected the various paramitas... Those cultivating the Buddha's Path are able to cultivate all the paramitas, all those methods which "lead to the other shore," to perfection. They do not just cultivate one kind, but cultivate various paramitas: giving, holding the moral precepts, patience, vigor, dhyana-samadhi, prajna-wisdom. They cultivate these Six Paramitas as well as the other myriad practices.

They entered and realized each of the Bodhisattva grounds of wisdom. They obtained all the different kinds of Bodhisattva wisdom—they reached this level of attainment, **and accomplished the unsurpassed Bodhi of all Buddhas.** Those people in the future will certainly become Buddhas. They will certainly accomplish the unsurpassed Bodhi of all Buddhas and obtain the Buddha fruition.

Upon their Parinirvana, called the 'great cessation,' which is when they obtained Nirvana's fruit of happiness, **their sharira were divided and distributed.** After their cremation what is left are *Sharira*, which are the Buddhas' adamantine relics that come from cultivating morality, samadhi, wisdom and the many other methods of practice.

I follow and rejoice in all of their roots of goodness. Samantabhadra Bodhisattva made a great vow. He said, "I will follow and rejoice in the merit and virtue created by all the Buddhas who gave their heads, eyes, brains, and marrow. I will also do the same."

Moreover, I follow and rejoice in the merit and virtue of all the different types of beings in the six paths of existence and the four kinds of birth in all the worlds of the ten directions. It does not matter whether their merit and virtue is great or small, or whether they are beings who come from any of the six paths of existence or born from any of the four kinds of birth, I will follow and rejoice in whatever merit and virtue they create. The six paths of existence are the realms of gods, humans, asuras, animals, hungry ghosts, and beings in the hells. These are the six paths of the revolving wheel of birth and death. The four kinds of birth are birth from a womb, from an egg, from moisture, and by transformation.

I follow and rejoice in their merit and virtue, **even if it is as small as a single particle.** Even if they are unable to accomplish great deeds and their acts of merit and virtue are as small as tiny atomic particles, I will still follow and rejoice in, that is, delight in learning from them while doing these deeds.

I follow and rejoice in all the merit and virtue of all the Shravakas, Pratyeka-Buddhas, that is all the living beings of the ten directions and the three periods of time who belong to the vehicle of the Hearers and the vehicle of the Pratyeka-Buddhas, that is those 'enlightened to conditions,' as well as **Learners and Those Beyond Learning in the ten directions and the three periods of time.** "Learners are those of the first, second, and third fruition of an Arhat who are on the stage of Learners. One who has reached the fourth fruition of an Arhat is called one at the stage "beyond learning."

I follow and rejoice in the vast, great merit and virtue, and will myself perform the meritorious deeds **of all the Bodhisattvas, who in their quest for Unsurpassed, Right and Equal Bodhi, cultivate measureless difficult ascetic practices.** Their aspiration is to attain the Unsurpassed, Right and Equal, Right Enlightenment, and they cultivate the most difficult ascetic practices. The merit and virtue created by all Buddhas' and Bodhisattvas' vows and deeds are vast and great.

So it is that even if the reaches of space, the realms of living beings, the karma of living beings, and the afflictions of living beings come to an end, still my following and rejoicing in merit and virtue are without end. My vow to follow and rejoice will be without end. **It continues in thought after thought without cease.** In each thought I will unceasingly bring forth this vow. It can never be cut off. **I never tire of this karma in body, speech, and thought.** I make this vow with my body, with my mouth, and with my mind; with the three karmas of body, mouth, and mind, I make this vow and there will never come a time when I become tired, nor will there ever be a time when I feel I have done enough. I will carry on this vow forever and never get lazy. You want to be vigorous. The more difficult it is, the more I to wish to do it.

To Request the Turning of The Wheel of Dharma

SUTRA:

Moreover, Good Man, to request the turning of the wheel of Dharma is explained like this. Within each and every smallest atomic particle in the Buddha kshetra-lands throughout the ten directions and the three periods of time, to the exhaustion of the dharma-realm and the reaches of space, there are vast Buddha kshetra-lands as many as the smallest atomic particles in ineffably ineffable numbers of Buddha kshetra-lands. In each and every land, in thought after thought, all Buddhas are accomplishing Equal and Right Enlightenment, their number as many as the smallest atomic particles in ineffably ineffable numbers of Buddha kshetra-lands. An ocean-wide assembly of Bodhisattvas surrounds each Buddha. Using all manner of skill-in-means with my body, mouth, and mind, I earnestly request that they turn the wonderful wheel of Dharma.

COMMENTARY:

I will now explain the principle of requesting the turning of the wheel of Dharma. **Moreover, Good Man, to request the turning of the wheel of Dharma is explained like this. Within each and every atomic particle in the Buddha kshetra-lands throughout the ten directions and the three periods of time, to the exhaustion of the dharma-realm and the reaches of space, there are vast Buddha kshetra-lands as many as smallest atomic particles in ineffably ineffable numbers of Buddha kshetra-lands.** In each smallest atomic particle are again ineffably ineffable Buddha-lands as numerous as the smallest atomic particles in vast Buddha kshetra-lands, and **in each and every land, in** thought after thought, there are all Buddhas accomplishing Equal and Right Enlightenment, their number as many as the smallest atomic particles in ineffably ineffable numbers of Buddha Lands. An oceanic assembly of Bodhisattvas, just as vast as the great ocean, surrounds each Buddha. Using all manner of skill-in-means with my body, mouth, and mind and all kinds of skillful words, I earnestly request that they turn the wonderful wheel of Dharma. I request them to turn the great wheel of Dharma of all Buddhas, Bodhisattvas, Shravakas, and Those Enlightened to Conditions throughout the ten directions.

SUTRA:

So it is that even if the reaches of space, the realms of living beings, the karma of living beings, and the afflictions of living beings come to an end, my constant request that all Buddhas turn the wheel of proper Dharma is without end. It continues in thought after thought without cease. I never tire of this karma in body, speech, and thought.

COMMENTARY:

I earnestly request the Buddhas to turn the wonderful Dharma wheel, which is the vow I made. **So it is that even if the reaches of space are ended**, when there is no more space, the realms of living beings are ended, when there are no more living beings, **the karma of living beings is ended**, when the karmic obstructions of living beings have come to an end, **and the afflictions of living beings are ended**, when the afflictions of living beings are no more, still **my** vow to constantly **request that all Buddhas turn the wheel of proper Dharma is without end**. There is no way my vow can end. It is without end.

My vow **continues in thought after thought without cease**. This vow continues through each thought continuously and is never cut off. **I never**

To Beseech the Buddhas to Remain in the World

SUTRA:

Moreover, Good Man, to beseech the Buddhas to remain in the world is explained like this. All Buddhas, Tathagatas, are as numerous as the smallest atomic particles in all Buddha kshetra-lands, throughout the ten directions and the three periods of time, exhausting the dharma-realm and the reaches of space. When they are about to enter Parinirvana, or when any Bodhisattva, Shravaka, One Enlightened to Conditions, Learner, and One Beyond Learning, including any Good Teacher wishes to enter Parinirvana, I ask them all not to enter Nirvana. I request that they remain in the world for as many kalpas as the smallest atomic particles in all Buddha kshetra-lands to benefit and delight all living beings.

So it is that even if the reaches of space, the realms of living beings, the karma of living beings, and the afflictions of living beings come to an end, my beseeching is without end. It continues in thought after thought without cease. I never tire of this karma in body, speech, and thought.

COMMENTARY:

Moreover, Good Man, to beseech the Buddhas to remain in the world is explained like this. I will now explain the meaning of the vow to beseech the Buddhas to remain in the world. **All Buddhas, Tathagatas, are as numerous as the smallest atomic particles in all Buddha kshetra-lands throughout the ten directions and the three periods of time, exhausting the dharma-realm and the reaches of space**, filling up all the dharma-realm, all of space, as well as all Buddha-lands. These Buddhas, Tathagatas, are as numerous as smallest atomic particles. **When they are about to enter Parinirvana**—after they have taught those who have affinities with them, the Buddhas prepare to enter Nirvana. When they are about to enter Nirvana, I will definitely beseech them not to enter Nirvana, but to always remain in the world, teaching and transforming living beings. Not only will I ask all Buddhas to dwell in the world forever, I will also ask **any Bodhisattva, Shravaka, One Enlightened to Conditions, Learner, and One Beyond Learning** not to leave the world. Those Arhats of the First Fruition, the Second Fruition, and the Third Fruition are still on the level of Learners, whereas those Arhats of the Fourth Fruition are on the level of Those Beyond Learning.

Including any Good Teacher who **wishes to enter Parinirvana...** Not only will I request all these enlightened sages, but I ask all good teachers, Dharma Masters who lecture the Dharma and the Sutras, not to leave the world. Following my vow, **I ask them all**, each and every one of them, **not to enter Nirvana** or at least not to do it so quickly. **I request that they remain in the world for as many kalpas as there are smallest atomic particles in all Buddha kshetra-lands.** I request that they stay with us for a period of time as long as the kalpas that are as numerous as the smallest atomic particles in all these Buddha kshetra-lands, **to bring benefit and delight to all living beings.** I wish that all Buddhas, Bodhisattvas, Shravakas, Those Enlightened to Conditions, and all Good Teachers remain in the world forever and bring benefit to all living beings.

So it is that I make my vow like this: **even if the reaches of space come to an end...** Basically, the reaches of space cannot come to an end. However, let's suppose that it could not exist anymore. **If the realm of living beings** comes to an end... Fundamentally the realm of living beings can never come to an end nor could it not exist anymore. But let's suppose that it could not exist anymore. If the karma, the karmic obstacles, **of living beings** comes to an end... Again, basically it is not possible for it to not exist anymore. If **the afflictions of living beings come to an end...** It is also not possible for these to be exhausted and no longer exist. However, suppose they all could come to an end, yet my vow to beseech all Buddhas, Bodhisattvas, Shravakas, Those Enlightened to Conditions, and Good Teachers to constantly remain in the world would still be endless. **It continues in thought after thought without cease**, in a continuum of thought that is never ever interrupted. **I never tire of this karma in body, speech, and thought.** The power of my vow is the same as what was mentioned before.

To Always Follow and Learn from the Buddhas

SUTRA:

Moreover, Good Man, to always follow and learn from the Buddhas is explained like this. It is like Vairochana Tathagata of this Saha World, who, from the time he first brought forth the Bodhi-mind, vigorously advanced without retreat. He gave up ineffably ineffable numbers of bodies and lives. He peeled off his skin for paper, split his bones to fashion pens, and punctured his skin to draw blood for ink to write out Sutras stacked as high as Mount Sumeru. He revered the Dharma to such an extent that he did not even cherish his own body and life.

COMMENTARY:

Moreover, Good Man, Samantabhadra Bodhisattva again called out to the Youth Good Wealth. What is the meaning of '**to always follow and learn from the Buddhas?**' It **is explained like this**. I will now explain it for you. **It is like Vairochana Tathagata of this Saha World.**

Saha is Sanskrit. It means "able to patiently bear, or bearable." This world is so full of suffering; it is really hard for all living beings to bear, yet they can still bear it. Why is this world full of suffering? In this world absolutely everything is suffering. Since even happiness is the cause of suffering, there is no real happiness. All the dharmas in this world are defiled and impure; therefore the world is all painful and suffering.

How is happiness the very cause of suffering? For example, most people like to wear new clothes, and putting on a new outfit is considered a very happy event. But when you are not careful and spill soup on it, or get it dirty some other way, you get afflicted.

People especially like to get rich. Although you acquire much wealth during your life, when you die you cannot take it with you. Nevertheless, while you are alive, you keep track of every cent. When you are without money, you devise ways to get it, and after you have it, you are afraid you will lose it. If you do not have any wealth, you eagerly seek for it and this is suffering. After you get it, you are afraid of losing it and this is also suffering. You don't feel that this is suffering. You worry about obtaining it or you worry about losing it. During your life you are afraid you will not get it. Once you get it, you are afraid of losing it. However, when you die, you cannot take along one penny. You tell me, is this suffering or happiness?

This is the case for these two things, which everyone in the world delights in. In the same way, all the other kinds of happiness are also causes for suffering. However, you have not yet realized this fact. Therefore, it is called the Saha World or the "bearable" world.

Vairochana Buddha is the **Tathagata of this Saha World, who, from the time he first brought forth the Bodhi-mind, vigorously advanced without retreat.** *Vairochana* is Sanskrit and means "purity," and it refers to the Dharma-body of the Buddha. Shakyamuni Buddha's Dharma-body is called Vairochana Buddha. When Shakyamuni Buddha first brought forth the Bodhi-mind he met the ancient Shakya and made offerings to him, vowing to be just like him. He was a potter then and made bricks, tiles, teacups, and so forth. When he saw the Shakya of old, he vowed to vigorously advance and never retreat. After that he was vigorous in body and mind, day in and day out and at all times, and was never lax or lazy in his cultivation.

He gave up ineffably ineffable numbers of bodies and lives. For an ineffably ineffable number of lives, he renounced his body and life and gave them away. For example, before Shakyamuni became a Buddha, he met Dipamkara Buddha and made an offering to him with his body. Dipamkara Buddha walking along the road, had come upon a large puddle of water; Shakyamuni, seeing an old Bhikshu coming, lay down in the water so that the old Bhikshu could walk across his body. This is how he gave his body, that is, used his body to help others.

Most of us would think that this is really stupid. Could he not have used boards and logs rather than his body to provide a way for the old Bhikshu to cross the water? That is pretty smart, but Shakyamuni Buddha did not think of such an ingenious method. If he had, then it is not certain that Dipamkara Buddha would have given him a prediction of Buddhahood because he would still have had a concern for himself. He still would have had an attachment to his body. Lying in the water showed that he was without a self and only wished to help and benefit other beings. He practiced the Bodhisattva path, and paying no attention to himself, he lay down in the mud to help an old Bhikshu walk across it.

Shakyamuni was a practicing ascetic at that time, but even though ascetics do not cut their hair or their beards, still they are not hippies. Do not think that Shakyamuni was a hippie. I saw an article written by a Chinese person who said that Confucius was a hippie. This is total rubbish, and only amounts to confusing the true with the false and spreading false statements.

Then Dipamkara Buddha gave Shakyamuni Buddha a prediction. He said, "In the future you will become a Buddha. You cultivate the Bodhisattva path in this manner, and I do too. Thus it is, thus it is. In a future life, you will become a Buddha and your name will be Shakyamuni."

This is how Shakyamuni Buddha was on the causal stage of practice. He renounced his body and life practicing giving. From an immeasurable number of kalpas in the past to the present, he did this in life after life. He practiced the Bodhisattva path so perfectly.

Vairochana Buddha is the pure Dharma-body Buddha. He pervades all places. Vairochana also means, "to pervade everywhere." The Buddhas' Dharma-body is neither present nor not present. There is nowhere that he is and nowhere that he is not.

What does it mean to say that there is nowhere that the Dharma-body Buddha isn't? If we say that there is nowhere that he is not, then he is everywhere, but why do we not see him? Since we do not see him, doesn't this mean that he is not present? No, that's not the case.

Whether we see him or not, he is still present. Because he pervades all places, it is said that there is no place where he is present, and there is no place where he is not present. He fills up the entire dharma-realm.

Someone may ask, "You say that he extends everywhere; does this include filthy places like toilets?" Not only does he exist in toilets, but he exists in places that are even more filthy. The Buddhas' Dharma-body exhausts the reaches of space and pervades the dharma-realm. The Buddhas' Dharma-body is not defiled or pure, not produced or destroyed, and does not increase or decrease. Therefore, he is present everywhere.

Shakyamuni Buddha gave his body and life in cultivating the Bodhisattva path to seek unsurpassed Buddhahood. **He peeled off his skin for paper.** He stripped skin from his body to use as paper. **He split his bones to fashion pens and punctured his skin to draw blood for ink.** To do what? **To write out Sutras.** He used his skin for paper, his bones for pens, and his blood for ink to write out Sutras.

Why didn't Shakyamuni Buddha go buy some paper, pens, and ink to write out Sutras? The principle here is the same as the one that applied when Shakyamuni Buddha used his body to make a bridge in the mud. You could explain this by saying that there was no paper in India at that time. For example, when the Sutras were compiled, they used palm leaves. They wrote out the Sutras on palm leaves. If one were to lay out the leaves upon which the *Dharma Flower Sutra* was written, they would stretch for about two and a half miles.

When Shakyamuni Buddha was practicing the Bodhisattva path and seeking the Buddha-dharma, science was not that advanced, and there was no such thing as paper as we know it, and certainly no such thing as a paper company. So paper could not be purchased anywhere. Unlike today, when paper is easily obtainable and books can be printed easily, things were not so convenient then. There was no place to buy paper, pens, or ink. So he used his skin for paper, his bones for pens, and his blood for ink to write out the Sutras.

In ancient times, science was not so advanced. In China, bamboo was used to write on before paper was invented. Bamboo was split and tied together to make writing tablets. In the past, the *Book of History*, the *Book of Poetry*, the *Book of Changes*, and all the other ancient classics, were written out on bamboo. While paper, pens, and inks exist at the present time, do not think that they always existed. In ancient times there was absolutely no place to purchase these things.

Besides the lack of a place to buy these things, there was another reason for him to use his skin, bones, and blood to write out Sutras. This shows that he had forgotten himself for the sake of the Dharma and did not fear pain and suffering. For the sake of the Dharma he feared nothing and renounced his blood, bones, and skin to write out Sutras. Because he was willing to make great sacrifices for the Buddha and his quest for the Dharma, he gave up his body.

Stacked as high as Mount Sumeru. He used his skin, bones, and blood to write out a stack of Sutras as high as Mount Sumeru.

He revered the Dharma to such an extent that he did not even cherish his own body and life. In Hong Kong now, there is a monk named Shou Ye. Some years ago he was the abbot of both the Guang Ji Hermitage Monastery at Wu Tai Mountain and the Bodhi Temple in Shanghai. Later he went to Vietnam and built a very large temple, but when the Vietnam War started, he returned to Hong Kong. He used his blood, obtained by cutting his tongue and other parts of the body, to write out the *Flower Adornment Sutra* in Chinese characters two inches high. You can say that this state is inconceivable. He specialized in reciting the *Flower Adornment Sutra*, bowing to the *Flower Adornment Sutra*, and practicing according to the *Flower Adornment Sutra* thus abiding in the Flower Adornment Bodhimanda. All of these represent the state of a Bodhisattva.

SUTRA:

How much the less did he cherish a king's throne, cities, towns, palaces, gardens, groves, or anything else at all. He also cultivated various kinds of difficult ascetic practices...

COMMENTARY:

In his past lives, Shakyamuni Buddha practiced various kinds of difficult ascetic practices and brought forth a great Bodhi-mind for the sake of benefiting all living beings. Therefore, he did not cherish his own body or life. **How much the less did he cherish a king's throne.** Since he did not cherish either his body or his life, how much the less did he cherish having the position of a king. If Shakyamuni Buddha had not renounced the life of a householder, he would have been a Wheel-Turning Sage King.

There are four kinds of Wheel-Turning Sage Kings: the Gold Wheel King, the Silver Wheel King, the Copper Wheel King, and the Iron Wheel King. The Gold Wheel King rules over all Four Continents, Purvavideha in the east, Jambudvipa in the south, Aparagodaniya in the west, and Uttarakuru in the north. The Silver Wheel King rules over all but the northern continent Uttarakuru. The Copper Wheel King watches over two continents, and the Iron Wheel King takes care of one continent. Shakyamuni Buddha, while about to take the throne of a king, renounced the householder's life to cultivate.

An emperor was the wealthiest person. Honored as the "Son of Heaven" in China, his wealth and blessings were as vast as the four seas. Shakyamuni gave up all of this to leave the home-life and practice the path. He renounced his country, his **cities**, his wife and children, all his **towns**, all his valuable **palaces**, and all his valuable **gardens** and **groves, or anything else at all**. He gave up everything he possessed.

He also cultivated various kinds of difficult ascetic practices, and was able to bear what is most difficult to bear. He renounced a king's throne to leave the home-life to cultivate various kinds of ascetic practices. This is really something that ordinary people can't do. The different kinds of austere practices that Shakyamuni Buddha cultivated in this life and in previous lives were extremely difficult to do.

SUTRA:

...Up to and including that he accomplished the great Bodhi beneath the Tree. Then he manifested all kinds of spiritual powers, gave rise to all kinds of transformations, made appear all kinds of Buddha bodies, and dwelled in all kinds of assemblies. Perhaps he dwelled amidst the assemblies in the Bodhimandas of all great Bodhisattvas. Perhaps he dwelled amidst the assemblies in the Bodhimandas of the

Shravakas and the Pratyeka-Buddhas. Perhaps he dwelled amidst the assemblies in the Bodhimandas of Wheel-Turning Sage Kings, lesser kings, and their retinues. Perhaps he dwelled amidst the assemblies in the Bodhimandas of kshatriyas, brahmans, elders, and lay people, up to and including dwelling amidst the assemblies in the Bodhimandas of the gods, dragons, others of the eightfold pantheon of spiritual beings, as well as humans, and non-humans and others. He dwelled in all kinds of assemblies such as these. His voice was full and perfect like a great thunderclap. He complied with the likes and desires of living beings and brought them to accomplishment, up to the time that he entered Nirvana.

In all these ways I will learn from the Buddhas. In the same way that I learn from the present World Honored One, Vairochana, so too I learn from all the Tathagatas in every particle in all Buddha kshetra-lands in the ten directions and the three periods of time, throughout the dharma-realm and the reaches of space. In thought after thought I will learn from them all.

So it is that even if the reaches of space, the realms of living beings, the karma of living beings, and the afflictions of living beings come to an end, still my learning from them is without end. It continues in thought after thought without cease. I never tire of this karma in body, speech, and thought.

COMMENTARY:

Up to and including that he accomplished the great Bodhi beneath the tree... "Up to and including" means that he passed through many stages in between. For example, after the Buddha meditated in the Himalayas for six years, he then went to sit beneath the tree—the Bodhi Tree.

When Shakyamuni Buddha went to the Himalayas, his parents at first sent five people to cultivate with him and act as his Dharma protectors. Three of these five, however, were unable to endure the suffering, and they soon ran off to the Deer Park to cultivate the path there.

The two remaining people stayed with Shakyamuni during the time he ate one sesame seed and one grain of wheat a day, until he became just skin and bones. At that time, a heavenly maiden came to him. Some say she was a heavenly maiden and others say she was a milk maid, but I do not think that the distinction is important. She appeared and gave the Buddha some rice gruel prepared with milk. The Buddha accepted her offering and ate it.

As he ate it, the two remaining ascetics who were still with the Buddha said, "He's finished. So far this prince has been able to undergo suffering and cultivate the spiritual path, but now he's taking milk from a milk maid. He can't cultivate the path if he does things like this."

So they left and abandoned the Buddha, saying, "You are unable to undergo suffering, so we can't cultivate with you." These two also left him to go to the Deer Park. So all five left.

Shakyamuni Buddha then was left alone in the Himalayas. He also was ready to move his location. It was then that he went to sit beneath the Bodhi Tree. The Bodhi Tree was very large, covering an area of approximately one square mile. When Shakyamuni Buddha saw it, he thought it was a good place, so he decided to sit beneath the Bodhi Tree and cultivate the path, resolving, "If I don't accomplish the path, then I won't get up from my seat." Then he sat in full lotus posture. At that time a youth named Auspicious gave him some auspicious grass, and Shakyamuni Buddha sat down on it to cultivate the spiritual path.

He cultivated the path for forty-nine days until he saw a bright star in the east and became enlightened. As it is said, "In the night he saw a bright star and enlightened to the spiritual path." And sighing three times he said,

> How amazing! How amazing! How amazing!
> All living beings have the Buddha-nature and can become Buddhas.
> It is only because of their false thoughts and attachments that they are unable to realize it.

Why is it that living beings do not become Buddhas? Because they have false thinking and attachments. So this is how Shakyamuni Buddha became enlightened under the Bodhi Tree when he gazed upon a bright star at nighttime.

Then he manifested different kinds of spiritual powers. He manifested the wonderful function of many kinds of spiritual powers. He **gave rise to all kinds of transformations**, and changes and brought forth all kinds of inconceivable states. And **made appear all kinds of Buddha bodies.** He brought forth the pure Dharma-body, Vairochana Buddha, the perfect Reward-body, Nishyanda Buddha, and hundreds of thousands of millions of Transformation-bodies of Shakyamuni Buddha. He manifested all these many different kinds of Buddha bodies, to the extent that he manifested bodies traveling throughout the ten directions becoming Buddhas. **And he dwelled in all kinds of assemblies.** He spoke Dharma for everyone in all the many Dharma assemblies.

Perhaps he dwelled amidst the assemblies in the Bodhimandas of all great Bodhisattvas. He spoke Dharma and lectured Sutras for all the great Bodhisattvas who gathered together. **Perhaps he dwelled amidst the assemblies in the Bodhimandas of Shravakas and Pratyeka-Buddhas.** He also explained the Sutras and spoke Dharma for the gatherings of those of the Two Vehicles, the Shravakas, and Pratyeka-Buddhas who had set up Bodhimandas. **Perhaps he dwelled amidst the assemblies in the Bodhimandas of Wheel-Turning Sage Kings, lesser kings, and their retinues.** Previously, I explained that there are four kinds of Wheel-Turning Kings: the Gold Wheel-Turning King, the Silver Wheel-Turning King, the Copper Wheel-Turning King, and Iron Wheel-Turning King. The Gold Wheel King rules over one set of four continents under heaven, and he possesses Seven Jewels. These are not the Seven Jewels of gold, silver, lapis lazuli, crystal, mother-of-pearl, red pearls, and carnelian.

What are they? The first is the Wheel Jewel. When the Gold Wheel King rides on his Wheel Jewel, he can go faster than a rocket. In two hours he can travel everywhere in the four continents under heaven and do all kinds of things. The Wheel Jewel is a flying wheel, which can travel on land and in space. It can even travel in the water or in fire.

The Wheel-Turning King's second jewel is the Elephant Jewel, the White Elephant Jewel. When the Wheel-Turning King rides on his elephant, he can move about very quickly.

His third jewel is the Dark Green Horse Jewel. This horse is a dragon horse, which can also travel on the earth, in water, and when it gallops rapidly it can travel through space.

The Wheel-Turning King also has the Wish-fulfilling Jewel, which is also called the Wish-fulfilling Pearl. This spiritual pearl manifests all kinds of transformations from spiritual powers as one wishes. Whatever the king wishes for will appear. This is the Wish-fulfilling Jewel.

The King's fifth jewel is called the Jade Woman. Whenever he wishes, a beautiful woman will accompany him.

He also has the Jewel of the Minister in Charge of the Treasury. For example, if the king wishes to use gold, wherever he goes he can have the minister dig open the earth and there will be gold inside. Whatever jewels he wishes to use, the minister can dig up the earth and find those jewels. Because of this Jewel of the Minister in Charge of the Treasury, he can always have his wishes fulfilled.

The Wheel-Turning King's seventh jewel is called the General Jewel. When he must deploy his military forces, he does not need to train a large number of soldiers. From within the General Jewel, he can call up as large an army as he wishes.

The Wheel-Turning King has these seven jewels. This king also has one thousand sons. Each one is a courageous and skillful warrior who is especially heroic.

"Lesser kings" are kings under the rule of the Wheel-Turning King. Retinues include those in these smaller countries in addition to those of the Wheel-Turning Sage King. The Buddha dwelled in the Bodhimandas of these assemblies.

Perhaps he dwelled amidst the assemblies in the Bodhimandas of kshatriyas, brahmans, elders, and lay people. "Kshatriyas" are the aristocrats in India, which include the kings and others in the ruling class. "Brahmans" are those who have pure thoughts and who cultivate pure practices. "Elders" are elderly people with great blessings, and "lay people" are all the laity. The Buddha dwelled in all of those assemblies, **up to and including that he dwelled amidst the assemblies in the Bodhimandas of the gods, dragons, others of the eightfold pantheon of spiritual beings, as well as humans, and non-humans.** He may also dwell in the Bodhimandas of the assemblies of gods, dragons, and the other spiritual beings of the eightfold pantheon, as well as humans and non-humans.

He dwelled in all kinds assemblies such as these. When he became a Buddha, he dwelled in all the various assemblies mentioned above. **His voice was full and perfect;** the perfect voice of the Buddha is **like a great thunderclap,** a great rumble of thunder resounding in the air. **He complied with the likes and desires of living beings and brought them to accomplishment.** He accorded with the delights of living beings and brought them all to maturity. That is he caused those living beings who had not yet planted the roots of goodness to plant the roots of goodness; those who had already planted the roots of goodness to increase them; and those who had increased their roots of goodness to bring them to maturity. He also caused those whose roots of goodness had matured to obtain liberation.

...Up to the time that he entered Nirvana. This includes all the things he did throughout his entire life and then entering Nirvana with its four virtues at the end of his life. **In all these ways I will learn from the Buddhas.** Just as he practiced all the many difficult ascetic practices and explained the Dharma in all Bodhimandas, so too, I will do the same. I will follow and study these many methods of practice.

In the same way that I learn from the present World Honored One Vairochana, the pure Dharma-body Buddha, who pervades everywhere, and who cultivated all methods of practice amidst assemblies in the various different Bodhimandas, **so too I learn from all the Tathagatas in every particle in all Buddha kshetra-lands in the ten directions and the three periods of time throughout the dharma-realm and the reaches of space.** I will do the same with respect to all Tathagatas. I will follow and learn from them, according to the vows I made previously. Thus I will always learn from the Buddhas. **In thought after thought,** in each and every thought, **I will learn from them all**. I will always follow and study these methods of practice of all Buddhas.

So it is that even if the reaches of space come to an end, I will continue with my study and practice in this way. This will be the case, even when the reaches of space no longer exist. When **the realms of living beings** come to an end, **the karma of living beings** comes to an end, **and the afflictions of living beings come to an end, still my learning from them is without end**. Even when the realms of living beings are exhausted, the karma of living beings is exhausted, and the afflictions of living beings are exhausted, my vow to learn from the Buddhas will never end. **It continues in thought after thought without cease**. I will learn from the Buddhas in thought after thought, and my study will never end. **I never tire of this karma in body, speech, and thought.** My body, speech, and thought will continue these deeds without ever tiring. There will never be a time when I become tired, lazy, or grow weary of the Dharma.

To Constantly Conform with Living Beings

SUTRA:

Moreover, Good Man, to constantly conform with living beings is explained like this. Throughout the oceans of kshetra-lands in the ten directions exhausting the dharma-realm and the reaches of space, all living beings have all kinds of differences. That is to say, there are those born from eggs, womb-born, moisture-born, born by transformation, as well as those who live in dependence upon earth, water, fire, or wind. There are also beings that dwell in space or live in plants and trees.

This includes all the many kinds of living beings, with diverse bodies, shapes, appearances, lifespans, clans, names, and mental natures. This includes their many kinds of knowledge and views, desires and pleasures, intentional activities and modes of deportment, clothing and diets. They dwell in many different villages, towns, cities, and palaces. They include gods, dragons, others of the eightfold pantheon of spiritual beings, as well as humans, non-humans, and others. There are beings without feet, with two feet, four feet, or many feet, with form or without form, with thought or without thought, and not entirely with thought and not entirely without thought.

I will conform with all these many kinds of beings. I will make offerings to and serve them in various ways, just as I honor my own father and mother and serve my teachers, elders, Arhats, up to and including the Tathagatas, equally without difference.

COMMENTARY:

Moreover, Good Man, to constantly conform with living beings is explained like this, said Samantabhadra Bodhisattva. "I will again explain for you the principle of constantly conforming with living beings. **Throughout the oceans of kshetra-lands in the ten directions**, in all the Buddha-lands of the ten directions, **exhausting the dharma-realm and the reaches of space, all living beings have all kinds of differences.** All the many kinds of living beings with all their differences are born due to the union of a myriad of conditions, and thus each one has its own special conditions. Therefore, they are of many different kinds. Living beings are not of just of one kind, but are of many different kinds and species.

That is to say, there are those born from eggs. The *Shurangama Sutra* says,

> *Birth from a womb comes about because of emotion. Birth from eggs comes about because of thought. Birth from moisture depends on a union, and birth by transformation depends on separation.*

Womb-born are creatures born from emotions. How are living beings born from wombs? Through emotional or sensual love. Birth from eggs takes place because of thought. For example, a mother hen sits on her eggs and constantly thinks about her baby chicks, and eventually she hatches them. **Moisture-born** beings come about because of a union of moisture and consciousness. Those **born by transformation** come about from separation and change. For example, a caterpillar becomes a butterfly or a mouse transforms into a bat. This is called birth by transformation, which depends on separation. This happens when it separates from its original body and then changes to become a body of another species.

As well as those who live in dependence upon earth, water, fire, or wind. There are also living beings who rely on the four elements—earth, water, fire, and wind, for their life. **There are also beings that dwell in space or live in plants or trees.** There are also living beings that live in space or on flowers, grasses, plants, and trees. **This includes all the many kinds of living beings, with diverse bodies, shapes**, their different shapes, their features and **appearances**, and their different **lifespans**, some long and some short. They also have their **clans**; many kinds of animals have clans. Tigers have their own clans; bears have their own clans; deer have their own clans; and so forth. All species have their own clans, and each clan has its own special **names**.

Living beings have their own **mental natures** as well. For example, the nature of tigers is that they like to harm living beings, while the deer's nature is to be kind and to eat only plants and not eat other living beings. Each living being's nature is unique. Some are bold and some are timid. Some run off when they see people. And others see people and want to eat them.

This includes their many kinds of knowledge and views. Their knowledge and views are different. Their various **desires and pleasures**. The things that they delight in are not the same. Their various **intentional activities**. The things they do are also different. **And** their many different **modes of deportment**. The way they walk, their attitude, and deportment are each different.

Even their **clothing** is different. People wear clothes, animals have skin as their clothing, while birds wear the clothing of feathers. **And diets.** Some living beings eat raw meat, whereas others eat grass; some eat dirt, whereas others eat many kinds of nourishment. **They dwell in many different kinds of villages.** Living beings live in a wide variety of places, such as villages, **towns, cities, and palaces**.

They include gods, dragons, others of the eightfold pantheon of spiritual beings, as well as humans, non-humans, and others. This includes all the gods, dragons, ghosts, spirits, gandharvas, asuras, kinnaras, garudas, and mahoragas. **There are beings without feet.** Some beings, like snakes, do not have feet. Some have two legs, some have four legs, and some have many legs. Some are **with form** and some are **without form.** Some are **with thought and** some are **without thought.** Some neither have thought nor lack thought. And some are **not entirely with thought and not entirely without thought.**

I will conform with all these many kinds of beings. I will change into all their many kinds of bodies to teach and transform all these different kinds of living beings. **I will make offerings to and serve them in various ways.** I will serve them in different ways and make offerings to them, **just as I honor my own father and mother.** I will constantly conform with all living beings and respect them in the same way I revere my parents, **serve my teachers, elders, Arhats,** who have "realized the fruition," **up to and including the Tathagatas equally without difference.** I will regard them all the same way that I regard the Buddhas, to whom I make offerings. I serve them all equally without difference or discrimination.

SUTRA:

I will be a good doctor for those suffering from sickness. I will show the right road to those who have lost their way. I will be a beacon of light for those in the dark night. And I will enable the poor and destitute to uncover hidden treasures. The Bodhisattva impartially benefits all living beings in this manner.

COMMENTARY:

There are many kinds of illnesses. Living beings have 84,000 kinds of illness and the Bodhisattva uses 84,000 kinds of good medicine to cure these illnesses. So the text reads, **I will be a good doctor for those suffering from sickness.** A good doctor is one who is a very skillful expert in the field of medicine. He treats the illnesses of other beings as he would treat his own illnesses. He uses all the possible different methods to cure the illnesses of living beings.

I will show the right road to those who have lost their way. Sometimes living beings take the wrong road. Although they have two eyes, sometimes they cannot tell which road is right and which road is improper. Sometimes they have gone astray and have taken the wrong road. If you know they have taken the wrong road, you should point out the right road for them to follow.

For example, today there are many young people who do not know the proper road to follow. Their minds are engrossed in laziness, drinking, and taking illicit drugs, and they go down the wrong road. At times like these the Bodhisattva uses different kinds of methods to lead them towards the proper road, so they do not take the wrong path.

I will be a beacon of light for those in the dark night. What is "the dark night?" Those who do not understand the Buddha-dharma are in the dark night, but after they understand the Buddha-dharma, they have seen the light. Why do I say this? People who do not understand the Buddha-dharma do everything in a confused way. Once they understand the Buddha-dharma, they realize the great, bright, and proper path. You should enable living beings who do not understand the Buddha-dharma to understand it and see the light.

And I will enable the poor and destitute to uncover hidden treasures. He enables them to obtain a treasure trove, which contains gold, silver, or other precious jewels found in the earth.

The Bodhisattva impartially benefits all living beings in this manner. Without discriminating, the Bodhisattva equally benefits and aids all living beings by teaching and transforming them.

SUTRA:

Why? If a Bodhisattva conforms with living beings, then he conforms with and makes offerings to all Buddhas. If he honors and serves living beings, then he honors and serves the Tathagatas. If he makes living beings happy, he makes all Tathagatas happy. Why? Because all Buddhas, the Tathagatas, take the heart of great compassion as their substance. Because of living beings, they bring forth the heart of great compassion. From the heart of great compassion, the Bodhi-mind is born. And because of the Bodhi-mind, Equal and Right Enlightenment is accomplished.

This is like a great king of trees growing in the rocks and sand of a vast wasteland. If its roots get water, the branches, leaves, flowers, and fruits will all flourish. The Bodhi-tree king growing in the vast wasteland of birth and death (Samsara) is the same. All living beings are the roots of the tree and all Buddhas and Bodhisattvas are its flowers and fruits. By using the water of great compassion to benefit living beings, one can realize the flowers and fruit of the Buddhas' and Bodhisattvas' wisdom.

COMMENTARY:

The previous text mentioned the Bodhisattva conforming with living beings. When living beings are sick, he is a good doctor for them, and when living beings mistakenly take the wrong road, he points out the proper road for them. Bodhisattvas are beacons of light for living beings in the dark of night and cause those who are suffering in poverty to find hidden treasures.

In this way, Bodhisattvas should benefit all living beings impartially. **Why? If a Bodhisattva conforms with living beings**, if a Bodhisattva who practices the Bodhisattva path constantly conforms with living beings, fulfilling their likes, **then he conforms with and makes offerings to all Buddhas.** If you conform with all living beings, just this is conforming with and making offerings to all Buddhas. Why? This is because there is no difference between these three: the mind, Buddhas, and living beings.

If he honors and serves living beings, then he honors and serves the Tathagatas. If you are respectful to and serve all living beings, then you honor and serve the Tathagatas; it is equivalent to honoring, respecting, and making offerings to the Tathagatas. **If he makes living beings happy, he makes all Tathagatas happy.** If living beings are happy, then the Tathagatas are happy, and so those who have left the home-life say,

> Guard your mouth, collect your mind,
> And do not transgress with your body.
> Don't trouble any living beings,
> And stay far away from non-beneficial ascetic practices.
> One who cultivates like this can rescue the world.

Do not cause any living being to become afflicted, and do not cultivate unbeneficial ascetic practices. Stay far away from them. If you are like this, then you can teach and transform living beings. If you can cause all living beings to be happy, then all the Buddhas, Tathagatas, will be happy too.

Why? Why is it that if all living beings are happy then the Buddhas are happy? It is because the Buddhas and living beings are one. Buddhas are living beings, and living beings are Buddhas; Buddhas are living beings who have become Buddhas, and living beings are beings who have not yet become Buddhas but will do so in the future. They are the same as the Buddhas, and in the future they will be equal and identical with the

Buddhas. Buddhism is different from all other religions in this regard because it is the most impartial.

Why is it that if living beings are happy, the Buddhas are happy? **Because all Buddhas, the Tathagatas, take the heart of great compassion as their substance.** What is the substance of all Buddhas? The heart of great compassion, and it is **because of living beings that they bring forth the heart of great compassion**. The Buddhas bring forth the heart of great compassion because of living beings.

From the heart of great compassion, the Bodhi-mind is born. Because they give rise to a heart of great compassion, the mind of enlightenment arises. **And because of the Bodhi-mind, Equal and Right Enlightenment is accomplished.** Because of the mind of enlightenment, they realize Equal and Right Enlightenment.

Next the text presents a simile. **This is like a great king of trees growing in the rocks and sand of a vast wasteland. If its roots get water, the branches, leaves, flowers, and fruit will all flourish.** In the sandy ground there stands a great king of trees. If the roots of this tree get water, the branches and leaves will flourish, and the flowers and fruits will be fragrant and sweet.

The Bodhi-tree king growing in the vast wasteland of birth and death (Samsara) is the same. We living beings are now in the vast wasteland or desert of birth and death. The Bodhi-tree king, that is, Shakyamuni Buddha, who obtained enlightenment beneath this tree, is like the king of trees described above in the rocks and sand of a vast wasteland.

All living beings are the roots of the tree. Why are living beings inter-related with the Buddhas? All living beings are like the roots of the tree, **and all Buddhas and Bodhisattvas are its flowers and fruit.** All Buddhas and Bodhisattvas are like the flowers that bloom and the fruits that ripen on the tree. **By using the water of great compassion to benefit living beings**, the Buddhas use the wisdom-water of great compassion to enable living beings to obtain benefit, and then **one can realize the flowers and fruit of the Buddhas' and Bodhisattvas' wisdom**. In this way the Buddhas and Bodhisattvas can accomplish the limitless and boundless flowers and fruit of wisdom.

SUTRA:

Why? If a Bodhisattva benefits living beings with the water of great compassion, he is able to attain Anuttara-Samyak-Sambodhi. Therefore, Bodhi depends upon living beings. If there were no living beings, no Bodhisattva could ever realize the Unsurpassed Proper Enlightenment.

Good Man, you should understand these principles in this way. When the mind is impartial towards living beings, one can accomplish perfect great compassion. By using the heart of great compassion to conform with living beings, one successfully makes offerings to the Tathagatas. In this way the Bodhisattva conforms with living beings.

So it is that even if the reaches of space, the realms of living beings, the karma of living beings, or the afflictions of living beings come to an end, my conforming with living beings is without end. It continues in thought after thought without cease. I never tire of this karma in body, speech, and thought.

COMMENTARY:

Why? Why is it the case that the Buddhas and Bodhisattvas are the flowers and fruits, and living beings are the roots of the tree? **If a** Buddha or **Bodhisattva benefits living beings with the water of great compassion...** What is the water of great compassion? It is the nature of the mind when one is kind and compassionate. One has kindness, compassion, and sympathy towards all living beings. It is for this reason that Guan Shi Yin Bodhisattva and all the other Bodhisattvas recite the Great Compassion Mantra to imbue the water of great compassion with spiritual power to benefit living beings.

Among the Forty-Two hands of Avalokiteshvara (Guan Shi Yin) Bodhisattva are the Willow Branch Hand and the Pure Bottle Hand. They are used together; the willow branch is dipped into the pure bottle to draw out the water of compassion. Avalokiteshvara continuously recites the Great Compassion Mantra to imbue the water of great compassion with spiritual power and dispense it from the pure bottle to benefit living beings. In the verse in praise of Avalokiteshvara Bodhisattva, there is a line that reads, "The sweet dew in the vase is constantly sprinkled everywhere." The liquid in the pure bottle is called both the water of compassion and sweet dew, and it is constantly sprinkled everywhere to benefit living beings.

The water of great compassion is used to benefit living beings so that **he is able to attain Anuttara-Samyak-Sambodhi.** Because Bodhisattvas use the heart of great compassion to benefit living beings, they advance in their position and are able to perfect Unsurpassed, Right and Equal, Proper Enlightenment. Anuttara-Samyak-Sambodhi is a Sanskrit term, which is translated as "the Unsurpassed, Right and Equal, Proper Enlightenment."

Proper Enlightenment is the fruit or stage of enlightenment realized by those of the Two Vehicles, the Shravakas and Those Enlightened to Conditions. This means that they have enlightened themselves, a state called Proper Enlightenment. Although they have enlightened themselves, they have not reached the stage of Right and Equal Enlightenment. The stage of enlightenment of Bodhisattvas is called Right and Equal Enlightenment. It is right and equal to the Buddhas. But even though they have obtained Right and Equal Enlightenment, they still have not obtained the Unsurpassed Enlightenment. Bodhisattvas are called those who are surpassed by others, and Buddhas are called those who are unsurpassed. Unsurpassed Enlightenment is the position or stage of enlightenment of the Buddhas.

To attain the Unsurpassed, Right and Equal Enlightenment is to attain the position of a Buddha. If Bodhisattvas do not benefit living beings, if they do not use the water of great compassion to teach and transform living beings, then they can never become Buddhas. How does one become a Buddha? A Bodhisattva must benefit living beings in order to become a Buddha. This is called benefiting oneself and benefiting others.

Therefore, Bodhi depends upon living beings. Where does Bodhi, the Way of enlightenment, come from? It comes from living beings. **If there were no living beings**, suppose there weren't any living beings, **no Bodhisattva could ever realize the Unsurpassed Proper Enlightenment.** Without living beings, no Bodhisattva could become a Buddha. Why? This is because there would be no place for them to create merit and virtue. Living beings create merit and virtue before the Three Jewels. What about Bodhisattvas? Bodhisattvas create merit and virtue before living beings. How do Bodhisattvas create merit and virtue before living beings? They do this by benefiting living beings, causing them to leave suffering and obtain happiness, causing them to put an end to birth and death, and causing them to turn away from confusion and return to enlightenment. This is what is meant by benefiting living beings.

Good Man, you should understand these principles in this way. You good people who cultivate the path should understand these principles and meanings. You should interpret this in the following way. **When the mind is impartial towards living beings.** With respect to the Buddhas, living beings, and the mind, these three are one, and the one is three. They are inconceivable. The Buddha is inconceivable, living beings are inconceivable, and the mind is inconceivable. Therefore, the three, the mind, the Buddha, and living beings, are not different. The Buddha, living beings, and the mind are of one substance. In an indiscernible way, they are one. **One can accomplish perfect great compassion.** If you can understand this principle, then you can perfect the heart of great compassion. **By using the heart of great compassion to conform with living beings, one successfully makes offerings to the Tathagatas.** If you use a mind of great kindness and compassion to comply with living beings, then you can accomplish the merit and virtue of making offerings to the Tathagatas.

In this way the Bodhisattva conforms with living beings. Bodhisattvas who cultivate the path and practices of a Bodhisattva conform with living beings in this manner.

In making the vow to conform with living beings, **so it is that even if the reaches of space, the realms of living beings, the karma of living beings, or the afflictions of living beings come to an end**—even if these four were to come to an end, still my vow to conform with living beings would never end. It cannot cease. Basically the reaches of space, the dharma-realm, living beings, living beings' karma, and the afflictions of living beings can never end. But even if they did, still I would continue my vow. Therefore, **my conforming with living beings is without end. It continues in thought after thought without cease.** Just as in the mind one thought after another continues without interruption, I will continue my vow like this in thought after thought without cease. **I never tire of this karma in body, speech, and thought.** My actions in body, mouth, and mind will continue, and I will never get tired. I will always practice and maintain this vow and act accordingly.

To Transfer All Merit and Virtue

Moreover, Good Man, to transfer all merit and virtue is explained like this. All of the merit from the first vow, to worship all Buddhas, up to and including the vow to conform with living beings, I transfer to all living beings throughout the dharma-realm and the limits of space. I vow to cause all living beings to always attain peace and happiness, and to be without any sickness or suffering. I wish that they will not succeed in doing any evil and that all the good karma that they would like to do will quickly be achieved. I will close the doors to the evil destinies and make known the right road to becoming a human, a god, or realizing Nirvana.

Suppose there are living beings who, because they accumulated a lot of evil karma, have evoked the retribution of all kinds of extreme suffering. I will undergo all this suffering on their behalf. I will enable all of these living beings to attain liberation and to ultimately realize unsurpassed Bodhi. The Bodhisattva cultivates transference in this way.

So it is that even if the reaches of space, the realms of living beings, the karma of living beings, or the afflictions of living beings come to an end, my transference of merit and virtue is without end. It continues in thought after thought without cease. I never tire of this karma in body, speech, and thought.

COMMENTARY:

This is Samantabhadra Bodhisattva's tenth vow, to transfer all merit and virtue. **Moreover, Good Man**, I will explain this again for you. **To**

transfer all merit and virtue is explained like this. What is the meaning of transferring all merit?

All of the merit and virtue from the first vow, to worship all Buddhas. The first vow is to worship all Buddhas; the second is to praise the Tathagatas; the third is to extensively cultivate making offerings; the fourth is to repent of karmic obstacles and reform; the fifth is to follow and rejoice in merit and virtue; the sixth is to request the turning of the wheel of Dharma; the seventh is to beseech the Buddhas to remain in the world; the eighth is to always and learn from the Buddhas, **up to and including** the ninth, **the vow to conform with living beings**. "All of the merit and virtue" means cultivating all the king of vows generates much merit and virtue. Is it the case that I should keep and use all this merit and virtue for myself? No.

Samantabhadra Bodhisattva said to the youth Sudhana, "**I transfer** all of the merit and virtue."

"To transfer" means "to give away." I don't want any of the merit and virtue that belongs to me. I will give it to others instead. Who is it given to? Samantabhadra Bodhisattva says he wishes to give it **to all living beings throughout the dharma-realm and the limits of space**. I will give all of my merit and virtue to all living beings. I don't want it for myself. So I will give it to all living beings in the dharma-realm.

I vow to cause all living beings to always attain peace and happiness. My wish is that all living beings are peaceful, happy, and obtain benefit at all times. **And** I vow that they will **be without any sickness or suffering** so that they will be without any sickness or suffering whatsoever.

I wish that they will not succeed in doing any evil and that all the good karma that they would like to do will quickly be achieved. If there are those who plan to engage in evil activities, my wish is that they will not succeed. However, I wish that they quickly accomplish all the good karma and wholesome things they would like to do. **I will close the doors to the evil destinies**, that is, the doors to the hells, the realm of hungry ghosts, the realm of animals, and the realm of the asuras, so that living beings do not fall into any of these realms. I vow to transfer my merit and virtue to living beings so that the doors to the evil paths of the hells, hungry ghosts, animals, and asuras are closed. **And make known the right road to becoming a human, a god, or realizing Nirvana.** This means to show them the right path to humans and gods. This is to clearly tell and explain to others how to become human beings, how to be born in the heavens, and how to attain Nirvana.

To be a person, you must receive and maintain the Five Moral Precepts. If you wish to ascend to the heavens, you must, in addition to cultivating the Five Moral Precepts, practice the Ten Good Karmas. If you wish to attain Nirvana, you must cultivate the Four Noble Truths, the Twelve Links of Conditioned Origination, the Six Paramitas, the myriad practices, and the Bodhisattva path, and then you can obtain permanence, happiness, true self, and purity, that is, the bliss of Nirvana.

Suppose there are living beings who, because they accumulated a lot of evil karma, have evoked the retribution of all kinds of extreme suffering. Living beings have created a mass of evil karma, that is they accumulate many different kinds of bad karma, and as a result, they must undergo the most severe suffering and pain. However I, Samantabhadra Bodhisattva, who have made this king of vows, **will undergo all this suffering on their behalf.** I will undergo suffering on living beings' behalf so that they will not have to undergo the retribution from their accumulated evil karma.

Look at the vow made by this Bodhisattva! He is so kind and compassionate! Having heard about Samantabhadra's vow, if we still do not cultivate, we are really foolish to the extreme. Samantabhadra Bodhisattva has vowed to undergo suffering on our behalf, so that now we do not have to bear so much suffering. But he never tells us how much suffering he has undergone on our behalf. He never says, "I've stood in for you and taken one day's worth of suffering, one year's worth of suffering, or one life's worth of suffering. I've suffered so much for you. You should at least invite me for a meal or for a cup of tea." He is not like this. He does not ask for thanks, nor does he ask you to invite him over to get something back for what he has done for you. When we read this passage of the Sutra, we should weep bitter tears and show our gratitude to Samantabhadra Bodhisattva.

I will enable all of these living beings to attain liberation so that they are unfettered and without any obstacles. None of these kinds of retributions of suffering will hinder them. I will enable them to obtain liberation **and to ultimately realize unsurpassed Bodhi**. They will finally achieve the Proper and Equal Bodhi, Right and Equal, Proper Enlightenment.

The Bodhisattva cultivates transference in this way. He transfers all of his merit and virtue to all living beings because that is what Bodhisattvas are supposed to do. Bodhisattvas benefit other people, and they do not just exclusively benefit themselves. Therefore, they do not want any of their merit and virtue, but wish to transfer and give it away to all living beings in the dharma-realm.

So it is that even if the reaches of space, if the limits of space could be exhausted, if **the realms of living beings**, if **the karma of living beings, or the afflictions of living beings come to an end, my transference of merit and virtue is without end.** Suppose these came to an end, my vow to transfer all merit and virtue would still never come to an end. Basically, the limits of space, living beings, the karma of living beings, and the afflictions of living beings cannot be exhausted. However, even if these things did no longer exist, my vow to transfer all merit and virtue would never be exhausted. **It continues in thought after thought without cease.** It would go on like the stream of thoughts that people have. **I never tire of this karma in body, speech, and thought.** I will cultivate these ten vows in my actions, in my speech, and in my thoughts, and I will never tire. I will never feel that it's too toilsome or that I'm too tired and wish to rest. I will never rest. Night and day I will be vigorous in cultivating the Dharma of these ten king of vows.

Now we understand the ten king of vows of Samantabhadra Bodhisattva. When we compare their measure to the size of the reaches of space, we find that although the reaches of space may no longer exist, these vows can never end. Samantabhadra Bodhisattva would continue to cultivate according to these vows.

These ten king of vows are not only cultivated by Samantabhadra Bodhisattva. If he were the only one who cultivated them, it would not be necessary to make them known in the *Flower Adornment Sutra*. He wishes to enable all of us living beings to follow them and put these ten king of vows into practice. And he wishes that we will bring forth vast and great minds that are equal in measure to all of space and the dharma-realm. Then we can transfer all of our own merit and virtue to all living beings in the dharma-realm. How big would you say is the body of these vows?

All living beings and the vows of Samantabhadra Bodhisattva combine to become one. Therefore, all living beings are Samantabhadra Bodhisattva. And all these Samantabhadra Bodhisattvas also teach and transform living beings. It is not the case that only Samantabhadra Bodhisattva is Samantabhadra Bodhisattva. Anyone who relies on these ten great king of vows of Samantabhadra Bodhisattva and cultivates them is Samantabhadra Bodhisattva. "Samanta" means "everywhere," and

"Bhadra" means "a worthy sage." That is, all living beings everywhere throughout the dharma-realm become worthy sages.

These King of vows of Samantabhadra Bodhisattva were not just prepared for Samantabhadra Bodhisattva, but they are methods that are taught for all of us living beings. This is because it is to be feared that we living beings might not understand how to cultivate. Samantabhadra brings forth the heart of great compassion and introduces us to these ten king of vows for the express purpose of teaching us how to cultivate, that is to tell us to rely on these ten great vows of Samantabhadra Bodhisattva in our cultivation. Therefore, after you have read this Sutra, you should not think that it concerns only Samantabhadra Bodhisattva and not yourself. This is a mistake. After hearing about these ten great king of vows, these methods of cultivation, we too, should make vows like these and practice according to them.

The Merit of these Practices and Vows

▼

SUTRA:

Good Man, these are the Bodhisattva, Mahasattva's ten great vows in their entirety. If Bodhisattvas can conform to and enter these great vows, then they will be able to bring all living beings to maturity. They will be able to comply with Anuttara-Samyak-Sambodhi. And they will be able to perfect Samantabhadra's ocean of practices and vows. Therefore, Good Man, this is the way you should understand the meaning of these vows.

Suppose a good man or good woman were to fill up worlds as many as the smallest atomic particles in measureless, boundless, ineffably ineffable numbers of Buddha-lands throughout the ten directions with the seven extremely wonderful jewels as well as the most supreme peace and happiness known to gods and humans; and gave these to all the living beings in all those worlds; and made offerings of them to all the Buddhas and Bodhisattvas in all of those worlds; and they did this continuously without cease for kalpas as numerous as the smallest atomic particles in all of those Buddha kshetra-lands. The merit and virtue acquired from this, when compared to the merit and virtue of a person who hears this king of vows pass by his ear but once, does not even equal one one-hundredth, one one-thousandth, or even one part in an upanishad.

COMMENTARY:

After Samantabhadra Bodhisattva had explained the ten great king of vows, he said, "**Good Man, these are the Bodhisattva, Mahasattva's ten great vows.** These ten are practiced by the Bodhisattva who cultivates the Bodhisattva path. *Mahasattva* is a Sanskrit term that means "a great Bodhisattva among Bodhisattvas."

All Bodhisattvas should cultivate these ten great vows as well. Therefore, I said that these ten great king of vows are not exclusively the personal cultivation of Samantabhadra Bodhisattva. All Bodhisattvas cultivate them, and all living beings can cultivate them too. The achievement of all Buddhas and Bodhisattvas comes from the practice of these ten great king of vows. And living beings who wish to become Buddhas should cultivate in accordance with them.

When you cultivate these ten vows, you must cultivate them "**in their entirety.**" They must be perfected and completed. You must act in accord with the vows that Samantabhadra Bodhisattva has made and not give up half way in your cultivation of them. You should not practice them a while and then decide that they are very difficult and change your mind. If you change your mind, then you are not cultivating the vows to perfection or completely. You should never change your resolve. Even if the reaches of space came to an end, or there are no more living beings, or the karma of living beings has been completely eradicated, or the afflictions of living beings are totally gone, still your cultivation of these vows should never end.

Moreover, Samantabhadra Bodhisattva says, "**If Bodhisattvas can conform to and enter these great vows:**" to conform to means to rely on these ten great king of vows to cultivate these ten great practices. To enter means to get inside these great king of vows. At this point the ten great vows are the same as the Bodhisattva who practices the Bodhisattva path, and the Bodhisattva who practices the Bodhisattva path is the same as these ten great king of vows. The Dharma and the person become one without distinction. This is the meaning of "to conform to and enter."

They will then be able to bring all living beings to maturity. If you can cultivate in accordance with these ten great king of vows, you will be able to bring all living beings to maturity. What does "to bring all living beings to maturity" mean? In your cultivation of the ten great king of vows, you cause living beings without the roots of goodness to plant the roots of goodness. For example, many living beings don't understand that having filial piety for one's parents is a good thing. When you are able to teach and influence them to have filial piety for their parents, it causes them to plant the roots of goodness. There is a saying,

> Of the ten thousand evils, lust is the worst;
> Of the hundred types of good, filial piety is foremost.

What makes people different from animals is that people understand how to have filial piety for their parents and to revere their teachers and elders. People are different from animals. Animals do not understand filial piety. However, it is said:

> The lamb kneels to get its mother's milk;
> The crow returns to feed its parents.

The young lamb kneels when it takes milk from its mother. And when the young crow grows up, it returns to care for its elder parents. From these examples we can see that filial piety is a fundamental quality of human beings. Those who do not have filial piety for their parents do not have the roots of goodness. One must have filial piety for one's parents, and then one certainly has the roots of goodness. For those who do not have the roots of goodness, you should cause them to plant the roots of goodness. And for those who already have the roots of goodness, you help them to increase their roots of goodness.

For example, when the Great Master, the Sixth Patriarch, was still living at home, he went to the mountains every day to gather firewood and then sold it at the marketplace. With the money he earned, he bought rice to support his mother. In this way he planted the roots of goodness.

Basically, the Great Master, the Sixth Patriarch, already had the roots of goodness. This is the state of a Bodhisattva.

One day after he had finished selling his firewood at an inn, he heard someone reciting the *Vajra Sutra*. When the person reached the line, "One should bring forth the mind which does not dwell anywhere," the Great Master had an awakening. This guest who recited the Sutra, gave him ten taels of gold. Some of it he used for his mother's welfare and what was left he used to go to Huang Mei to seek the Dharma. This helped him plant the roots of goodness and also helped him perfect the karma of the path that leads to enlightenment.

One helps living beings who already have the roots of goodness to make them become even greater. And one helps those who have already increased their roots of goodness to reach maturity. "To mature" means "to perfect the karma of the path that leads to enlightenment." For a living being to come to maturity means that he or she becomes a Buddha. This means the fruition of Buddhahood reaches maturity. Therefore, the text says, **they will then be able to bring all living beings to maturity.**

They will be able to comply with Anuttara-Samyak-Sambodhi. "To comply with" means that they rely on this path or road to cultivate. What do they cultivate? They cultivate Anuttara-Samyak-Sambodhi, the "Unsurpassed, Right and Equal, Proper Enlightenment." Unsurpassed Enlightenment surpasses the state of the Bodhisattvas. Right and Equal Enlightenment surpasses the state of those of the Two Vehicles and Proper Enlightenment surpasses the state of common worldly people. So this is to transcend the state of an unenlightened common person and enter the state of an enlightened sage. The achievement of Anuttara-Samyak-Sambodhi refers to the fruition of a Buddha. **And they will be able to perfect Samantabhadra's ocean of practices and vows.** If you cultivate these ten great king of vows, you can achieve and perfect the ocean of Samantabhadra Bodhisattva's practices and vows. Samantabhadra Bodhisattva specializes in granting the wishes of all living beings, giving them whatever they seek.

Samantabhadra Bodhisattva once was a food server in the dining hall of a monastery. Those monastics that have renounced the householder's life assemble in the refectory for their meal and the tables are arranged in two long rows separated by about 3 to 4 feet facing one another. In front of each person are two bowls, one for rice, and the other for vegetables.

When Samantabhadra Bodhisattva served as a food server, he carried small bottles of soy sauce, hot sauce, pepper, and other condiments around his waist. He would walk before each person, and if the person wanted salt, he would give him salt; or if he wanted soy sauce or oil, he would give him that. He gave them whatever they wanted. This is how he fulfilled the wishes of living beings.

But satisfying the wishes of living beings is not all that easy to do. For example, someone might want salt, but as soon as he gave him salt, the monk would say, "Hey! I don't want that much. You gave me too much."

When he came to the next person who wanted salt, he would give him a little less, and the monk would say, "Give me more! You act like I'm eating your salt. This salt belongs to the assembly. You're too stingy." Still, he always tried to comply with everyone's demands. This is how difficult it was for Samantabhadra Bodhisattva to satisfy the wishes of living beings.

Living beings are strange. If you give them a lot, they say it is too much, and if you give them a little, they say it is not enough. If they don't say anything and you give them some, then they say they don't want any. And if you do not give them anything, they will say that you are looking down on them, that you are being unkind to them. You can see, then, that it was not easy for Samantabhadra Bodhisattva to fulfill the wishes of living beings.

Since that is how living beings are, should you decide not to try to fulfill their wishes and just ignore them? On the contrary, the more difficult they are, the more you should do this hard work. If people scold you, hit you, or look down on you when you cultivate these difficult practices, they are testing you to see if you are sincere. Therefore, those who cultivate the path should not fear difficulty. The more difficult things are, the more you should resolve to do them. For example, if you sweep the grounds and someone scolds you by saying, "From morning to night you do nothing but sweep the ground. What do you think you're doing? What's the use of sweeping the grounds?" You should just not pay attention to them.

"Well, then, if your sweeping irritates people, should you intentionally sweep the grounds every day to cause them to get mad?" you ask. Of course not! But, in general, when you cultivate the path, and if your cultivation is correct, then even if people scold you, you should ignore them. If you are practicing something that is incorrect, however, then you should quickly change. Everything is like that.

And they will be able to perfect Samantabhadra's ocean of practices and vows. In the ocean of Samantabhadra's practices and vows, there are many kinds of practices in addition to these ten great king of vows. The strength of his practices is as big as the great ocean, and so we should completely fill up or fulfill this ocean of vows. **Therefore, Good Man**, because of what I have just said, **this is the way you should understand the meaning of these vows.** You should understand the meaning of these vows in accordance with my explanation of them.

Suppose a good man or good woman who cultivates the five moral precepts and the ten good karmas **were to fill up worlds as many as**

the smallest atomic particles in measureless, boundless, ineffably ineffable numbers of Buddha-lands throughout the ten directions, with the seven extremely wonderful jewels... That is, he or she filled up all these world systems as numerous as smallest atomic particles. "Extremely wonderful" means the very best of the seven jewels: gold, silver, red pearls, carnelian, and so forth. In general, these seven jewels are the most valuable things that exist.

...As well as the most supreme peace and happiness known to gods and humans, together with the foremost happiness of gods and humans, the most wonderful bliss, **and gave these to all the living being in all those worlds**, if they gave this bliss as a gift to all the living beings in as many worlds as are discussed above.

There are three kinds of giving:

1) the giving of wealth;
2) the giving of Dharma;
3) the giving of fearlessness.

Of the first kind, the giving of wealth, there are two kinds, internal and external. Internal wealth includes your body, mind, nature, and life. One vows, "I will give things of my own; I will give my eyes to people, or my ears, my nose, my tongue, or my head, my brains, or my marrow." External wealth includes one's country, cities, spouse, and children. One who truly practices giving gives away his whole country to others. He does not want to be a king. Nor does he want any cities that belong to him. Suppose everything in San Francisco, a large city, belongs to me. I wish to give everything away to other people.

Men find it most difficult to give up their wives or girlfriends. If you are able to give up what you basically cannot give up, then that is true giving. If you cannot give them up, then that is not giving.

There once was a woman who heard me say that giving a wife to others is a form of giving, so she asked if she could give away her husband. This is probably the first time anyone has given away her husband. I told her, "You must first find someone else for him; if you can't find anyone to accept him, how can you give him away? You can't throw him out in the street and call it giving." Later I said, "You don't really have a mind of giving. You still can't give him up." And in fact, she did not give him away after all. "Giving wealth" means that one can renounce one's valuables and give them all away.

The second kind of giving is the giving of Dharma. "Of all the kinds of offerings, the offering of Dharma is supreme." The giving of Dharma is also called offering the Dharma. To lecture Sutras, speak Dharma, teach living beings, and turn the wheel of Dharma are all forms of giving the Dharma. Giving Dharma is better than giving wealth, but the Dharma you give should accord with the conditions of living beings it is intended for, so that when they hear the Dharma, they will progressively understand the Buddha-dharma and then become enlightened.

The third is the giving of fearlessness. Some may have an unexpected accident or disaster, or see a ghost, a demon, or other weird entities or bandits, and forget everything and become scared out of their wits. At that time, you console them, "Don't be afraid. Recite Homage to Guan Shi Yin Bodhisattva, and Guan Shih Yin Bodhisattva will protect you. Don't be afraid." If you explain this so that they can understand, they will then recite the name of Guan Yin Bodhisattva and as soon as they do, they will naturally lose their fear and regain their composure. Or they can recite the name of Amitabha Buddha, and they will very quickly be far from fear. This is called the giving of fearlessness.

I have briefly described these three kinds of giving. You should practice them in cultivating the Bodhisattva path.

If they gave these jewels and bliss as a gift to all the numerous living beings in as many worlds as are discussed above, **and made offerings of them** as has been described **to all the Buddhas and Bodhisattvas in all of those worlds**—if they gave all kinds of offerings to the Buddhas and Bodhisattvas in all of those worlds, **and did this continuously without cease for kalpas as numerous as the smallest atomic particles in all of those Buddha kshetra-lands.** If they gave these gifts constantly, passing through as many kalpas as there are smallest atomic particles in that many Buddha-lands, making gifts not for just one or two days, but continuously and without rest for as many great kalpas as there are smallest atomic particles in these numerous worlds, **the merit and virtue acquired from this...** The merit and virtue acquired by these people who practice giving would be very great indeed!

When compared to the merit and virtue of a person who hears this king of vows pass by his ear but once... A person who hears these ten great king of vows of Samantabhadra Bodhisattva recited, not explained, but simply recited so that they pass by his ear but once, will gain merit and virtue which surpasses the merit and virtue of the person described above who made all those gifts. As it is said, "You hear it one time and it plants an eternal seed for the path." Once you hear it, you have a seed for Bodhi forever. If you compare this person's merit and virtue with the merit and virtue derived from giving in the measureless and boundless numbers of worlds for such a long time as measureless and boundless numbers of kalpas, the merit of the latter, compared to the merit of a person who hears the great vows but once, **does not even equal one one-hundredth.** The merit and virtue derived from all this giving does not equal one one-hundredth of the merit and virtue derived from hearing these ten great king of vows, nor **one one-thousandth.** The giving does not equal one one-thousandth, **or even one part in an upanishad.** An upanishad refers to the essence of a particle, and it is even smaller than an atomic particle. The merit and virtue derived from giving all the unsurpassed gifts for many kalpas of time does not equal one upanishad's amount when compared to the merit and virtue gained from hearing these ten great king of vows.

Why is the merit and virtue derived from these ten great king of vows so great? If you give wealth, you can only save a person's body and life. However, giving these ten great king of vows is the giving of Dharma. One may cultivate Samantabhadra's Contemplation or Samantabhadra's Repentance, which are the ten great king of vows. When one cultivates this kind of contemplation, then the one becomes infinite, and the infinite becomes one. The one becomes the dharma-realm, and the dharma-realm becomes one. Worshiping one Buddha is worshiping all Buddhas of the dharma-realm. And worshiping all Buddhas of the dharma-realm is worshiping one Buddha. The first vow is to worship and revere all Buddhas, and the merit and virtue derived from this practice is infinite and inexhaustible. The merit and virtue is especially great. If you cultivate this Dharma, then day-by-day your Bodhi seeds will grow, and before long you will accomplish the fruition of Bodhi. Therefore, the merit and virtue is especially great.

SUTRA:

Moreover, if a person, with a mind of deep faith in these great vows, receives and upholds, reads and recites them from memory, or even writes out a single four-line verse, he or she can quickly eradicate the karma of the five Avīci offenses. All of the world's illnesses that afflict the body and mind, as well as the various kinds of suffering and distress, up to and including all the bad karma equal in number to the smallest atomic particles in Buddha kshetra-lands will all be wiped away.

COMMENTARY:

Moreover, if a person—it is not certain, but there may be such a person **who with a mind of deep faith...** Deep faith is not shallow. One brings forth a mind of genuine and proper faith, which means a mind that really has no doubts. **In these great vows...** One has faith in Samantabhadra Bodhisattva's ten great king of vows. Whoever **receives and upholds reads and recites them from memory**, that is one who relies on this Dharma to cultivate. He recites this chapter on the Practices and Vows of Samantabhadra Bodhisattva every day. "To read" refers to using a book to read the text and "recite them from memory" means to recite the vows from memory without looking at the text. **Or even writes out a single four-line verse**. Or if you cannot read or recite the text, perhaps you can write it out with a pen. This is not talking about writing out the entire text, but just writing a single four-line verse. For example, you might write out,

> To worship all Buddhas;
> To praise the Tathagatas;
> To extensively cultivate make offerings;
> To repent of karmic obstacles and reform.

Someone only writes out four lines of verse or the names of the vows like this.

Can quickly eradicate the karma of the five Avīci offenses... Quickly does not refer to a fixed period of time. It may be that it is eradicated by writing it once a day, twice a day, or many times a day. Very quickly they are eradicated. The five Avīci offenses are five karmic offenses that lead to the Avīci hell. In this hell, one person sees that his body totally fills it up. If there are many people in this hell, each person sees his own body totally filling it up, yet they do not obstruct one another. Time spent in this hell is also uninterrupted. From the time someone first enters it until the time he leaves, there is no break in the suffering he undergoes as retribution for his offenses. His suffering is uninterrupted, his lifetime is uninterrupted, time is uninterrupted, and the retribution he undergoes is uninterrupted.

All of the world's illnesses that afflict the body and mind. Some people become ill in body, and some people become ill in mind. Illness of the body refers to the sicknesses we may contract, and illnesses of the mind refers to the suffering in our minds when we are not happy.

As well as the various kinds of suffering and distress. If you are sick, you undergo suffering and distress, and if you suffer and are afflicted, then you are not happy. **Up to and including all the bad karma equal in number to the smallest atomic particles in Buddha kshetra-lands will all be wiped away.** Every kind of evil karma can be wiped away. But to do so, you must have a mind of deep faith. If you do not have a mind of deep faith, but only wish to try it out to see if it works, you will not invoke a response. Why? This is because the Buddhas and Bodhisattvas do not appreciate living beings coming to test them. They can test you, but you cannot say, "I don't believe the Dharma spoken by the Buddha, so I think I'll try them out to see if they work." You should sincerely put it into practice and not just test it out to see if it works.

SUTRA:

All the demon-armies, the yakshas, rākshasas, kumbhāndas, pishāchas, bhūtas, and so forth that drink blood and devour flesh, all these evil ghosts and spirits, will stay far away from this person. Or they will make a resolve to draw near and protect him.

Therefore, if a person recites these vows, he goes throughout the world without any obstruction, like the moon in the sky that emerges from

clouds. All Buddhas and Bodhisattvas will praise him. All people and gods should venerate him. All living beings should make offerings to him.

This good man is well able to be reborn as a human and will perfect all of Samantabhadra's merit and virtue. Before long, he will be just like Samantabhadra Bodhisattva, obtaining a subtle and wonderful physical body replete with the thirty-two hallmarks of a great man.

If he is born among humans or gods, he will always live in a superior family. He will totally destroy the evil destinies and he will be far apart from all bad friends. He will be able to vanquish all those on heterodox paths. He will be completely free from all afflictions. He's just like the lion king, able to subdue all beasts. Such a person is worthy of receiving the offerings of all living beings.

COMMENTARY:

All the demon-armies. In this world there are many heavenly demons and those on paths outside of Buddhism. Why don't they show themselves? They hide away because the Buddha-dharma is in the world, but if there was no Buddha-dharma here, they would openly appear in the world.

What are these "demon armies?" The word "demon" in Chinese (魔) is derived from the Sanskrit *mara*, which means "murderer" or "one fond of killing." Mara likes to kill any living being he sees. The demonic armies include demon kings, demon citizens, demon children, and demon women. Demon women are especially beautiful; however they also delight in killing.

The yakshas can travel very fast. There are flying yakshas, yakshas that travel on the ground, and yakshas who travel in space. They are also called those that are brave and strong. They are brave and skilled in fighting and extremely cruel and evil. They have no other ability than harming human beings.

Rākshasas is a Sanskrit word which carries the meaning of "fearsome" ghost. Both the yakshas and rakshasas are mentioned in the *Shurangama Mantra: yao cha jie luo he,* (line 247), and *luo cha si jie luo he,* (line 248). *Yao cha* is yaksha, and *luo cha si* is rākshasa. Reciting the *Shurangama Mantra* prevents these demons from harming people and in fact causes them to protect people. Reciting *yao cha jie luo he, luo cha si jie luo he* can get rid of the misfortune of an untimely death. It prevents these very ominous and dangerous situations.

Kumbhāndas are barrel-shaped ghosts. They are also called ghosts that have the shape of a winter melon. And they are yen mei (spellbound when asleep) ghosts. They are skilled at yen mei. What is yen mei? When people are asleep, they cast a spell on them to prevent them from talking no matter how hard they try to talk. They can also paralyze people so that they can't move or do anything at all.

Pishāchas are also a kind of ghost. This ghost is called a ghost that eats a person's vital energy as well as the vital energy of the five grains.

Bhūtas, and so forth. Bhūtas are another type of ghost. I don't remember if I explained this before. It means a ghost with a huge body. His body is extremely large. It's as large as Mount Sumeru.

These two ghosts, bhūtas and kumbhāndas, are also found in the **Shurangama Mantra: bu duo jie luo he, jiu pan cha jie luo he**. The kumbhānda ghost is also called the ghost that rides in vehicles or on horses. Together with bhūtas they can prevent accidents and they can also get rid of disasters connected with city walls. For example, if a city's walls are crumbling and you aren't careful, you could be crushed to death. However, if you recite the *Shurangama Mantra,* you could prevent this disaster. In the same way, you can prevent car accidents, accidents on horseback, and other disasters. These two ghosts can protect people and get rid of these kinds of difficulties. In the *Shurangama Mantra* we find the names of these ghost kings, and if you recite this mantra, not only will they refrain from hurting you, they will protect you.

That drink blood and devour flesh, all these evil ghosts and spirits... These ghosts either drink people's blood or they eat their flesh. These are evil ghosts and spirits. **Will stay far away from this person**. However, if you recite the ten great king of vows of Samantabhadra Bodhisattva, then these evil ghosts will go far away from you.

Or they will make a resolve to draw near and protect him... If they do not wish to go far away from you, they may decide to draw near to protect you and become your Dharma protector. **Therefore, if a person recites these vows, he goes throughout the world without any obstruction.** A person who recites these ten great king of vows, will not be hindered wherever he travels in the world. He does not have any obstructions whatsoever. He will be able to destroy all obstructions.

One will be **like the moon in the sky that emerges from clouds**, like the bright moon appearing in the sky without being blocked or obstructed by clouds. You'll be like the moonlight shining wherever you go. **All Buddhas and Bodhisattvas will praise him.** In addition to this all the Buddhas and Bodhisattvas of the ten directions will praise such a person, and **all people and gods should venerate him**. All humans and gods respect one who recites these ten great king of vows. **All living beings should make offerings to him.** All living beings should make offerings to the person who recites these ten great king of vows.

This good man, the good man who recites these ten great king of vows, **is well able to be reborn as a human.** In each life he will be able to attain a human form. **And will perfect all of Samantabhadra's merit and virtue.** He will be able to cultivate and perfect the merit and virtue of Samantabhadra Bodhisattva. **Before long, he will be just like Samantabhadra, obtaining a subtle and wonderful physical body.** He will very quickly obtain a subtle and wonderful body, like Samantabhadra Bodhisattva, **replete with the thirty-two hallmarks of a great man**, just like the fine features of the Buddhas.

If he is born among humans or gods, if he is born in the human realm or in the heavens above, **he will always live in a superior family.** Wherever he goes, the family in which he is born will always be a great one. It will be the most powerful, most noble, and the wealthiest family. **He will totally destroy the evil destinies.** He's able to destroy all the four evil destinies of the hells, hungry ghosts, animals, and asuras, **and he will be far apart from all bad friends.** Good friends will always draw near to him and bad companions will be left far behind.

He will be able to vanquish all those on heterodox paths. He will have the power to subdue all adherents of heterodox or non-Buddhist paths. **He will be completely free from all afflictions.** The worst problem that people have is all their afflictions, but now one can be liberated from all afflictions. **He's just like the lion king, able to subdue all beasts.** He's able to subjugate all animals. As soon as the lion roars, the myriad beasts are frightened. **Such a person is worthy of receiving the offerings of all living beings.** He will deserve to receive the offerings of all living beings.

SUTRA:

Further, when a person is on the verge of death, at the very last kṣaṇa-instant of life, when all his sense-faculties deteriorate, all of his family departs from him, and all of his power and influence are diminished

and lost; when his ministers, great officials, everything in his inner and outer court, his elephants, horses, carts, and precious jewels, hidden treasures, and all things such as these can no longer accompany him, then this king of vows alone will never leave him. At all times, these vows will be before him guiding him. In a single kṣhaṇa-instant, he will be reborn in the Land of Ultimate Bliss.

Upon arriving there, he will immediately see Amitabha Buddha, Manjushri Bodhisattva, Samantabhadra Bodhisattva, the Bodhisattva Who Contemplates With Self-Mastery (Avalokiteshvara), Maitreya Bodhisattva, and others. The physical features of these Bodhisattvas, who are all around him, are dignified and majestic; their merit and virtue perfect.

COMMENTARY:

Further, when a person who reads and recites Samantabhadra Bodhisattva's ten great king of vows **is on the verge of death, at the very last kṣhaṇa-instant of life, when all his sense-faculties deteriorate**. A kṣhaṇa is a very, very short moment of time; and at the last kṣhaṇa, all of a person's sense-faculties, his eyes, ears, nose, tongue, body, and mind, disperse. That is the moment when the sense-faculties scatter and deteriorate: the eyes can no longer see; the ears cannot hear; the tongue cannot taste; the nose can no longer detect smell; and the body loses the sense of touch. All the sense-faculties no longer function, and **all of his family departs from him,** the dying person. All of his relatives and friends separate from him, because he has already died.

And all his power and influence are diminished and lost. When a person dies, all his awesome virtue, power, and influence are completely lost including **his ministers** and **great officials**. If you are a king, then you have a prime minister and all kinds of great ministers, as well as

everything in his inner and outer court, great palaces, and countries. "Inner court" refers to wives and wealth, and "outer court" refers to all material wealth such as **his elephants, horses, carts, and precious jewels, hidden treasures, and all things such as these can no longer accompany him.** When you are on the verge of death, nothing will go along with you. **Then this king of vows alone will never leave him.** Only the ten great king of vows of Samantabhadra Bodhisattva will stay with you. Because they are in your Eighth Consciousness, there is no way they can leave you.

At all times, these vows will be before him, guiding him. In all places and at all times, they will be in front of him, so that **in a single kshana-instant**, in a very short instant of time, **he will be reborn in the Land of Ultimate Bliss. Upon arriving there, he will immediately see Amitabha Buddha.** After arriving in the Western Pure Land of Ultimate Bliss, one sees Amitabha Buddha.

Going west, the Land of Ultimate Bliss is trillions of Buddha-lands away. Amitabha Buddha is the Teaching-Master of the Land of Ultimate Bliss. His name is Sanskrit, and it means "measureless life" and "measureless light," because both his life and his light are infinite; therefore he is called the Buddha of Measureless Light and Life.

Manjushri Bodhisattva's name means "wonderful virtues" and "wonderfully auspicious." So this is Wonderfully Auspicious Bodhisattva. **Samantabhadra Bodhisattva** is the Bodhisattva who is the host for this chapter, the *Chapter on Samantabhadra's Practices and Vows*. **The Bodhisattva Who Contemplates With Self-Mastery (Avalokiteshvara)** is the Bodhisattva Who Observes the Sounds of the World (Guan Shi Yin). **Maitreya Bodhisattva, and others.** Maitreya Bodhisattva's name in Sanskrit means "clan of kindness." He is also called Ajita, which means "invincible;" no one can defeat him. In the future, Ajita Bodhisattva, who is Maitreya, will be the next Buddha in our Saha world, the fifth Buddha of the Worthy or Bhadra Kalpa.

When will Maitreya Bodhisattva become a Buddha? There are certain people of heterodox paths who say that he has already come into the world and become a Buddha. Actually Maitreya Bodhisattva's appearing in the world is still a long way off. Quite a long time must pass before he becomes a Buddha. Presently our world is in a period of "kalpa decrease." During this time the average lifespan of human beings decreases by one year every one hundred years and the average height of a human being also decreases by one inch. This continues until the average lifespan is ten years, and people are no more than a foot tall, about the size of today's dogs. Although they will be small, their evil thoughts will be great. The smaller they become, the meaner they get.

At this time when the average human lifespan is ten years, a few days after people are born, they will understand sexual desire and will engage in sexual activity just like dogs and pigs do now. At that time, they will be able to kill one another with only a blade of grass. So people will kill each other. "I kill you, and you kill me." This mutual slaughter will occur because there will be too many people in the world. They will be as numerous as ants. People will be everywhere. If a person survives and is not killed, he or she will still die at the age of ten.

From this point on, a period of increase will begin. The average human lifespan will increase by one year every hundred years, and the average height will also increase by one inch. When the average age reaches eighty-four thousand years, another period of decrease will begin. When the average age reaches eighty thousand years, Maitreya Bodhisattva will come into the world and become a Buddha. Therefore, those people on heterodox paths who say that Maitreya Bodhisattva is already in the world are talking as if in a dream.

The physical features of these Bodhisattvas, who are all around him, are dignified and majestic. The physical bodies of all these Bodhisattvas that he sees will be upright and dignified, and **their merit and virtue perfect.** These Bodhisattvas, with their perfect appearances and complete merit and virtue are all around him.

SUTRA:

This person will see himself born from a lotus flower and will receive a prediction for future Buddhahood from the Buddha. After receiving this prediction, for numberless quadrillions of nayutas of kalpas throughout ineffably ineffable numbers of worlds in the ten directions everywhere, with the power of wisdom, he will accord with the minds of living beings and bring them benefit.

Before long, he will sit in a Bodhimanda, vanquish the demon armies, accomplish Equal and Proper Enlightenment and turn the wonderful wheel of Dharma. He will cause living beings in worlds as many as the smallest atomic particles in Buddha kshetra-lands to bring forth the Bodhi-mind. According with their basic natures, he will teach and transform them until they are brought to accomplishment. To the end of the oceans of kalpas of the future, he will greatly benefit all living beings.

COMMENTARY:

This person born in the Land of Ultimate Bliss **will see himself born from a lotus flower.** A person who has read, recited, received and upheld, and written out Samantabhadra Bodhisattva's ten great king of vows will be born in the Western Land of Ultimate Bliss in a lotus flower. **And will receive a prediction for future Buddhahood from the Buddha.** In the Western Land of Ultimate Bliss, there are only men, no women.

Everyone is born by transformation from a lotus flower, not from the body of flesh and blood of a father and mother. There is a saying: "When the flower blossoms, one sees the Buddha." When one's lotus flower blossoms, one will see a Buddha appear before himself, seated in a lotus flower. Amitabha Buddha will then foretell the time when one will become a Buddha.

After receiving this prediction, once one has received a prediction for their future Buddhahood, **for numberless quadrillions of nayutas of kalpas throughout ineffably ineffable numbers of worlds in the ten directions everywhere, with the power of wisdom, he will accord with the minds of living beings and bring them benefit.** For so many nayutas of kalpas, in so many worlds, with the power of his own wisdom he will comply with the hearts of living beings and benefit them.

Before long, he will sit in a Bodhimanda. He will very quickly in a short period of time sit in a Bodhimanda and become a Buddha. He will **vanquish the demon armies**, all the heavenly demons and those on heterodox paths, and will **accomplish Equal and Proper Enlightenment.** That is, he will become a Buddha. Then he will **turn the wonderful wheel of Dharma**, which is another way of saying that he will teach and transform living beings. He will speak the Dharma to rescue them. **He will cause living beings in worlds as many as the smallest atomic particles in Buddha kshetra-lands to bring forth the Bodhi-mind. According with their basic natures, he will teach and transform them until they are brought to accomplishment.** He will accord with living beings and use ingenious expedient methods to teach and transform them and bring their fundamental natures to maturity. **To the end of the oceans of kalpas of the future, he will greatly benefit all living beings.** He will benefit all living beings for countless eons, exhausting the limits of future time.

SUTRA:

Good Man, if these living beings hear or have faith in these great king of vows, or receive, uphold, read, recite from memory, or extensively explain these vows for others, all the merit and virtue they obtain can only be known by the Buddha, the World Honored One, and by no one else.

Therefore, all of you who hear this king of vows should harbor no doubts. You should attentively accept these vows. After accepting them, you should be able to read them. After reading them, you should be able to recite them from memory. After reciting them from memory, you should be able to uphold them and even write them out and extensively explain them for others. In a single thought, these people will be able to accomplish all of their practices and vows.

COMMENTARY:

Good Man! Samantabhadra Bodhisattva again calls out, "This person who practices good deeds." **If these living beings hear or have faith in this great king of vows, or receive, uphold, read, recite from memory, or extensively explain these vows for others, the merit and virtue they obtain…** "These" living beings refers to those who receive, maintain, read, and recite *The Practices and Vows of Samantabhadra Bodhisattva Chapter*. If you hear or have faith in these ten great king of vows or if you can receive them with your heart, put them into practice with your body, read them from the text, or recite them from memory, and explain them extensively for others, then the merit and virtue so obtained **can only be known by the Buddha, the World Honored One, and by no one else.** Only the Buddha can comprehend this. Only the Buddha, the World Honored One, knows how great this merit and virtue is. None of the other Bodhisattvas or Arhats can fathom the magnitude of this merit and virtue.

Therefore, all of you who hear these king of vows of Samantabhadra Bodhisattva **should harbor no doubts.** You must make sure to not have any doubts. "The mind of a cultivator of the path should never have doubts. As soon as doubts arise, he will go astray." If you want to cultivate the path, you cannot have doubts about the Dharma spoken by the Buddha. If you do, you can easily go down the wrong road, and you will not obtain any benefit.

You should attentively accept these vows. You should earnestly and honestly receive and maintain these ten great king of vows. **After accepting them, you should be able to read them.** After you accept their meaning, you should read these ten great king of vows from the text. **After reading them, you should be able to recite them from memory.** Having read them, you should be able to recite them from memory without looking at the Sutra text. **And after reciting them from memory, you should be able to uphold them.** After you are able to recite them from memory, you should protect and maintain these ten great king of vows **and even write them out and extensively explain them for others.** You should use a pen to write them out, and then you constantly explain these ten great king of vows for others.

In a single thought, in such a short period of time as one thought, **these people will be able to accomplish all of their practices and vows.** All of one's cultivation and one's hopes and vows will be accomplished. That is, all of one's merit and virtue will be accomplished, and all of one's vows will be fulfilled.

SUTRA:

The blessings that one will amass are measureless and boundless. One will be able to rescue living beings from the great ocean of afflictions and suffering, causing them to make good their escape, so that all of them are reborn in Amitabha Buddha's Land of Ultimate Bliss.

COMMENTARY:

Previously I explained that one who can read, recite, and write out the ten great king of vows of Samantabhadra Bodhisattva and proclaim them extensively for others can fulfill all his practices and vows in as short a time as a single thought. Now the text says **the blessings that one will amass are measureless and boundless**. In his cultivation of Samantabhadra Bodhisattva's practices, all of the blessings that he has attained when accumulated together are measureless and boundless. They cannot be calculated with numbers, nor can their limits or boundaries be found.

One will be able to rescue living beings from the great ocean of afflictions and suffering. Those Bodhisattva's who bring forth the Bodhi-mind and cultivate Samantabhadra Bodhisattva's practices can rescue living beings in the great ocean of suffering and afflictions.

Although we common people have afflictions, we are not aware that afflictions are suffering. If you have afflictions, you suffer. However, if you are free from afflictions, then you have no suffering. Those people who cultivate the practices of Samantabhadra Bodhisattva can rescue all living beings from the great ocean of suffering and afflictions, so that they leave suffering and obtain happiness, thus **causing them to make good their escape**. One can liberate all living beings from the ocean of suffering, so that they reach the Other Shore of Nirvana. Where will they go? Where will they be reborn? That is, in what world or land will they be reborn? **So that all of them are reborn in Amitabha Buddha's Land of Ultimate Bliss.**

Although the name "Amitabha Buddha" consists of only a couple of words, the entire Buddha-dharma is included within these words. Shakyamuni Buddha spoke every Sutra after being requested to speak the Dharma by someone. In the *Vajra Sutra* it was Subhuti who requested the Dharma, and Shariputra requested the Dharma in the *Dharma Flower Sutra*. The only exception was the *Amitabha Sutra*. No one requested the Buddha to speak the *Amitabha Sutra*. It was spoken without request. Why? Because, no one understood this Dharma. The Pure Land Dharma door appears to be very simple, but actually the words "Amitabha Buddha" encompass all the Sutras in the Three Treasuries and the Twelve Divisions of the Buddhist canon. A few decades ago I wrote this verse:

> *Amitabha Buddha is the king of the ten thousand dharmas,*
> *Which totally contains the Five Periods and the Eight Teachings.*
> *A practitioner need only uphold and recite it single-mindedly*
> *And he will certainly reach the unmoving field of serenity and light.*

A few decades ago I was moved while reciting the Buddha's name, and so I wrote this verse. You may see "Amitabha Buddha" as only being a Buddha's name, but if you recite his name, you can understand all dharmas; and thus the verse says, "Amitabha Buddha is the king of the ten thousand dharmas." In the second line, "the Five Periods" are:

In the second line, "the Five Periods" are:

1. the Flower Adornment Period;
2. the Agama Period;
3. the Vaipulya Period;
4. the Prajna Period;
5. the Dharma Flower-Nirvana Period.

"The Eight Teachings" are:

1. the Storehouse;
2. the Pervasive;
3. the Exclusive;
4. the Perfect;
5. the Sudden;
6. the Gradual;
7. the Secret;
8. the Unfixed.

The words "Amitabha Buddha" contain the Five Periods and the Eight Teachings; thus "A practitioner need only uphold and recite it single-mindedly." All that cultivators need to do is to recite Amitabha Buddha's name with a concentrated mind, and they "will certainly reach the unmoving field of serenity and light." You will certainly reach the Pure Land of Eternal Serenity and Light, which is the unmoving Bodhimanda.

Shakyamuni Buddha spoke about Amitabha Buddha without being asked. No one requested him to speak, yet he spoke the *Amitabha Sutra*. Some people think that reciting Amitabha Buddha's name is a practice for old ladies and that people with wisdom should not cultivate this method. This is a mistake! Whether you are wise or unintelligent, you can cultivate the practice of reciting Amitabha Buddha's name. This Dharma door benefits beings of all three capacities: superior, average, and inferior capacities. They all derive benefit. All are blessed, and so everyone can cultivate this method. It's not just for old ladies.

Why recite Amitabha Buddha's name? We living beings in the Saha World have the closest affinities with the Guan Shi Yin Bodhisattva. Guan Shi Yin Bodhisattva reveals the Universal Door and has thirty-two response-bodies. Amitabha Buddha has even greater affinities with all living beings because he is the teacher of Guan Shi Yin Bodhisattva and Great Strength Bodhisattva and is the Teaching-Master of the Land of Ultimate Bliss.

How is it that we have affinities with Amitabha Buddha? In a past life, when he was cultivating on the causal stage of practice before becoming a Buddha, Amitabha Buddha was a Bhikshu named Fa Zang (Dharma Treasury). Bhikshu Fa Zang made Forty-Eight Great Vows and each vow was for the purpose of leading living beings to the Land of Ultimate Bliss to become Buddhas.

The Bhikshu Fa Zang vowed, "In the future, when I become a Buddha, there will only be men and no women in my world." Everyone knows that without women there can be no men, and that without men, there can be no women. Everyone must have a father and mother to be born. If there are only men in the Land of Ultimate Bliss, can men give birth to children? No. If not, where do the children in the Land of Ultimate Bliss come from?

The children are born from lotus flowers. Beings born in the Land of Ultimate Bliss first enter a lotus bud. When we recite the name of Amitabha Buddha, our lotus bud grows. When we recite once, our flower grows a little. When we recite again, it grows a little more. The more we recite, the larger the bud grows, until the lotus gets as big as a carriage wheel. When we are on the verge of death, Amitabha Buddha comes in person to take us to the Land of Ultimate Bliss. Then he puts our spirit-nature into that lotus flower. When the lotus flower opens, your Dharma-body appears. Therefore, the saying goes, "When the flower opens, one sees the Buddha." When the lotus flower opens, a Buddha is born. Since everyone who becomes a Buddha is a man and not a women, the Land of Ultimate Bliss has only men and no women.

How far away is the Land of Ultimate Bliss? It's a hundred billion Buddha-lands away. It's a very long distance from us. Amitabha Buddha said "After I become a Buddha, my land will certainly only have men and not have any women." So all people in his land are born by transformation from lotus flowers. There is a verse that says:

I vow to be born in the Western Pure Land,
Where the nine grades of lotus flowers are my parents.

The "nine grades of lotus flowers" are our parents. Each of the nine grades are further divided into nine grades, making a total of eighty one grades. What are the nine grades? They are the highest superior grade, the middle superior grade, the lowest superior grade; the highest medium grade, the middle medium grade, and the lowest medium grade; and the highest inferior grade, the middle inferior grade, and the lowest inferior grade. Each of these nine grades of lotus flowers is again divided into nine grades, which gives a total of eighty-one grades. All of us living beings who recite Amitabha Buddha's name can be born in the Western Land of Ultimate Bliss.

When Amitabha Buddha was the Bhikshu Fa Zang, one of his Forty-Eight Vows is as follows: "When I become a Buddha, any living being throughout the ten directions who recites my name will be born in my land." He vowed that they all would be born in his land. And when they go to his land, they will be "born by transformation from a lotus flower and realize Anuttara-Samyak-Sambodhi." They will attain the Unsurpassed, Right and Equal, Proper Enlightenment. Since Amitabha Buddha made this vow, if we of the Saha world recite "Namo Amitabha Buddha" at the end of our lives, he will come and extend his hand to take us. When you look at the image of Amitabha Buddha, one hand is held out. This is an expression of his wish to lead you to the Land of

Ultimate Bliss. That is, he uses his hand to pull you off to the Land of Ultimate Bliss. It is said,

> Amitabha is foremost of the Buddhas of the ten
> directions and the three periods of time.
> In nine grades he rescues living beings.
> And his awesome virtue is inexhaustible.

Therefore, you should not look upon Amitabha Buddha too lightly.

In the future during the Dharma Ending Age, the Dharma will no longer exist; it will be destroyed. Now the Sutras have words. However, in the Dharma Ending Age the words of the Sutras will disappear by themselves. Why? Because living beings will not have any blessings. Their karmic offenses will be too heavy. So they will not have the opportunity to read the Sutras. We need not discuss the future, even today some people whose eyes are without any disease cannot see clearly when they read Sutras. They see it in a muddled way because they have obstructions. What kind of obstructions? These are the same karmic obstructions that living beings in the Dharma Ending Age will experience. Although they have eyes, they cannot read the Buddha-dharma clearly. In the future, all the Sutras of the Buddha-dharma will no longer exist.

Which Sutra will disappear first? The *Shurangama Sutra* will disappear first, and after it no longer exists, the other Sutras will continue to be extinguished until the only one left is the *Amitabha Sutra*. At that time this Sutra alone will exist in the world for one hundred years, and it will save measureless numbers of living beings. But after one hundred years, it too will be gone, and all that will remain will be the words "Namo Amitabha Buddha," which will survive for another hundred years. The living beings who will recite "Namo Amitabha Buddha" and be rescued will be very many indeed. They will be measureless and boundless in number. After this period of one hundred years, the word "Namo" will be gone, leaving only "Amitabha Buddha." At that time people who understand the Buddha-dharma will recite "Amitabha Buddha, Amitabha Buddha," frantically seeking for the Buddha to save their lives. After another hundred years, the words "Amitabha Buddha" will also disappear, at which time the Buddha-dharma will be totally extinct.

Why did Shakyamuni Buddha explain the *Amitabha Sutra* without being requested? Because this Sutra is extremely important and because it will be the last Sutra to remain in the world when the Dharma vanishes. So those of us who study the Buddha-dharma must never look lightly on the practice of reciting Amitabha Buddha's name.

When practicing Chan meditation, for example, people investigate: "Who is reciting the Buddha's name?" If we are able to do this, it confirms that in the past we have recited the name of the Buddha, and as a result we will be able to investigate "Who is reciting the Buddha's name." If you have not recited the name of the Buddha before, then how could you investigate "Who is reciting the Buddha's name" now. Therefore, examining the topic "Who is reciting the Buddha's name?" shows that we had recited the Buddha's name in past lives. However, some have recited a lot, and some have recited a little; some have recited earnestly, and some have recited in a muddled manner. Now that we have encountered this Dharma, we should not take it lightly and ignore it. We should pick it up and continue the work that we had already done in the past by reciting "Namo Amitabha Buddha." If you recite "Namo Amitabha Buddha," you can be reborn in the Land of Ultimate Bliss. In this land one will "endure none of the sufferings but enjoy every bliss."

SUTRA:

At that time, Samantabhadra Bodhisattva Mahasattva, wishing to restate his meaning, contemplated everywhere in the ten directions and spoke these verses.

COMMENTARY:

At that time, Samantabhadra Bodhisattva, this **Mahasattva,** this great Bodhisattva, **wishing to restate his meaning, contemplated everywhere in the ten directions and spoke these verses.** He wished to explain his meaning again, in order to explain it a little more clearly. He contemplated the basic natures and causes and conditions of living beings everywhere throughout the ten directions. Then he spoke these verses. Look how kind and compassionate Samantabhadra Bodhisattva is! Since he's afraid that we might not understand the Sutra, he explains it again in verse form.

Verses

SUTRA:

Before the lions among men throughout the worlds of the ten
   directions and the three periods of time,
With pure body, speech, and thought I worship them all,
   omitting none.

With the awesome spiritual power of Samantabhadra's
   practices and vows,
I appear everywhere before all Tathagatas.
One body manifests bodies as many as particles in a
   kshetra-land,
Each one worships Buddhas as many as particles in a
   kshetra-land.

In each particle there are Buddhas as numerous as particles,
And in each of these places there is an assembly of
   Bodhisattvas.
Each particle throughout the infinite Dharma Realm is
   the same.
I deeply believe they are all filled with Buddhas.

Each body using the ocean of all sounds
Everywhere gives voice to infinite and wonderful words,
That, throughout all kalpas of the future,
Praise the deep ocean of the Buddhas' merit and virtue.

COMMENTARY:

The first vow of Samantabhadra Bodhisattva is to worship all Buddhas, and the second is to praise the Tathagatas. This section of text discusses these two vows. **Before the lions among men throughout the worlds of the ten directions and the three periods of time.** "Throughout" means that everything is included. North, south, east, west, northeast, southeast, northwest, southwest, and above and below make up the ten directions.

Monasteries and temples are called "the permanent residences for those from the ten directions." This means that they are places where members of the Sangha from the ten directions reside. How can Sangha members come from above and below? Among the Sangha, there are many worthy sages who have realized the First, Second, Third, or Fourth Stages of an Arhat. Or perhaps they are Bodhisattvas. Sages who have realized these stages of enlightenment can come from above and below. The Buddhas also dwell throughout the ten directions. Therefore, monasteries are called "the permanent residences for those from the ten directions."

These permanent residences for those from the ten directions are places where Sangha members reside. Among one hundred monks, one true cultivator of the path can certainly be found. And there is certainly one Arhat among one thousand monks. However, you do not know which one it is. You don't know which one is the Arhat. Therefore, in the large monasteries when the Dharma Masters go to the dining hall to eat, there might be several hundred or several thousand monks. The number of monks is not fixed. Among three thousand monks there will be three Arhats.

However, you don't know which ones they are. Arhats aren't going to make themselves known to you. They appear in many different shapes and forms. They may manifest in a body of great awe-inspiring virtue. Their awesomeness inspires fear, and their virtue deserves veneration.

Or they may appear to be very foolish and even filthy, so that one look at them is enough.

Yet, one does not realize that these are Arhats. When you are face to face with one, you cannot recognize him. However, after he's left you think, "Oh! That was an Arhat" Then you may try to find him, but you will not be able to do so. If you look for an Arhat a second time, you will not be able to see him. That's the way Arhats are. Bodhisattvas are also like this. Therefore, it is said, "Face to face with Guan Shi Yin, one does not recognize him." Even though you meet Guan Shi Yin (Avalokiteshvara) Bodhisattva in person, you don't recognize that it is Guan Shi Yin Bodhisattva.

A long, long time ago, on Tian Tai Mountain in China, a magistrate of a prefecture, much like a governor of today, visited Guo Qing Monastery and talked with the Abbot there. He said, "In ancient times past, Bodhisattvas and Arhats constantly appeared and lived among the people. But now, although there are many monks, I have not seen a single Arhat or Bodhisattva."

The Abbot, whose name was Feng Gan, replied, "Oh, so you wish to see Bodhisattvas and Arhats? That's very easy. Back in the kitchen here at Guo Qing Monastery, the one who cooks the food is Manjushri Bodhisattva, and the one who boils the water and serves the food is Samantabhadra Bodhisattva." The magistrate asked, "What are their names?"

"One is Han Shan, and the other is Shi De," replied the Abbot.

"I'm going to see them," the official said.

"Okay," said the Abbot. "If you want to see them, then go ahead."

The magistrate went to the kitchen looking for Manjushri and Samantabhadra Bodhisattva. He asked, "Who are Han Shan and Shi De?"

A monk there pointed and said, "Those two." When the magistrate looked, he saw two ugly looking monks who had not shaved their heads or face. With their long hair and beards, they looked much like hippies. The only difference is that hippies are followed by demonic ghosts, whereas these two emitted golden light. Present-day hippies radiate a black energy from their bodies.

If you had the spiritual power of the Heavenly Eye, you would see that the greater the demonic energy hippies have, the more black energy they have. And you will see that behind them, they are followed by demonic ghosts. Without the spiritual power of the Heavenly Eye, of course, you would not know about this. However, there is one test you can perform to know whether this is the case. What is the test? If you get close to hippies that have demonic ghosts with them, they will stink. Their stench will be very strong. They themselves are not aware of this, but if you are not a hippie, you will be able to detect the strong smell from their bodies.

The magistrate bowed to Han Shan and Shi De. Although they were disheveled, unkempt, and rather filthy, he had faith in the Abbot, and believed what he said about them being Manjushri Bodhisattva and Samantabhadra Bodhisattva. When he bowed, Han Shan and Shi De demanded, "What are you doing? Why are you bowing to us?"

The magistrate replied, "The Abbot told me that one of you is Manjushri Bodhisattva and the other one is Samantabhadra Bodhisattva. Please be kind and compassionate and rescue me."

When they heard this they said, "Feng Gan talks too much. He's a troublemaker, and a blabbermouth!"

They then started backing up. As they retreated, the magistrate advanced forward. The two backed up towards the cliff called Moon Light which had a steep stone face or wall. The magistrate saw that when they reached the stone wall, a door opened up and they disappeared into it. The magistrate rushed to enter with them, but the door closed before he could do so.

Just before they disappeared, the magistrate said, "Be kind and compassionate and rescue this disciple."

Han Shan and Shi De replied, "You don't even bow to Amitabha Buddha! Why are you following us?"

The magistrate asked, "Who is Amitabha Buddha?"

Han Shan and Shi De answered, "The Abbot Feng Gan is a transformation-body of Amitabha Buddha who has come into this world to teach and transform living beings. Why don't you bow to him? What are you coming after us for?"

As soon as the magistrate heard this he thought, "Oh, originally the Abbot is a transformation-body of Amitabha Buddha!" He could not get into the stone wall because the door that had opened for Han Shan and Shi De had already closed. So he went back to see the Abbot, to bow to him and ask to be rescued.

However, when he arrived back at the Abbot's quarters, he found that the Abbot had also passed on and entered Nirvana while sitting in meditation. The magistrate returned, but the Abbot had already left. So there was nothing he could do.

He thought, "I had the opportunity right before me, and I missed it. I didn't recognize what was right in front of my face. Manjushri Bodhisattva has run off, Samantabhadra is gone, and Amitabha Buddha has entered

Nirvana." Fortunately, after the magistrate recovered from his grief and disappointment, he cultivated diligently and made good progress.

Before all the lions among men throughout the worlds of the ten directions and the three periods of time. The three periods of time are the past, present and future. The "lions among men" refers to the Buddhas. So this means the Buddhas of the three periods of time. **With a pure body, speech, and thought**. Samantabhadra Bodhisattva says that I use the purest and most sincere karma of body, mouth, and mind. The three karmas of body, mouth, and mind are pure. **I worship them all, omitting none**. Throughout all the worlds in the ten directions and in the three periods of time, I bow to all the lions among men. I bow to all the Buddhas of the ten directions and the three periods of time.

With the awesome spiritual power of Samantabhadra's practices and vows. My strength alone is not sufficient to worship all the Buddhas everywhere in the ten directions and the three periods of time. However, because I cultivate the great awesome spiritual power of Samantabhadra's practices and vows, he aids me. In the past Samantabhadra Bodhisattva had these practices, made these vows, and thus has this kind of awe-inspiring spiritual power. **I appear everywhere before all Tathagatas**. Now when I bow to one Buddha, I am bowing to all Tathagatas. I am able to appear everywhere before all Tathagatas and bow to them. **One body manifests bodies as many as particles in a kshetra-land**. One of my bodies manifests bodies as numerous as the minutest particles in all the Buddha-lands. **Each one worships Buddhas as many as particles in a kshetra-land.**

I manifest bodies as numerous as the particles in a kshetra-land and they worship Buddhas everywhere as numerous as the particles in a kshetra-land. It is not that I am capable of doing this myself, rather this is entirely due to the help of Samantabhadra Bodhisattva. He enables me to have this kind of state. When I bow to one Buddha, I bow to immeasurable Buddhas. And bowing to immeasurable Buddhas is the same as bowing to one Buddha. This is the same as what occurs in the five Avīci (Unhindered by Space or Time) Hells. These hells are unhindered and, in this case, the cultivation of Dharma is unhindered. This is the cultivation of the Contemplation of the Dharma Realm. In this contemplation, one person bows to all Buddhas everywhere. You are bowing right before each Buddha and simultaneously bowing before all the Buddhas of the ten directions and the three periods of time. This is like the Avīci Hells, but this is not the Avīci Hells. Rather it is the unhindered state of the Dharma Realm. The Dharma Realm is like this, but it is not like being in the Avīci Hells.

In each particle there are Buddhas as numerous as particles. In each particle there are Buddhas as many as particles. **And in each of these places there is an assembly of Bodhisattvas.** Within each place there is an assembly of Bodhisattvas, Arhats, Shravakas, Those Enlightened to Conditions, Bhikshus, Bhikshunis, and all living beings. **Each particle throughout the infinite Dharma Realms is the same.** Dharma Realms are infinite and inexhaustible, and the minute particles are also inexhaustible. **I deeply believe they are all filled with Buddhas**. I deeply believe all Buddhas completely fill up worlds as numerous as all the minutest particles in the inexhaustible Dharma Realms.

Each body using the ocean of all sounds. Each of my bodies brings forth an ocean of all sounds to praise the Buddhas. **Everywhere gives voice to infinite and wonderful words.** All of them everywhere emit an inexhaustible number of subtle and wonderful sounds to laud and praise them. **That throughout all kalpas of the future**, exhausting all kalpas of future time. **Praise the deep ocean of the Buddhas' merit**

and virtue. They praise the Buddhas' extremely deep merit and virtue, which is measureless and boundless like a great ocean.

SUTRA:

> Using the most supreme and wonderful flower garlands,
> Songs and music, incense pastes, parasols, and canopies,
> And other most supreme adornments such as these,
> I make offerings to all Tathagatas.
>
> With the most supreme clothing and superior incense,
> Powdered and burning incense, lamps, and candles,
> Each one heaped as high as Wonderful High Mountain,
> I make offerings to all Tathagatas.

COMMENTARY:

We just discussed the vow to praise the Tathagatas, and now we will explain the third vow, to extensively make offerings. **Using the most supreme and wonderful flower garlands.** When making offerings to the Buddhas, you should use the very best things. You should not offer the Buddhas the things which you don't want. Rather you should give many superior offerings, the very best and most wonderful objects. When offering flowers, only use wonderful flowers. "Garlands" are wreaths made up of flowers strung together. These belong to the category of offerings like pennants and canopies.

Songs and music, incense pastes, parasols, and canopies. You may also use all kinds of songs and tunes to praise the Buddhas. "Incense pastes" are rubbed onto things so that they smell very fragrant. These too, are offered to the Buddhas. "Canopies" are like beautifully adorned umbrellas with tassels. These precious coverings can be seen if you have opened your Heavenly Eye, for there are many precious canopies, banners, and flags suspended in space. Bodhisattvas make offerings like these to all the Buddhas. **And other most supreme adornments such as these.** As was just explained, they use all kind of precious things to make canopies and other adornments like these. **I make offerings to all Tathagatas.** I make offerings to all Tathagatas everywhere as numerous as minutest particles.

With the most supreme clothing and incense: I also offer the finest clothing and incense to the Buddhas. **Powdered and burning incense, lamps, and candles** include incense that is burned, like sandalwood, and oil lamps that are lit and offered before the Buddhas.

Each one heaped as high as Wonderful High Mountain. I make these offerings using the Dharma Realm contemplation. When I offer these adornments, I contemplate that they are as great as Mount Sumeru, or as voluminous as the waters of the great sea.

I make offerings to all Tathagatas. I offer all these precious objects to all Buddhas, that is, all the Tathagatas of the ten directions.

SUTRA:

> With a vast, great mind of supreme understanding,
> I have deep faith in all Buddhas of the three periods of time.
> With the power of Samantabhadra's practices and vows,
> I make offerings to all Tathagatas everywhere.

COMMENTARY:

This verse explains that this way of making offerings is **vast and great**. The offerings are vast and great, and I understand the mind of making these great offerings is a **mind of supreme understanding**, which is inconceivable and beyond the understanding of ordinary people. However, I understand it.

The mind with which I make offerings is an offering of the Dharma Realm. With a mind of the Dharma Realm I make offerings to the Buddhas of the Dharma Realm, and the Buddhas of the Dharma Realm enter this mind of the Dharma Realm." This describes the mind of supreme understanding.

I have deep faith in all Buddhas of the three periods of time. To have deep faith means to have true faith which is an inexhaustible faith. This means that even when the karmic obstructions of living beings are extinguished, when the afflictions of living beings are extinguished, when the realms of living beings no longer exist, and when the reaches of space up to and including the Dharma Realm cease to exist, still my mind of faith will never be extinguished. This is the meaning of "I have faith in all the Buddhas of the three periods of time." That is, to have a very deep and profound faith in all Buddhas of the past, present, and future.

With the power of Samantabhadra's practices and vows. Because I rely entirely on the power of the practices cultivated and vows made by Samantabhadra Bodhisattva, **I make offerings to all Tathagatas everywhere.** I can make offerings on the scale of the Dharma Realm to all Buddhas of the Dharma Realm everywhere.

SUTRA:

> **All the evil karma I have created in the past,**
> **Caused by beginningless greed, hatred, and delusion,**
> **Produced by my body, speech and thought,**
> **I now repent and reform of it all.**

COMMENTARY:

These verses speak of repenting and reforming of karmic obstructions. Why should you want to repent and reform? Because, "Offenses that are so great that they fill the heavens are destroyed once one repents of them." Regardless of what kind of offense karma you have, it is only to be feared that you will not repent of it. As soon as you repent and reform, your offense karma will be destroyed.

In China Confucius said,

> Don't be afraid to correct your faults.
> If you can correct your faults, they will cease to exist.
> Foolish people think they have no faults,
> The noble person changes his faults.

"Don't be afraid to correct your faults." If you fear correcting your faults, then your faults become greater and more severe. "If you can correct your faults, they will cease to exist." However, if you can change your faults, then you will be without any faults. If you wish to hide your faults or cover them up, not wanting people to know about them, then your faults will become more severe and greater. Most foolish people say that they have no faults. "Foolish people think they have no faults." Inferior people gloss over their faults. They have faults, but they conceal them. They don't want other people to know about them. But noble people wish to change their faults. They are happy to change their faults. Sages lessen their faults, which means they reduce or decrease their faults. As for Buddhas and Bodhisattvas, they have no faults at all.

The text reads, **all the evil karma I have created in the past**. "Past" refers to everything that has come before the present time. In past lives for measureless numbers of kalpas up to the present, in each life I have created evil karma. Why have I created so much evil karma? Because of beginningless greed, hatred, and delusion. Where did this creation of evil karma come from? It all is **caused by beginningless greed, hatred, and delusion**. For kalpas without beginning up to the present, my mind has given rise to greed, anger and delusion. With a greedy mind, one never feels satisfied and one creates many karmic offenses. If a person's greed is not fulfilled and they do not get what they want, they give rise to afflictions and hatred. Why do afflictions arise? Afflictions arise because of delusion. In the beginning one had a greedy mind. The basis of greed is delusion, which is ignorance, and everything comes from ignorance.

My evil karma is **produced in body, speech, and thought**. Killing, stealing, and sexual misconduct are done by my body. Greed, hatred, and delusion are created by my mind. And my mouth engages in irresponsible speech, false speech, harsh speech, and divisive speech. These ten evils are produced by my body, speech, and thought karma. **I now repent and reform of it all**. I want to repent and reform of all of these ten evil deeds that I have done. I want to change my faults and start anew.

Delusion is a kind of attachment. No matter what one does, one has attachments. Those who are greedy for wealth have attachment to wealth. Those who are fond of sex have attachment to sex. Those who like writing compositions are attached to writing, and those who like to write poetry have attachment to poetry.

I will tell you about a monk poet. This monk liked to write poetry and had an attachment to it. He liked to befriend literary people. If a learned person came to his temple he would be welcomed. Those who were not learned were not welcomed. This attachment was so severe that if a learned person could write two poems, he would be allowed to stay and eat in his temple. However, if a visitor could not write poetry, he was not only refused meals and lodging, but was not even allowed to enter the door.

You can see how because of his attachment, this monk encountered a demonic obstacle. One day at dusk, a person arrived at the temple. Because there was no other village nearby, the traveler wanted to spend the night. The young novice who answered the door said, "If you wish to stay here, you will have to meet certain requirements set forth by my master. You must write two poems or you may write one poem and one ode, or you may write an essay. Then you will be allowed to stay here. Can you write an essay, poetry, or odes?"

The visitor answered, "I can write them all." In fact this person was illiterate. But it was already dark, and he needed a place to spend the night. He thought, "After I eat a couple of meals, then we can talk about this."

The young Shramanera went to his master and said, "The person at the door says he can write essays, poetry, songs, and odes."

"Let him stay," his master replied. So the Shramanera welcomed him in and cooked him a very good meal. The traveler probably had not eaten for several days, because he really ate a lot. He did not worry about writing poetry or essays, but just thought that he would eat the meal first and then talk about the writing later. After he ate his fill, what do you think happened? The little novice gave him a pot of tea. Then he locked the traveler's door from the outside. Why? He was afraid the guest would run away, and he wanted to see his writing the next morning.

So the traveler spent the night there, but because he had eaten too much, he had to go to the toilet during the night. There was no toilet in his room. Yet when he tried to open the door, he found it was locked from the outside. He had eaten so much that he had diarrhea. In this predicament he had no other alternative, because he was unable to get out of the room. So he used a flower vase as a toilet. He filled up one flower vase, and then he filled a second flower vase. After that he drank the tea in the teapot. Then he had to go again. So he used the teapot as a toilet too and made a mess.

The next morning the novice unlocked the door and gave the guest some breakfast. Then after he had finished eating, the novice asked him, "Did you write any poems last night?"

The guest replied, "I wrote two poems.[39] They are in the flower vases." The novice thought that since he had written two poems, he was free to leave, and so he opened the gate and let the visitor out.

After the traveler had departed, the novice's master asked, "Did the person that came yesterday compose any poems?"

The young novice replied, "Yes, and he put them in each of the flower vases."

The master said, "Bring them here so I can read them."

The novice went to the room in which the traveler had spent the night. When he reached into one of the flower vases, he pulled out a handful of excrement. Then he reached into the other flower vase, and again pulled out a handful of excrement. And then he thought to use the tea in the teapot to wash his hands. So he tried to drink some of the tea first, but instead he drank the diarrhea. Just then he heard the old monk call out for him to bring the poems. So the novice came into the room and showed him the two handfuls of excrement [which also sounded like two poems].

After this incident with this visitor, the old monk did not accept guests anymore. Because the visitor had filled up two flower vases with his diarrhea, the old monk was able to conquer his attachment. Afterwards, he did not ask people to write poetry anymore, either.

---

39. In Chinese, the characters for "writing poetry," *zuo-shi*, have the same sound as "going to the toilet," and the characters for "a poem," *i-shou shi*, sound the same as "a handful of excrement," *yi-shou shi*. Therefore the question in Chinese, "Did you write any poems?" also sounds like, "Did you go to the toilet?"

SUTRA:

> **All living beings in the ten directions,**
> **Learners and Those Beyond Learning in the Two Vehicles,**
> **And all Tathagatas and Bodhisattvas,**
> **I follow and rejoice in all their merit and virtue.**

COMMENTARY:

This verses discusses the vow to follow and rejoice in merit and virtue. **All living beings in the ten directions**. Everyone knows what the ten directions are, but you might not understand what living beings are. Living beings are produced from a combination of numerous conditions. For example, becoming a human being is not easy. To become a human being you have to do what people are supposed to do. What are the things that people are supposed to do? You have to learn the path that is walked by people. You have to learn how people speak and to learn to behave the way good people behave. Then you can become a person. If you emulate the way ghosts behave, then you will become a ghost in the future.

Living beings are produced from the combination of numerous conditions. This means that they are created by the present single thought in their minds. If your present single thought is to become a Buddha and cultivate the Buddha's Path, then in the future you will become a Buddha. This is created by your mind. If your present single thought is to practice the path of the Bodhisattva to benefit other people, to benefit yourself and others, and to enlighten yourself and others, then you can become a Bodhisattva. If you have the thought to cultivate the vehicle of the Shravaka, then you will attain the fruition of an Arhat. This is the vehicle of the Shravaka. If you wish to cultivate the vehicle of Those Enlightened to Conditions and achieve their levels of attainment, then you can become One Enlightened to Conditions. If you wish to ascend to the heavens, then follow the five moral precepts and do the ten types of good. If you wish to be a human being, then you must hold the five moral precepts, which prohibit killing, stealing, sexual misconduct, lying, and taking intoxicants. Then you can become a human being.

If you want to become an *asura*, then you should fight with people every day and harbor a lot of hatred. Then you can become an *asura*. If you want to become an animal, then do stupid things. Then you can become an animal. If you want to become a hungry ghost, then do dark secretive things, things that you do not want people to see. Then you can become a ghost. If you wish to fall into the hells, create more karmic offenses. Then you can go to the hells.

Everything is made from the mind alone. This Sutra says:

> *If one wishes to understand*
> *All the Buddhas of the three periods of time,*
> *One should contemplate the nature of the Dharma Realm:*
> *Everything is made from the mind alone.*

Basically there are no heavenly palaces, no hells, no Buddhas, no Bodhisattvas, and no human beings. There is nothing at all. Why do they exist? They are created by the present single thought of our mind. Thus the Ten Dharma Realms come into existence. And all the different kinds of forms and appearances exist. If we did not give rise to a single thought, this is the same as the mind not existing. Then, as it is said,

> *With no mind and no thoughts,*
> *Blessings are boundless.*
> *With selfish desires and distracting thoughts,*
> *There are transgressions.*

If you have no mind and no thought, then you have boundless blessings. If you have selfish desires, which are greed, then you create offenses. Therefore it is said, "All living beings have the Buddha nature." All living beings have the Buddha Nature, and yet all living beings do not have the Buddha nature. How can one say that they do not have the Buddha nature? If you do not cultivate, you do not have it, but if you do cultivate, you do have it. You can also say that if you cultivate, you have it, and if you don't cultivate you have it. When you cultivate your Buddha nature is the way it is, and if you don't cultivate your Buddha nature is still the way it is. Still another way to explain it is that if you cultivate you don't have it and if you don't cultivate you don't have it. What does this mean? You should not have any attachment. If you have attachment then you say, "I have the Buddha nature." If you don't have any attachment, then having it is like not having it. It does not exist, yet it doesn't not exist. You shouldn't be attached.

What I just said sounds like a joke, but it is for the purpose of breaking people's attachments. If we are without attachments, we can become Buddhas. Why is it that we have not become Buddhas? It's just because we have attachments. Therefore, we should get rid of our attachments, and then we can become Buddhas.

The text says, "I rejoice in and follow all the merit and virtue of all beings in the ten directions," **Learners and Those Beyond Learning in the Two Vehicles.** The "Two Vehicles" are Shravakas and Those Enlightened to Conditions. "Learners" comprise the first three stages of an Arhat. These are called the stages of learning. The fourth-stage Arhat is the position "beyond learning."

And all Tathagatas and Bodhisattvas. This refers to all the Tathagatas as well as all the Bodhisattvas. **I follow and rejoice in all of their merit and virtue.** I rejoice in and follow all the merit and virtue of the

Shravakas, Those Enlightened to Conditions, Learners, and Those Beyond Learning as well as the merit and virtue of the Buddhas and Bodhisattvas. I will follow and rejoice in even as much as a small atomic particle of merit and virtue, and I will also do the same for as much merit and virtue that is as great as Mount Sumeru. It is not the case that if the merit and virtue is small, I will not rejoice in and follow it, but if it is great, I will. Whether the merit and virtue is great or small, I will rejoice in and follow it. There is a saying,

> Don't do an evil deed just because it seems small,
> And don't neglect doing a good deed, because it seems small.

Do not think that just because an evil action seems insignificant it is okay to do. And don't think that just because a good action is insignificant, it doesn't need to be done. You should know that every mountain is composed of an accumulation of minute particles. Although a single minute particle is so small, if you gather together a lot of them, they become a mountain. And although a single good deed might be small, if you do many of them, they become measureless and boundless.

SUTRA:

> **All the Lamps of the World throughout the ten directions,**
> **Those who first realized Bodhi,**
> **I now request and beseech them all**
> **To turn the wheel of the unsurpassed, wonderful Dharma.**

COMMENTARY:

All the Lamps of the World throughout the ten directions. The ten directions include everything; they are the Dharma Realm, and the Dharma Realm is the ten directions. The "Lamps of the World" are the Buddhas. They are bright lamps for the world.

Before when there was no Buddha in the world, it was dark, and there were heterodox and deviant teachers who proclaimed their teachings. What are deviant teachers? Deviant teachers are those whose knowledge and views are improper. They lead people to enter demonic states. They are unable to teach people proper knowledge and views, and instead teach people improper knowledge and views. Improper knowledge and views are equivalent to darkness, whereas proper knowledge and views are light.

I have said this many times before:

> One who is confused transmits his confusion to another,
> Through this one transmission, two become confused.
> The teacher falls into the hells,
> And his disciple tunnels into the hells as well.

When a deviant teacher proclaims his teachings, he'll tell you that if you take some drugs you can attain the "void." And he will certify you, saying, "This is the void. The void is just like this. You are certified to a particular stage of enlightenment. You have already reached the Four Dhyanas." The Fourth Dhyana is nothing special, and neither are the First, Second, or the Third. They are very ordinary. However he even says, "You now have obtained the void. You are the same as the Buddha. Being a Buddha is not much different from this." He causes people to have improper knowledge and views and guides them down the wrong road. This is called confusion.

What is meant by confusion? He himself does not understand. He's befuddled and bewildered. That's called confusion. Confusion is being all mixed up. They don't understand anything at all, so they are in a muddled state. And there are others who wish to learn this muddled state from them. This is the meaning of "One who is confused transmits his confusion to another. Through this one transmission two become confused." One person teaches the other and then two people are confused. The teacher doesn't understand anything, and now both of them don't understand anything.

Why does he not understand anything? If a confused person transmits his confusion to another person, isn't it the case that they both become confused? This is the case of the blind person leading the blind. He himself is blind; he doesn't have the sense of sight. He leads others down the wrong road. And others who can't see believe that he can see. Who would have known that the person leading cannot see the road either? However, he wishes to cheat people and lead them down the road just the same. This is the meaning of "through this one transmission, two become confused."

The teacher falls into the hells, because the teacher is confused and does not understand how to cultivate. He is muddled and bewildered, so he runs off into the hells. His disciple believes that his teacher certainly could not take a wrong road, so he follows behind him. However, the door to the hells is already closed. So he acts like a pig who uses his mouth to dig with the hope of getting through the door. This is what is meant by, "And his disciple tunnels into the hells as well."

After he breaks in, he sees his teacher, who says, "What are you doing here?"

The disciple responds, "You are my teacher, so I of course, as your disciple, followed you here. What is this place?"

The teacher answers, "I'm still not quite sure. I don't know which Buddha-land this is."

After a while, the hungry ghosts and yakshas come and say, "As a teacher you didn't teach your students very well. All you did was lie to your disciples and cheat people. Okay! Now you can go to the Hell of Pulling Out Tongues." So he falls into the Hell of Pulling Out Tongues.

As for the disciple, he did not cheat people, but because he also did a lot bad things, he now is put into a pot of oil to be fried for a while. The disciple screams, "Oh! This is really terrible. Since you cheated people, you fall into the Hell of Pulling Out Tongues. You deserve this because of your transgressions and because you misled people. I followed you, learned your confused teaching, and created many offenses. So now I must be fried in this pot of oil. This punishment is very hard to endure!"

His teacher replies, "I don't have a mantra to recite now. I have no way to get out of this. I can't save you. And I can't even save myself."

This teacher took along his confused disciple with him when he fell into hell to undergo suffering. This is the meaning of "one who is confused transmits his confusion to another." When an improper teacher speaks, he causes people to go astray and fall into the hells. If we wish to cultivate, we should find a Good Teacher. A Good Teacher is one with wisdom and intelligence. If we wish to learn the Path, we should follow wise teachers and not follow deluded teachers. The principles of wise teachers are always proper, and they will not lead people down improper paths.

Before the Buddha came into the world, there were only confused teachers who transmitted their confusion to others. But when the Buddha came into the world, he was like a sun or a shining lamp. So the Buddha illuminated the world with his light, and so the text says, "Before all the Lamps of the World of the ten directions."

Those who first realized Bodhi. Who first realized Bodhi? Everyone is the one who first realized Bodhi. What is "Bodhi?" You have heard Dharma Masters who lectured on the Sutras explain it as meaning "enlightened to the Path." What is enlightened to the Path? You become enlightened to not doing any evil activities and instead do all kinds of good. This is enlightenment or being enlightened to the Path. If you only know how to do evil and not do good, you are also enlightened to a path. However, this is being enlightened to an evil path. To understand how to do good and not do evil is to be enlightened to the Path.

Enlightening to the Path is to progress step by step. What is meant by to progress step by step? It's like a piece of bamboo, which is made up of sections- one on top of the other to form a single stalk of bamboo. Each section is higher than the previous one. Bodhi is the same way. Each step is higher than the previous step. So you progress step by step from being a common person to becoming a Buddha. This is to progress or ascend step by step. This is Bodhi. However, if you descend step by step, it means that you have enlightened to an evil path. If you ascend step by step you will become enlightened to the good path. So it is said, "The superior person ascends, while the inferior person descends." The inferior person goes downwards, while the superior person goes upwards.

"Those who first realized Bodhi" are those who first became Buddhas. How did the very first Buddha become a Buddha? We know that reciting Sutras is cultivation. Reciting mantras is cultivation. And practicing the Bodhisattva path of the Six Paramitas and the myriad practices is also cultivating. But before the very first Buddha, no one knew about the Six Paramitas and the myriad practices, or how to cultivate. There were no Sutras to recite or mantras to recite, so how did one become a Buddha?

It is said that if you can recite the Shurangama Mantra from memory, then for seven lives you can be as rich as a great oil baron. When some people hear this, they devote themselves completely to reciting the Shurangama Mantra from memory in order to be as rich as an oil baron for seven lives. For example, yesterday I talked about Nelson Rockefeller's grandfather, John D. Rockefeller. Some people recite the Shurangama Mantra just to seek blessings and honor, but they are making a mistake. It is true that if you can recite the Shurangama Mantra from memory, then at the very least, for seven lives you can have as much money as the great oil barons. However, the reason we recite is not to acquire wealth but to become Buddhas. If you can recite the Shurangama Mantra from memory, then you can obtain Bodhi. You can ascend higher step by step. Each step is higher than the previous one. If you wish to be like a great oil baron, then you have worldly blessings and honor.

Now we're talking about world-transcending blessings and honor which are real blessings and honor. Only if you have roots of goodness will you be able to recite and memorize the Shurangama and Great Compassion Mantras. Without roots of goodness, you will not even be able to hear the names of the Great Compassion and Shurangama Mantras. You can see this by counting the following: How many people have ever heard the Shurangama Mantra? How many people have ever recited it? How many people have ever heard of the Great Compassion Mantra, and how many people have ever recited it? Today I see there are some people teaching others how to recite the Shurangama Mantra. This is one of the best classes for cultivating the Path. You should teach all those who wish to study it so that they are able to recite and uphold this mantra. You should explain the benefits of this practice to everyone. If you can recite and uphold by memory the Great Compassion Mantra or the Shurangama Mantra, the result in the future will be inconceivable. Not only can you be a great oil baron, you can also become the king of a country. This is most inconceivable.

We recite mantras and Sutras to accomplish Bodhi. What Sutras and mantras did the one who first attained Bodhi recite? The one who first became a Buddha, an immeasurable number of kalpas ago, at the time when this world first began to develop, was originally a Buddha, so he did not need to recite anything. Why was he originally a Buddha? Well actually, one cannot say that he was the first one to become a Buddha. Haven't I said that whoever accomplished his karma of the Path is the one who first realizes Bodhi? If one does not accomplish his karma of the Path, then he/she is not one who first realized Bodhi. The very first Buddha was there originally. Take the Heavenly Lord as an example. The idea of a Heavenly Lord is taken from Buddhism. Some people changed the meaning of the Buddha and called him the Heavenly Lord. The first one to realize Bodhi was the very first Buddha.

I now request them all, that is, all the Buddhas of the three periods of time and the very first Buddha. Now we are requesting and beseeching them. What are we beseeching them to do? **To turn the wheel of the unsurpassed, wonderful Dharma.** I request them all to remain in the world and to turn the wheel of the wonderful Dharma. "To turn" means to set in motion. "Unsurpassed" means that there is nothing higher than it. The wheel of wonderful Dharma is the inconceivable wonderful Wheel of Dharma. Didn't I tell you before? To lecture the Sutras is to turn the Wheel of Dharma; to teach the Dharma is to turn the Wheel of Dharma; to recite Sutras is to turn the Wheel of Dharma; to uphold mantras is to turn the Wheel of Dharma; to print Sutras is to turn the Wheel of Dharma; and even to operate a mimeograph machine is to turn the Wheel of Dharma. It is true. When you turn a mimeograph machine it prints, but if you do not turn it, it does not print. Is this not wonderful? This is a representation of turning the wheel of wonderful Dharma, a visible example of turning the Wheel of Dharma.

In actuality, however, the wheel of wonderful Dharma basically cannot be seen, nor can you conceive or think of it. You try to see it, but it cannot be seen. The wonderful Wheel of Dharma is such that "the path of words and language is cut off." It can't be spoken of. "The location of the mind's activities is extinguished." You try to find a pathway for your mind to follow, but it doesn't exist.

The mouth wishes to speak, but it is inexpressible;
The mind wishes to express it, but thoughts have vanished.

You wish to speak but there are no words to explain it. And your mind wishes to think about it, but pathway of thought has perished. This is to really turn the wondrous, inconceivable Wheel of Dharma.

For example, you now say you have not seen any Buddha in this world. First of all, this is because you have not visited very many places. You might reply that you have been all over the world, but you did not see any Buddha turning the wonderful Wheel of Dharma. You may have traveled all around the world, but have you been into space? There are Buddhas turning the Wheel of Dharma in space. If you want to see the Buddhas turning the Wheel of Dharma, then go into space. We now have rocket ships, which can go to the moon, but it is not for sure that people will be able to see them. If they do not see them, does this mean that they do not exist? No. There are many more than you can see. It is not for sure that you can see the wheel of wonderful Dharma being turned. Second, in the heavens there are Buddhas turning the Wheel of Dharma. You cannot see them either. Therefore, even though you are not able to see them, you cannot say that they do not exist.

There is no place where the wheel of wonderful Dharma is not being turned. If you understand, then absolutely everything is turning the wheel of wonderful Dharma. If you do not understand, then if they are turning the wheel of wonderful Dharma, you cannot recognize that they are turning it. If you are enlightened, you can see that of all the myriad phenomena of the universe—the world of primary retribution, and the world of dependent retribution—are turning the wheel of wonderful Dharma. So it is said,

> *On the tip of a single hair, appear kshetra-lands of the Jeweled King.*
> *Seated in a minute particle, he turns the Great Wheel of Dharma.*

When one person heard my explanation about the Heavenly Lord, he really agreed with me. He said, "What you say is correct. The Heavenly Lord is the Buddha, and the Buddha is the Heavenly Lord. Basically they are one and the same, but they have different names. It is just like one person has many different names. Isn't this what you mean?"

No. When I spoke of the Heavenly Lord, it was meant as an analogy. It is not that the Heavenly Lord is the Buddha and the Buddha is the Heavenly Lord. Do not think that you are so smart and that you have become enlightened. Why? I will explain the differences between the Heavenly Lord and the Buddha for you.

The Heavenly Lord lives in a heaven and rules over it; he is the Lord of the Heaven of the Thirty-three, also known as the *Trayastrimsha Heaven*. In the Shurangama Mantra, he is referred to as *yin tuo luo ye* (Indra), in line twenty-nine, which reads *Na mo yin tuo luo ye*. This line means "to take refuge with Indra."

In the past, the Heavenly Lord was a woman who saw a Buddha statue in a temple. The temple was in ruins, and the Buddha statue was exposed to the elements without a roof over its head or walls to protect it. It was much like a vagabond without any place to live, meditating out in the open. When this woman saw the Buddha image exposed to the wind and rain, she made the resolve to rebuild the temple. She could not do this by herself. So she got thirty-two other women together to help her. They finished rebuilding the temple. When their lives came to an end, they were all reborn in a heaven. The woman who led the project became the Lord of this heaven, and that is how the Heavenly Lord came to be. The Buddha on the other hand has no beginning and no end. So when I spoke about the Heavenly Lord previously, I was referring to him metaphorically.

In Christianity it is said that the Heavenly Lord created everything, that he created all myriad things of the world. Who created the Heavenly Lord?

"No one. He created himself," is the answer given.

If the Heavenly Lord created himself, why is it that we cannot create ourselves? Do you need to wait for the Heavenly Lord to create you? This is simply a very foolish notion that shows a total lack of wisdom. Christians also say that only the Heavenly Lord can be the Heavenly Lord, and that no other living being can become the Heavenly Lord. Didn't I tell you before, that the Heavenly Lord then is a lonely Heavenly Lord? He is the only one who can be the Heavenly Lord. Let him be this way. He has become one who is isolated and all alone. People in this world need to have good friends, but since no one else can become the Heavenly Lord, he becomes very special and different from everyone else. I feel that it is better not to be this kind of the Heavenly Lord. It is not very meaningful.

In Buddhism, the Heavenly Lord is a Dharma protector. When he is before the Buddha, he is not entitled to have a seat, but can only stand. Why? He has a status similar to that of the Dharma Protector Wei Tuo who is the Venerated Celestial Bodhisattva and Chie Lan Bodhisattva. Why is it that the Heavenly Lord, who only teaches a heterodox teaching, does not admit that the Buddha is superior to him? This is because he is selfish. He is like the head of a countryside village or a district. Village heads are found in rural areas, not the city. Since none of the country people have ever experienced life in an urban area, the village head can tell them, "I'm the greatest person in the world. You should follow what I say, and that is all you need to do." The country people have no experience with the outside world, having always been in the countryside, and so they believe the village head. They think he is the greatest and highest person. The Heavenly Lord of Christianity is like this.

He also says, "Only I am honored. I am the highest." In actuality you should explain the reason for such a claim in an open and forthcoming way. What's explaining this in an open and public way? It is not reasonable to say that this issue can't be openly discussed. For example, if someone asks, "What does the Trinity mean?" The answer is, "You cannot ask this. If you ask this it is a sin, an offense against the Heavenly Lord." This is a policy of keeping the people ignorant. This is teaching the people, "If you don't understand, don't ask; because if you ask, you have broken the law." This policy prevents the citizens from being knowledgeable, because if they have knowledge they will rebel.

The Heavenly Lord does not teach others to learn the Buddha-dharma for the same reason. He thinks, "Don't study the Buddha-dharma, because if you do and you become a Buddha, you'll be higher than me." Based on the principle that I just explained, all of you should not think that you have become enlightened. The enlightenment that you have attained is originally false. You've had a false enlightenment, not a true enlightenment.

SUTRA:

> If there are Buddhas who wish to enter Parinirvana,
>   I beseech them with utmost sincerity,
> Wishing that they long remain in the world
>   for as many kalpas as there are particles in kshetra-lands,
> To benefit and bring happiness to all living beings.
> All of the blessings from worshipping, praising,
>   and making offerings,
> From beseeching the Buddhas to remain in the world
>   and turn the Wheel of Dharma;

And from all the roots of goodness gained from following and rejoicing, and repentance and reform, I transfer to living beings and to becoming a Buddha.

COMMENTARY:

If there are Buddhas who wish to enter Parinirvana, I beseech them with utmost sincerity. Some people do not want to enter Nirvana. They say, "Nirvana is death. Buddhism calls death Nirvana." In fact, Nirvana means "not produced and not destroyed;" it is the Pure Land of Eternal Serenity and Light. It is neither produced nor destroyed, neither increasing nor decreasing, neither impure nor pure. It is the place where all Buddhas dwell.

The world we now live in is called "the land where common people and enlightened sages dwell together." This is because in this world there are common people, enlightened sages, which includes the Buddha, Bodhisattvas, Shravakas, and Those Enlightened to Conditions who all live together.

The place where those of the Two Vehicles dwell is called the "Expedient Land with Residue." Why is it called expedient? Although that place is acceptable, it is still not ultimate Nirvana. Rather it is a one-sided truth. It is the one-sided truth of Nirvana with Residue.

Bodhisattvas dwell in the "Beautified Land with True Rewards." Bodhisattvas roam about at their leisure with spiritual powers, they purify Buddha lands, and they teach and transform living beings.

The place where only Buddhas dwell is called the Pure Land of Eternal Serenity and Light.

If you study the Buddha-dharma, and somebody asks you, "What are the four lands?" You should know them. For example, a certain person said that he had already become a Buddha, so then I asked him, "In what land do you live?" He could not answer. He basically did not have any place for himself, so what kind of Buddha had he become? He became a Buddha that does not even know where he dwells. He goes around saying, "Everyone is a Buddha." However, if you ask him what land he lives in, he's speechless. He does not have anything to say.

"Who gave you your prediction? When you become a Buddha, what will be your name?" He cannot answer these questions either. This proves that he is a counterfeit Buddha.

For example, to say that a ghost is a Buddha is false and a fake. Or another example might be that one sells apples labeled as the highest grade. However, they are not really of the highest grade. These are counterfeit. When you become a Buddha, you should know where you're going and what your name will be. Shariputra had studied with Shakyamuni Buddha for over forty years. Then the Buddha gave him a prediction of Buddhahood, saying that he would be called Flower Light Buddha. If you say you are a Buddha, then what is your Buddha name? If you do not know, then you are not a Buddha. I say this is a counterfeit Buddha or a false Buddha. There are all kinds of false things in this world, even false or counterfeit Buddhas.

This is when the Buddhas have rescued and transformed the living beings that they should have rescued. That is, they have taught and transformed living beings for measureless numbers of kalpas and completed their task of saving them. This is called "having finished transforming those with whom they have affinities." Then they wish to enter Nirvana. However, if the Buddhas enter Nirvana and go to the Pure Land of Eternal Serenity and Light, then Samantabhadra Bodhisattva says, **If there are Buddhas who wish to enter Nirvana, I request with utmost sincerity...** I, with utmost earnestness and sincerity, request that they not enter Nirvana, but rescue more living beings. **Only wishing that they remain in the world for a long time, as many kalpas as there are particles in kshetra-lands.** I only wish that that they dwell for a long time in the world for kalpas as numerous as particles in kshetra-lands. **To benefit and bring happiness to all living beings.** That is, all living beings that exist are benefited and all are taught and transformed.

All of the blessings from worshipping, praising, and making offerings. This line refers to the vows that were spoken of previously, to worship all Buddhas and to praise the Tathagatas. It also refers to the vow to extensively make offerings. "Blessings" refers to making offerings to those with blessings. Some texts read, "To make offerings to the Buddhas," but the meaning is the same. Making offerings to the Buddha is the same as giving offerings to those with blessings, because the Buddhas have perfected blessings and wisdom; they are the doubly perfect ones, perfect in blessings and wisdom.

From beseeching the Buddhas to remain in the world and turn the Wheel of Dharma. With a sincere mind, relying on the power of Samantabhadra Bodhisattva's ten great King of Vows, I request that the Buddhas remain long in the world and constantly turn the wondrous wheel of Dharma.

And from all the roots of goodness gained from following and rejoicing, and from repentance and reform. The merit and virtue that comes from following and rejoicing and from repenting and reforming produces all kinds of roots of goodness. Once you repent and reform, your karmic offenses are lessened and your roots of goodness increase. **I transfer to living beings and to becoming a Buddha.** The text means, "I will not keep my roots of goodness for myself, but I transfer them to all living beings of the Dharma Realm. All my merit and virtue belongs to living beings of the Dharma Realm. And all the offenses of living beings in the Dharma Realm can be given to myself alone, so that I will take on the burden of their offenses." This is called undergoing suffering on behalf of living beings. Therefore the text says that I transfer it to living beings and the path of the Buddhas. That is, all of my merit and virtue is dedicated to living beings and the path of the Buddhas.

SUTRA:

> I follow and learn from all the Tathagatas
> And cultivate the perfect practices of Samantabhadra.
> I make offerings to all the Tathagatas of the past,
> The Buddhas of the present throughout the ten directions,
>
> And to all the Teachers of Gods and Humans of the future.
> May all my aspirations be fulfilled.
> I wish to learn from all the Buddhas of the three periods
>   of time
> And quickly attain great Bodhi.

COMMENTARY:

I follow and learn from all the Tathagatas. I wish always to study with the Buddhas, to eternally learn the Buddha's Path from all Buddhas. **And cultivate the perfect practices of Samantabhadra**. And I will cultivate and study Samantabhadra Bodhisattva's perfect practices. **I make offerings to all the Tathagatas of the past**. I make offerings to all the Buddhas of the past and **the Buddhas of the present throughout the ten directions**.

And to all the Teachers of Gods and Humans of the future. The future teachers of gods and men are the Buddhas. **May all my aspirations be fulfilled**. That is, may all my hopes and wishes, and all the things I take pleasure in, be fulfilled and accomplished. **I wish to learn from all the Buddhas of the three periods of time**. I wish to constantly learn and practice the Buddha-dharma with all Buddhas of the three periods of time, **and quickly attain great Bodhi.** I'll very quickly attain the path of Enlightenment that is great Bodhi.

SUTRA:

> **In all the kshetra-lands throughout the ten directions,**
> **Vast, pure, and wonderfully adorned,**
> **The assemblies surround the Tathagatas,**
> **As they sit beneath their royal Bodhi trees.**
>
> **May all living beings in the ten directions**
> **Be without worry, and always have peace and happiness,**
> **Obtain the Proper Dharma's profound benefit,**
> **And may their afflictions be eradicated without remainder.**

COMMENTARY:

In all the kshetra-lands throughout the ten directions. "All" includes the ten directions of the Dharma Realm—north, south, east, and west, northeast, southeast, northwest, southwest, above, and below, and all the kshetras lands, that is all the Buddha lands. That are **vast, pure, and wonderfully adorned.**

Because the entire great expanse of the ten directions of the Dharma Realm is meant, the line of text says, "vast." Pure means it is extremely pure without the slightest bit of defilement. "Wonderfully adorned," means that these kinds of inconceivable, subtle and wonderful things adorn the ten directions of the Dharma Realm.

The assemblies surround the Tathagatas. All the assemblies throughout the Dharma Realm—the oceanic assemblies of Bodhisattvas, the oceanic assemblies of Shravakas, the oceanic assemblies of Those Enlightened to Conditions, the oceanic assemblies of Bhikshus, Bhikshunis, Upasakas, and Upasikas, the oceanic assemblies of gods, dragons, and the rest of the eightfold pantheon of spiritual beings surround the Tathagatas, which are all the Buddhas. **As they sit beneath their royal Bodhi trees**. Every one of the Buddha lands of the ten directions has a Bodhi tree, and each Buddha accomplishes the path beneath that Bodhi Tree.

May all living beings in the ten directions be without worry and always have peace and happiness. I will transfer merit to them and vow that all living beings in all the worlds throughout the ten directions will be apart from all worry, grief, suffering, and affliction, and always obtain peace and happiness. **Obtain the Proper Dharma's profound benefit**. I vow that they will all obtain the extremely profound and wondrous Dharma of Prajna—this kind of benefit. **And may their afflictions be eradicated without remainder.** They eradicate all afflictions, so that not the slightest bit remains. To destroy all afflictions without remainder means that not even a hairsbreadth of afflictions remains.

Speaking about this is very easy, but doing it is very difficult. You say that you want to rid yourself of afflictions and then think that you can be without any afflictions, but your afflictions still arise. You might wish to cut off your afflictions, but you cannot. It is not known how many great kalpas you have had intimate connections with your afflictions. Therefore, although you may want to leave them, you cannot separate from your afflictions. Why can't you separate from your afflictions? Because you have no wisdom; you are deluded. Only people with wisdom can destroy all their afflictions without remainder.

When we listen to the Sutras and hear the Dharma, we study our inherent wisdom. Although we call it "studying our inherent wisdom," we do not acquire this wisdom by means of study. This wisdom is something we already have by nature. However, we have forgotten it. For a long time we have not used this profound prajna-wisdom, so we have forgotten it. Now because we hear the Sutras and the Dharma, we remember our inherent wisdom, and once it is remembered, delusion and afflictions go away. Then, even if you don't try to get rid of them, they cannot exist anymore.Where do afflictions and ignorance reside? They reside in darkness. If you have light, then the darkness will go away. What is light? Light is wisdom. What is darkness? Darkness is ignorance. If you have no ignorance, you will have no afflictions. Then you will give rise to real wisdom. Why do people have afflictions? It's just because they lack understanding. If they have understanding, they will not have any afflictions.

SUTRA:

> When I cultivate for the sake of Bodhi,
> In all destinies I will gain the knowledge of past lives.
> I will always renounce the householder's life and cultivate the
>   pure moral precepts,
> Unbroken, undefiled, and without outflows.

COMMENTARY:

When I cultivate for the sake of Bodhi. If you want wisdom, you must cultivate; if you do not cultivate, you will not have wisdom. Take a look at people who are intelligent. In past lives they have cultivated the spiritual path. Or perhaps in past lives they read many Sutras, or perhaps they cultivated a lot of ascetic practices, and so now in their present life they are intelligent. However, these types of ascetic practices are not the ascetic practices of sleeping, eating, and being lazy. Take someone who is lazy; it is not easy and it involves a lot of suffering. One does nothing at all. You must have some samadhi to be lazy like this. If you do not have any samadhi, and you try to be lazy, you will feel uncomfortable when you are sitting, and uneasy when you are standing.

There are many ways to cultivate Bodhi. Some practice Chan meditation, giving, upholding the moral precepts, patience, vigor, Dhyana-samadhi, or Prajna-wisdom. There are various different practices.

Explaining this brings to mind a historical case that I will tell you about. When did this take place? This story occurred ten thousand years ago and involved an old cultivator. How can we know what took place over ten thousand years ago? Of course we can. Archaeologists know what happened tens of thousands of years ago. How much the less, do Buddhists with the Five Eyes and Six Spiritual Powers know this. They can easily know what took place millions of years ago.

This case involves an old cultivator of the path. How did he cultivate? He practiced meditation. When he first began meditating, he had unbearable pain in his legs. When he sat for a while his legs hurt so much that he could not take the pain and so he fought with it. "You don't like the pain? Well, I like it." He negotiated with his legs. Then his legs said, "I can't take it." He replied, "You can't take it? That's your problem. I'm not going to pay attention to you."

And he continued to meditate. In the very beginning he sat in meditation for half an hour and was able to withstand the pain. Then he switched his legs and continued to train himself in meditation. Then he began sitting for an hour, then an hour and a half, then two hours, and continued to increase the length of his meditation periods. Finally he could sit for several days at one time, then several months, and then he could even sit for several years. In the end he finally defeated the pain in his legs. After he defeated his pain, he sat for very long time, and he never wanted to get up from meditation. He just wanted to meditate in one place and sat for a few decades. Then after several decades he switched his legs. Then he continued to meditate and decided to wait until Shakyamuni Buddha came into the world. He wanted to help him spread the Buddha-dharma.

When Shakyamuni Buddha came into the world, he saw that this old cultivator really liked to meditate and enter samadhi. He would never get up. It was just as if he were in a long sleep, and he slept for thousands of years. His clothes became all worn out, his face was covered with silt, and birds built nests on his head. It reached the point to where although he was a person, he was more like a statue made of clay. It is not known exactly how many years he sat there.

In the Tang Dynasty, a Dharma Master, Xuan Zang, made a pilgrimage to India to collect Sutras. The Chinese have a saying, "The Tripitaka Master of the Tang Dynasty went to the West to gather the Sutras." During his travels he happened upon this old cultivator whose clothes were in tatters and who was covered with an inch of dirt. If it wasn't an inch, it was at least a half an inch of dirt. His head, face, and body were covered with an incredible amount of dirt.

Dharma Master Xuan Zang took out a small hand bell and rang it in front of his face. "Ding!" The old cultivator said, "Mmmmmm!," and woke up from his sleep. "What are you doing?" he said.

Dharma Master Xuan Zang retorted: "What are *you* doing?"

The old cultivator said, "I'm waiting for Shakyamuni Buddha, the Red Sun Buddha, to come into the world so I can help him to spread the Buddha-dharma."

Dharma Master Xuan Zang said, "You've slept too long. You've slept for several thousand years. In fact, more than a thousand years have passed since Shakyamuni Buddha entered Nirvana. It's been a long time, and you're still sitting here not knowing what has happened. You didn't even know that Shakyamuni Buddha entered the world."

The old cultivator said, "No problem. I'll just meditate until the White Sun Buddha appears in the world. I'll wait for Maitreya Bodhisattva to come, and then I will help him teach and transform living beings."

Having said as much, he prepared to enter into samadhi again. He was used to being in samadhi and was about to enter samadhi again when Master Xuan Zang called to him, "Oh, elder fellow meditator, don't enter samadhi again. Although Shakyamuni Buddha has entered Nirvana, his Dharma still exists in the world. You can help me spread the Buddha-dharma."

The old cultivator said, "Help you? How can I help you spread the Buddha-dharma? Who are you, anyway?"

Dharma Master Xuan Zang said, "I'm from the land of Tang [China], and my name is Xuan Zang. I'm on my way to India to collect the Buddha's Dharma jewels, and when I return to China, I will need someone to help me spread the Buddha-dharma. You've been meditating in one place for so many years and doing nothing; this is just too pitiful. Why don't you help me spread the Buddha-dharma?"

The old cultivator said, "I can help you."

Dharma Master Xuan Zang said, "Yes, but now you'll have to change. You can't use the body you are in now. I don't think your body could even stand up. You've been sitting for so long that your legs have probably stuck together and won't want to separate. So you'll have to change your house. Move to a new house."

The cultivator said, "Where should I move to?"

Dharma Master Xuan Zang replied, "Move to Chang An, the capital of China, and go to the palace with the yellow tile roof. When I come back from India, I will come and get you."

The cultivator said, "Okay, I can do that. I believe what you say, and I'll help you spread the Buddha-dharma." Then he went off to Chang An to be reborn.

Originally Dharma Master Xuan Zang had told him to be reborn in the house with the yellow tile roof. What do you think happened? The old cultivator mistakenly thought he said the house with the green tile roof. So when he saw the house with green tiles, he went there instead by mistake. Whose house did he go to? He went to the home of General Yu Chi. General Yu Chi had a dark complexion whereas General Shu Bao Qin had a yellow complexion. And so the old cultivator became the son of General Yu Chi's older brother.

When Dharma Master Xuan Zang left Chang An, the Emperor Tai Zong had asked him, "When will you return? When you return, send me a message ahead of time, so I can make arrangements to welcome you back."

Dharma Master Xuan Zang replied, "Take a look at this pine tree. The branches of this pine tree are now pointing west. When they point east, I will return." He was referring to a large pine tree outside the Imperial Palace gate.

During the next fourteen years, Emperor Tai Zong often looked at the pine to see if the branches had turned to face east, and one day it happened. Is it not strange that a tree could do this? As an efficacious response the tree was able to change in such an extreme way. Emperor Tai Zong said, "Dharma Master Xuan Zang is probably coming back today. Let's quickly go outside the city to welcome him. When he left, he said that the branches on this pine would point to the east when he was about to return, and today they are pointing to the east." So everyone went to the outskirts of the city to welcome Dharma Master Xuan Zang and escort him home.

When Dharma Master Xuan Zang saw the Emperor Tai Zong, he was extremely happy, and said, "My emperor, I congratulate you."

The Emperor retorted, "Why are you congratulating me? Nothing special has happened."

"The year I left, a prince should have been born into your family."

"No, no prince has been born. You've been gone for so many years, but I haven't had a son during that time."

When Dharma Master Xuan Zang heard this he thought, "Strange, I told the old cultivator to be born as a prince. How is it that he never came? This is strange." Then he said, "Wait until tonight and I will meditate on this and see where this person went."

Emperor Tai Zong did not know what he was talking about. Dharma Master Xuan Zang had spoken words that were incomprehensible to him, so the emperor did not pay much attention. That night, Dharma Master Xuan Zang meditated and contemplated the causes and conditions surrounding the old cultivator's rebirth. As soon as he began his investigation, he saw that the old cultivator had run off to the household of General Yu Chi, and that he was now a young boy of fourteen. He had grown very big and tall, and from morning till night he misbehaved. Previously the old cultivator had expended an excessive amount of effort in following the moral rules. Now that he was born into the household of General Yu Chi, he did not follow moral behavior at all. How did he misbehave? He ate meat, drank alcohol, and messed around with women. He could do whatever he wanted to do. This was because General Yu Chi's household had power, money, and status. So no matter what he did, no one dared to supervise and control him.

Dharma Master Xuan Zang saw that he had gone to the wrong destination ending up in the household of General Yu Chi. The next day Dharma Master Xuan Zang told the emperor, "Yesterday I said that you had given birth to a new prince, but this person took the wrong road. I told him to be reborn to become your prince, however, he went to the household of General Yu Chi. Now you should issue an imperial edict commanding him to renounce the householder's life to become a monastic. This is because previously he made an agreement with me to come here and help me propagate the Buddha-dharma."

As soon as the Emperor Tai Zong heard this he said, "Okay." Then he made a proclamation, which was an order or command from the emperor, requiring General Yu Chi's nephew to become a monastic. When General Yu Chi received this order, he said to his nephew, "The Emperor wants you to become a monk."

"That's totally unreasonable!" the boy replied. "How can the Emperor tell me to renounce the householder's life to become a monastic? I haven't had enough fun playing around. How can I become a monk?"

General Yu Chi said, "You can't do that! If you don't become a monk when the emperor tells you to do so, you will be beheaded. If you do not obey the emperor's orders the consequences will be unimaginable. You'll be executed."

"Well, if that's the case, I'll go see the emperor myself and try to reason with him," replied the nephew.

The next day, General Yu Chi went to see the emperor and said, "My nephew, whom you have ordered to become a monk, would like to have a personal audience with your majesty to discuss this."

Dharma Master Xuan Zang knew in advance that the boy would not want to become a monk. He had already told the emperor, "Tomorrow, General Yu Chi's nephew will come to try to reason with you. He will give you his criteria for becoming a monk. Whatever his conditions are, agree to them. Whatever he would like to do is okay."

The emperor replied, "Okay. We can see what happens tomorrow."

The next day General Yu Chi's nephew came to see the emperor. The emperor said, "I now believe in the Buddha-dharma, and I feel that renouncing the householder's life to become a monk is the best thing one can do. Therefore, I want you to become a monk and propagate the Buddha-dharma."

The boy said, "If I become a monk, there are three things that I cannot do without. If you agree to these three conditions, then I will become a monk. But if you do not agree to them, then even if you wish to execute me, I still won't become a monk."

Now take a look at this! He actually had no regard for his own life! Emperor Tai Zong said, "What are your three conditions?"

He replied, "What I like most is drinking wine. Those who renounce the householder's life to become monastics are not permitted to drink wine. However, since I am becoming a monk by imperial decree, I'm an exception to his rule. I want to be able to drink wine. After I become a monk, no matter where I go, I must be followed by a cart full of wine."

The Emperor said, "I permit your first condition. What is the second condition?"

"Concerning my second condition, I really like to eat meat. Those who are monastics are vegetarians, but I cannot be a vegetarian. I have to eat meat. I can't do without eating meat for even a day. So I must be followed by a cart of meat wherever I go."

The Emperor Tai Zong said, "Okay. It's but a small matter and creates no problems. I give you my permission to do this. Do you have any more conditions?"

"Yes, I still have one more condition."

"What is it?" asked the emperor.

"Monks don't have wives. However, I'm an exception. You've commanded me to become a monk. So I'm forced to renounce the householder's life. Nevertheless, I cannot give up women. Therefore, wherever I go I want a cart full of beautiful women to follow me. I must have these three carts: a cart of wine, a cart of meat, and a cart full of beautiful women. If you agree to my three conditions, then I will reluctantly become monk. However, if you don't agree to even one of these conditions, then I won't become a monk."

Emperor Tai Zung thought, "He's really depraved!" However, Dharma Master Xuan Zang had told him to agree to any of his conditions. Then he said, "Okay. I permit you to have a cart full of beautiful women. If you agree to become a monk, these will be permitted. Now that I've agreed to your conditions, can you become a monk?"

The nephew of General Yu Chi thought, "I'll have three carts of the things that I like the most. Okay. I can become a monk."

Although his wishes were granted, he was still quite depressed. And he was unhappy when he became a monk. To become a monk by imperial decree is quite honorable and it's a rather exciting public event. His monastic ordination was held at Da Xing Shan Monastery, built by Dharma Master Xuan Zang. The distance from the front mountain gate to the abbot's quarters was about three or four miles. The monastery could house tens of thousands of people. When someone renounces the householder's life to become a monastic by imperial decree, in the large monasteries they ring the bell and beat the drum. For example, here in our temple we have a bell and drum. Whenever there are special Buddhist events, we beat the drum and ring the bell. After hearing this sound, the Dharma protectors and good spirits will come to guard and protect the event. Therefore, one cannot just casually ring the bell and beat the drum or fail to do these things as one pleases. When there is a Dharma assembly, these things must be sounded. This is not only to notify people, but to also give the order and notification to all the Dharma protectors as well.

At that time the bell and drum were struck at Da Xing Shan Monastery. One person rang the bell, "Clang, clang!" and one person beat the drum, "Boom, boom!" The nephew of General Yu Chi reached the back of the monastery, and when he heard the sounds of the bell and drum, he suddenly was enlightened. "Oh! Before I was the old cultivator!" Then he waved his hand towards the carts that were behind him and said, "All of you go back. I don't want you. Now, I have enough. I don't want you." All three carts retreated. The one with beautiful women returned back, the one with wine ran off, and the one with meat disappeared. He entered Da Xing Shan Monastery to renounce the householder's life to become a monk. And he was called the Three-Cart Patriarch.

He was also called Dharma Master Kui Ji. Dharma Master Kui Ji taught the Consciousness Only doctrine. He was extremely intelligent. Regardless of what Sutra it was, he only had to hear it once and he had it memorized. And if he read it once, he could remember it as well. Once a Sutra had passed by his eyes, he never forgot it. This shows how brilliant he was. These are the causes and conditions that led him to cultivate the path. During the Tang Dynasty Dharma Master Kui Ji made a very great contribution to spreading the Buddha-dharma.

When I cultivate for the sake of Bodhi, that is when seeking the enlightened way of Bodhi and cultivating the path. **In all destinies, I will gain the knowledge of past lives.** Regardless of what destiny it is, even within the four evil destinies, which are the asuras, animals, hungry ghosts, and hells, I will know my past lives. I will attain the spiritual power of recollecting one's past lives.

I will always renounce the householder's life and cultivate the pure moral precepts. We should not think that it is easy to renounce the householder's life to become a monastic. Becoming a monastic is not easy.

Don't say that renouncing the householder's life is an easy thing to do.
It comes about because of planting seeds of Bodhi in many lives.

Don't think that anyone can just casually become a monastic. When some people go to take the Bhikshu precepts at Bao Hua Mountain, they must first pass by a certain mountain cave. Some don't make it past this cave, because a demonic obstacle may arise or they might even die. They die right there. Others have no trouble taking the Shramanera precepts, but when they get ready to take the Bhikshu precepts, they go crazy and cannot be ordained. There are many people like this. Why does this happen? This is because they have insufficient virtuous practice.

We just finished discussing the Three Cart Patriarch. In previous lives he cultivated for who knows how many years. Yet when he was reborn in China in the current life, he became confused. When he was to renounce the householder's life to become a monastic, he wanted a cart of wine, a cart of meat, and a cart of women. However, when he heard the sounds of the bell and drum, he became awakened and realized that originally in his past life, he had been a cultivator of the path. Then he was able to help Dharma Master Xuan Zhang propagate the Buddha-dharma.

He investigated the Consciousness Only School. At that time there was a Dharma Master who was even more eminent. Who was this Dharma Master? Vinaya Master Dao Xuan, who specialized in upholding the moral precepts. He was never careless in the Four Deportments of walking, standing, sitting, and lying down. When he walked, he did so with a deliberate manner. What was it like?

"He walked like a breeze," like "the gentle breeze that blows so lightly, no waves form on the water." This is a very gentle breeze that sweeps across the water and there are no waves. If the wind is strong, waves will arise. If the wind is light, there will be no waves. That is the way one should walk.

"He stood like a pine tree." When he stood up, he stood as straight as a pine tree.

"He sat like a bell." Wherever he sat, his posture was erect just like a bell.

"He laid down like a bow." He reclined just like a bow.

In the Four Major Awe-inspiring Deportments of walking, standing, sitting, and lying down he conducted himself especially well. He did not casually talk with his mouth, or casually look at things with his eyes, nor did he casually listen to sounds with his ears. If it was not in accord with proper etiquette, he would not look at it. If it was not proper etiquette, he would not listen to it. If it was not proper etiquette, he would not say it. And if it was not proper etiquette, he would not do it. He did not speak or act in an unprincipled way.

Because he held the moral precepts so sincerely and well, he invoked a response from a god who made offerings of food to him. He ate only one meal a day. He did not have to prepare his own meal, because a god from the heavens above called Lu Xuan-cha made an offering of food to him each day.

The Three-Cart Patriarch, Dharma Master Kui Ji, had eaten every different kind of food to be found in the human realm. He had eaten all the various kinds of meat when he was a layman, and after he had become a monk, he had eaten the most flavorful types of vegetarian food. Having already eaten all of these, he got a bit greedy. What was he greedy for? "I have never tasted the food and drink of the gods. Vinaya Master Dao Xuan receives offerings of food from a god. I think I'll go to his place to get a meal." He had a very high position, because he had become a monk on imperial command, and further he was a National Master. He could do whatever he pleased. So he decided to visit Vinaya Master Dao Xuan early one morning to avail himself of a meal.

When he arrived, and Vinaya Master Dao Xuan had received him, he said, "I've eaten everything except the food and drink of the gods. When the god brings you your food today, don't eat the whole thing yourself, but share some with me"

Vinaya Master Dao Xuan said, "All right. I'll share it with you. Wait here."

Dharma Master Kui Ji waited until after noon, and still the god had not come. Not only did he not get to eat heavenly food that day, he did not even get any human food to eat. Why? Vinaya Master Dao Xuan was not equipped to prepare food. He did not have a kitchen, rice, flour, oil, salt, or vegetables; he did not have anything at all. The only thing to eat was dirt. There was a lot of dirt there on Zhong Nan Mountain. They might also have been able to eat wild plants or the leaves of trees.

So there wasn't anything to eat. Then Dharma Master Kui Ji became a little perturbed. "The truth of the matter is, it seems to me that you are just deceiving people. You claim that gods offer food to you, but we didn't get anything to eat at all. I've come here, but I've not observed a single god offer you any food."

Vinaya Master Dao Xuan did not reply. He thought, "If you say I'm a cheat, then I'm a cheat. If you say I'm a liar, then I'm a liar. I don't need to argue about it." Because he maintained the moral precepts, he did not like to talk too much.

After a while, it got dark. It was about twenty miles from the top of Zhong Nan Mountain to the bottom, and it was not possible to leave at night. Once one descended the mountain, it was another twenty miles to Chang An. So Dharma Master Kui Ji had to spend the night there.

What do you think happened? As soon as he reclined on the bed, he fell asleep and began snoring like thunder. The sound of the breathing through his nose was as loud as thunder. Vinaya Master Dao Xuan gave rise to some false thinking. Basically, old cultivators who uphold the moral precepts do not think like this. What did he think? "National Master! Although you are a National Master, you have no spiritual cultivation whatsoever. How could you sleep like this? It's really annoying." In his mind, he had these thoughts.

After he had these thoughts, he noticed a louse on his body. Sometimes people who have become monastics do not bathe very often, and their bodies become very dirty and attract lice. When a louse bit Vinaya Master Dao Xuan, he took it off his body and dropped it on the ground. After a while, another louse bit him, so he dropped that louse on the ground as well. He only slept a little bit throughout the night, while Dharma Master Kui Ji slept through the entire night snoring like thunder. Vinaya Master Dao Xuan tried to sit in meditation, but was unable to enter samadhi. So he ended up thinking all night long.

In the morning, Vinaya Master Dao Xuan could not take it anymore, and he complained, "Last night, how could you sleep like that? The way you sleep is totally improper. Your snoring sounds just like thunder, and you kept me from entering samadhi all night long. I meditated but couldn't enter samadhi."

How do you think Dharma Master Kui Ji replied? He said, "You say I don't have any cultivation? You're really the one who can't cultivate." The two of them argued back and forth.

Vinaya Master Dao Xuan said, "How do you know I can't cultivate?"

Dharma Master Kui Ji said, "You are an old cultivator who maintains the moral precepts and doesn't kill any living beings. However, didn't you pick two lice off your body last night? The first louse you threw down on the ground in a mean way. You killed it. You dropped the second louse on the ground more gently, but you broke his legs. Both of these lice, the one that was dead and the one that was still alive, went to King Yama to bring a grievance against you. They said that the old cultivator who holds the moral precepts committed the act of killing. I had to go and negotiate on your behalf. I said that you did this unintentionally, and that the lice should not seek revenge. Then King Yama told them to go off to rebirth. So finally the grievance was resolved."

When Vinaya Master Dao Xuan heard this he said, "Huh? I picked those lice off very slowly last night, and no one knew it. How did you know? This is strange."

Dharma Master Kui Ji was unhappy and said, "I'm leaving! Gods don't bring food to you. You're just deceiving people!" And he left.

After he had gone, the god Lu Xuan-cha came before noon and brought some food. Vinaya Master Dao Xuan in a very unhappy way said, "Why didn't you bring food yesterday? I went hungry for the whole day. And furthermore, there was a special guest for lunch. Why didn't you come with food?"

Lu Xuan-cha said, "Dharma Master, please be compassionate and forgive me. Yesterday when I came with the offerings for you, there was a golden light for fifteen miles in every direction. I wanted to go into this light, but I couldn't open my eyes. I couldn't tell north from south or east from west. I couldn't see anything except the golden light. Then I asked the local spirit who watches over the area, and he told me that there was a 'Bodhisattva in the flesh' at your place; so there was a golden light everywhere for fifteen miles all around. Therefore I couldn't come. Please forgive me."

When Vinaya Master Dao Xuan heard this he said, "No wonder! Dharma Master Kui Ji is a Bodhisattva in the flesh! This is an inconceivable state. I said he couldn't cultivate, and that he snored like thunder. He was just intentionally being that way. In fact his state is much higher than mine. Gods can't even get close to him."

After that, Vinaya Master Dao Xuan cultivated more intensely, and Dharma Master Kui Ji never again wished to eat the food offered by the gods. He didn't have this false thought anymore. These two experienced cultivators were eminent Sangha members of that period.

I will always renounce the householder's life and cultivate the pure moral precepts. I just discussed Vinaya Master Dao Xuan and Patriarch Kui Ji, who both had attained the inconceivable state of a Bodhisattva.

Ordinary people could not compare to them. As we now cultivate the practices and power of the ten great King of Vows of Samantabhadra Bodhisattva, we should also vow to always leave the home-life.

In renouncing the householder's life, we leave the home of afflictions, the home of the Three Realms of Existence, and the home of ignorance. What does it mean to leave the home of afflictions? Everyone has afflictions. You should put your afflictions down and let them go. That's what is meant by leaving the home of afflictions. The Three Realms of Existence includes the Realm of Sensual Desire, the Form Realm, and the Formless Realm. If you can leave the home of the Three Realms of Existence, then although you still live in the Realm of Sensual Desire, you will not have any sexual desire. Even though you have not reached the Form Realm, for you forms and appearances are empty, and even the Formless Realm is empty. This is the meaning of leaving the home of the Three Realms of Existence.

In leaving the home of ignorance, you break through ignorance which is the fundamental affliction. If you are able to eradicate ignorance, then the wisdom of the Enlightened Way of Bodhi will become perfected. This is the meaning of leaving the home of ignorance, the third of the three kinds of leaving home.

In China, not everyone who renounces the householder's life to become a monastic is able to cultivate. There is a custom in China concerning a child who has many illnesses as soon as he is born. In this case the parents take the child to many doctors, but he cannot be cured and will certainly die. Then, the parents think, "Since our child is going to die anyway, let's give him to the monastery so he can leave the home-life and become a novice monk." Now, it is often the case that after the child leaves the home-life his illnesses are cured, and he does not die. He leaves the home-life to avoid death. This kind of person definitely has the roots of goodness, but I'm afraid that such a person may be confused. How is he confused? He doesn't want to cultivate. He has the roots of goodness, but he has forgotten them. Therefore, it is not for sure that he will be able to cultivate. However, there is still a chance that he might. So this is the situation where a person goes to the monastery to leave home when he is very young.

Then there are those who leave the home-life because of the stress and strain in their life. They may come from a very poor household, and they leave home because they have heard that it is very easy to get food and clothing. These people leave the home-life for food and clothing.

Others decide to leave the home-life because they are old and have no one to take care of them. After they leave home and become a monk, they then take a young disciple who will have filial respect towards them because a disciple should be respectful towards his teacher. For example, he should offer whatever he eats to his teacher first, and no matter what the circumstances, he must always have respect and venerate his teacher. Before such a person became a monk, he did not have any sons or daughters so he leaves the home-life and then finds a young disciple who will take care of him. This kind of person leaves the home-life so that he will be taken care of in his old age, and it is not for sure that he will be able to cultivate.

Some people are forced to leave home due to circumstances. What does it mean to be forced by circumstances to leave home? The Patriarch Kui Ji is an example of such a case. Circumstances compelled him to leave the home-life. However, he was able to cultivate.

In China there was a law which said that regardless of what offenses a person has committed, even if he is a murderer, an arsonist, or a bandit, when he becomes a monastic, the government will not prosecute him.

These are people who leave the home life to avoid being punished for breaking the law. It is also not certain that these types of people can cultivate.

There is one kind of person, however, who can cultivate. Who? These are the people who bring forth the Bodhi-mind to truly resolve the problem of birth and death. So there are many reasons for leaving home, and you cannot say, "Oh! How can this person be a monastic? This person has such a big temper and great afflictions." There are different kinds of left-home people who become monastics for various different reasons. Now the text reads, "**I will always renounce the householder's life and cultivate the pure moral precepts.**" I cultivate and maintain the pure moral precepts.

Unbroken, undefiled, and without outflows. I cultivate the pure, precious moral precepts. And I uphold the pure, precious moral precepts, just like precious pearls. "Unbroken" means I have never broken or violated the moral precepts. "Without outflows" means that within the Vinaya or moral precepts there is no defect.

SUTRA:

> Gods, dragons, yakshas, kumbhandas,
> Including humans, non-humans, and others,
> In the languages of all living beings,
> With every voice I will speak the Dharma.

COMMENTARY:

Gods, dragons, yakshas, kumbhandas. Now we are discussing gods, dragons, yakshas, kumbhandas, and all the other ghosts. How do dragons become dragons? They are "zealous with the vehicle, but lackadaisical with the moral precepts." In the past they cultivated the Dharma of the Great Vehicle and were extremely vigorous, but at the same time they neglected the moral precepts, feeling that moral precepts were very common and ordinary. They felt it didn't matter if they held the moral precepts or not. Because of this, they were reborn as dragons. Being zealous with the vehicle they become dragons that have spiritual powers. However, because they were lackadaisical about the moral precepts, they fell into the path of animals. Dragons are still animals.

The list of gods, dragons and yakshas also includes asuras, kinnaras, mahoragas, garudas, and so forth. Kumbhandas are a type of ghost that are wider than they are tall. They are more than three feet tall and their width is at most, five feet. They do not have a head or feet, and are shaped like a millstone. Some say they are shaped like a winter melon. These ghosts wait for people to go to sleep, and then they do their mischief. What mischief do they do? They specialize in possessing people in their sleep. What is meant by "possessing people in their sleep"? The person can open their eyes and see things, but cannot speak or move. The person wants to move, but he can't. He tries to speak, but he cannot make a sound. Some people suffocate. They try to breathe and are unable to do so. They then will die. So kumbhanda ghosts can be very harmful. In this Sutra however, the kumbhandas are not so harmful. The ten great King of Vows of Samantabhadra Bodhisattva have influenced and transformed them so that they may become Dharma protectors. **Including humans, non-humans, and others, in the languages of all living beings:** all beings, regardless of whether they are gods, asuras, humans, or all the other types of living beings—in all of their languages, **with every voice I will speak the Dharma.** I will use all the various languages to speak Dharma for all living beings. Whatever type of living being I meet with, I will speak Dharma in that living being's own language.

SUTRA:

> I will diligently cultivate the pure paramitas,
> And never forget the Bodhi-mind.
> I will extinguish obstructions and defilements
>   without remainder,
> And will accomplish all the wondrous practices.

COMMENTARY:

I will diligently cultivate the pure paramitas. To diligently cultivate means not to be lazy and to be unafraid of toil or fatigue. To always be vigorous is to diligently cultivate. At all times one vigorously practices the pure, undefiled paramitas. Paramita is a Sanskrit word that means, "to reach the other shore". One cultivates from this shore of Samsara to reach the "other shore" of Nirvana.

And never forget the Bodhi-mind. Life after life I will never forget to bring forth the Bodhi-mind. What is the Bodhi-mind? It is the mind to diligently seek for the Buddha's Path. You do not want to forget this mind. In life after life you don't forget it.

I will extinguish obstructions and defilements without remainder. I will destroy all of the obstructions. Obstructions include, the obstruction of retribution, karmic obstruction, and the obstruction of afflictions. Defilements refers to all afflictions. When you have afflictions, it is like having defilements or impurities. "Without remainder" means there are no afflictions whatsoever.

And will accomplish all the wondrous practices... Now we are talking about wondrous practices. Today Guo Miao has come. Her mother said that in the future when she gets married, she should do so in the Buddha hall. You should tell her that in the future she should come to the Buddha hall to practice the path or Dhyana meditation or to put an end to birth and death. These are wondrous practices. To have achievement in whatever practice you cultivate, is called wondrous practice. You accomplish this kind of inconceivable state. What does inconceivable mean? It is beyond human expectations. You cannot imagine it, yet to your surprise you attain it. That's what is meant by wondrous. There is no way that you can think about it. It is inconceivable. That is called wondrous. Not only can you not conceive of it with your mind, you cannot describe it. It's a kind of subtle, wondrous and inconceivable practice. What is the subtle, wondrous, and inconceivable practice? It's investigating Dhyana and becoming enlightened. If you can become enlightened, then you have accomplished all the inconceivable wondrous practices.

SUTRA:

From all delusions, karma, and demonic states,
Within the worldly paths, I will attain liberation.

COMMENTARY:

From all delusions, karma, and demon-states. What are "delusions" and "karma?" Delusion is confusion or doubt. There are three kinds of delusion: view delusions, the delusions of thought, and the delusions like dust and sand. View delusions are coarse delusions, the delusions of thought are subtle delusions, and the delusions like dust and sand are called the delusion of ignorance.

What are view delusions? "When you encounter a state, you give rise to thoughts of greed and craving." Thoughts of craving are delusion. And when you have a lot of delusions, you become confused and lack understanding.

What is the delusion of thought? Because you do not understand reason, you give rise to improper discriminating thoughts. This is delusion of thought.

The delusions like dust and sand are extremely many. They are as numerous as the smallest atomic particles or as many as the grains of sand in the Ganges River. The ignorance we have in our minds was originally very little, but it has increased to a great amount. For this reason, it is called delusions like dust and sand: one's ignorance is as numerous as the minutest particles in the world and the grains of sand in the Ganges River. For example, in your life you may unexpectedly encounter a state and give rise to thoughts of greed and craving. Although this is considered delusion of views, fundamentally it comes from ignorance. Why do you give rise to thoughts of greed and craving? Where do these thoughts come from? If you seek for their source, you will find ignorance. Ignorance, therefore, is the source of birth and death or Samsara. We have not ended birth and death because ignorance obstructs us. These are three kinds of delusion.

How many types of delusion of views are there? There are eighty-eight kinds of delusion of views. How many kinds of delusion of thought are there? There are eighty-one. When one has realized the First Stage of an Arhat, one has cut off the eighty-eight view delusions. When one has realized the Second Stage of an Arhat, one has cut off the eighty-one thought delusions When one has realized the Third Stage of an Arhat, one cuts off the delusions like dust and sand. When one has realized the Fourth Stage of an Arhat, one destroys ignorance. And when ignorance is destroyed, the Dharma Nature is revealed.

However, he has not destroyed ignorance completely. Even the Bodhisattva of Equal Enlightenment has still not destroyed "ignorance concerning the characteristic of origination." This one last tiny bit of ignorance has not yet been destroyed. If one can destroy this final tiny bit of ignorance, one realizes Wonderful Enlightenment. Wonderful Enlightenment is the enlightenment of a Buddha. But because one has not yet destroyed this tiny bit of ignorance, one is still a Bodhisattva.

"Karma" refers to the good and evil karma that you create. There is a saying, "Even for hundreds of thousands of kalpas, the karma one creates is never forgotten." There is no way that the karma that you have created can disappear. If you do good, then you have good karma; if you do bad, then you have bad karma. Karma is always with you. The verse continues, "When the causes and supporting conditions come together, the results must be undergone by yourself."

When the conditions come together, when the time is right, you must undergo retribution. Undergoing your just reward means that you must undergo what is coming to you. If you have planted good causes, you will receive a good reward, but if you have planted bad causes, you will get a bad reward. If you do wholesome deeds, you will get good in return, but if you do evil, you will get evil in return. Therefore it is said:

> Even for hundreds of thousands of kalpas, the karma one creates is never forgotten.
> When the causes and supporting conditions come together, the results must be undergone by yourself.

I will now give you an example of how causes and conditions are at work. There was once a man who was very rich. How did he get rich? He was a rice merchant. In China, rice was sold by the pound and was measured using a scale or standard sized containers. The wealthy man added water to his rice to increase its weight and size. To one hundred pounds of rice he added ten to twenty pounds of water. The rice looked quite good, because it was larger and weighed more. However, when it dried out, it shrank so that there was not very much rice. He made a lot of money doing business like this.

He also sold liquor in the same way. He thought, "If a person drinks liquor, I should make money off of him. If he has the money to buy a drink, there's no reason why I shouldn't get a little more of it. If he doesn't have money, of course, then he can't buy it." At that time there was sorghum liquor. To every quart of this liquor he added about 20% water. So with every 10 quarts of liquor he made a lot of money.

This wealthy man had three sons. Because he loved gold and silver, he named his eldest son Gold and his second son Silver. What did he name his third son? He named him Karmic Obstructions. It is not known how rich he was. He made an excessive amount of money.

When he became old, he contracted an illness and was on the verge of death. He sought out a doctor to cure him, but the doctor threw up his hands and said he was at a loss to help him. He said, "I have no way to help you. You can only bide your time. If you have good things to eat, go ahead and enjoy them. Your time is near."

The man thought, "I have so much money it seems pointless to die like this. I'll have to discuss this with my sons and see which one will go along with me when I die. My eldest son is my favorite."

He called his eldest son Gold to him and said, "Do you know that for my entire life I have cared for you the most?"

His son said, "I know. You've been very good to me. As my father you have given me so much money and you have accumulated so much wealth—all of which will be mine in the future. I know you've been very good to me."

His father said, "I care for you so much and now that I'm about to die, I can't bear to leave you. Could you go along with me when I die?"

His eldest son said, "Your illness has made you mixed up and confused. How can I die with you? Are you joking with me? Please don't joke like this. You must really be telling a big joke."

His father said, "No! I'm serious. I'm not joking. Really, can you die with me or not?"

The eldest son said, "No I can't. You're asking me to die with you. You arranged for me to get married, so now I have a wife and a son. If I die, what will become of them?"

His father said, "During my entire life I cared for you so much, and yet when I ask you to accompany me in death, you refuse. Okay. Well, if you won't come along, just forget it." He wanted to get his second son, so he told Gold, "Quickly go tell Silver to come and see me."

Then he talked to Silver. "I have treated your elder brother a little bit better than you, but I've discovered that he does not have the least bit of filial respect towards me. I feel that you always have a lot of filial respect, and that you are very obedient to your father. Now, I'm about to die. Can you go along with me when I die?

Silver replied, "If Gold won't die with you, how could I possibly do it? I can't do this. If you are going to die, then hurry up and die. However, you can't tell me to die with you." Then he shook his arm and said, "Father, you are senile. You are truly an ignoramus. I'm still young. I haven't enjoyed my life enough, and you ask me to die with you. That's totally ridiculous. Having old people like you living in the world is simply a waste." Not only would this son not die with his father, but he scolded him as well.

The wealthy man said, "If you won't die with me, tell my youngest son to come." And he called for his third son, Karmic Obstructions.

"Karmic Obstructions, I'm about to die. Can you accompany me in death?"

Karmic Obstructions replied, "Of course. I'd be most happy to do this. I'll accompany you and serve you wherever you go."

Then the rich man thought, "He's really not too bad. At least I have one son who will be buried with me." Then he felt very satisfied.

But what happened when Karmic Obstructions went with his father? They went to see King Yama and King Yama asked the man, "When you were alive, did you add water to your rice and liquor before selling them?"

The wealthy man replied, "No. I would never do such a dishonest thing."

Can you guess what Karmic Obstructions said when he heard his father's reply? He said, "Yes, you did. Every time you sold rice or liquor, I saw you add water to them. King Yama is correct. How come you don't admit this?"

His son had gone along to testify as a witness to all the bad things his father had done. There was nothing his father could say. As a result, he was about to fall into the hells.

He said to his son, "You came along to testify against me, to say that I committed karmic offenses, not to say that I did virtuous deeds. If I had known you were going to be like this, I would have never asked you to accompany me. It would have been a lot better if you had never come. Now I've ended up in the hells. Even though I don't have a defense lawyer, I could have spoken on my own behalf and King Yama would not have known of my bad deeds. But you testified against me." Then the wealthy man was quite despondent. Therefore it is said,

You can't take anything with you (when you die).
Neither Gold nor Silver will be willing to go.
Only your Karma will follow you.

You can't take any of the myriad things that exist with you. Gold and Silver are unwilling to go. Only Karmic Obstructions will go along with you.

When King Yama is interrogating you,
Karma will tell it as it actually is.

When King Yama asks you what you did during your life, your karmic obstructions will verify what is true and what karma was actually done. Karmic obstructions are very fierce. What is the meaning of karmic obstructions? Karma is all the things that you do. If you do good, then you have good karma. If you do evil, then you have evil karma. The good that you do is called good karma, and the evil that you do is called evil karma. It is bad karma that constitutes your karmic obstructions.

Explaining this reminds me of another short story. It occurred when I was very young, while I was still a Shramanera (novice monk). At Chinese New Year, people always write matched couplets on red paper and hang them on either side of the main entrance of the monastery or their residence. This is called "writing scrolls for the New Year." If you look downstairs at the entrance of our building (the lecture was giving at the Buddhist Lecture Hall on Waverly Place in San Francisco in 1969), there is red paper posted on either side of the door, which is what I am talking about here. In the monastery someone might write, "May everything be auspicious in accord with your wishes" or some other auspicious words or verse.

At that time I wrote the four characters, "Wisdom like the sea" very quickly and with a lot of strength and power. When a fellow Dharma brother, who was also a Shramanera, saw these four words, he really liked them. And he recited, "Wisdom like the sea, wisdom like the sea, wisdom like the sea," over and over again. When I had heard him do this so many times, it really irritated me, and so I said, "The force of your karma is like the sea."

When he heard this he got very upset. He was so angry he wanted to hit me. He said, "*How* do you know the force of my karma is like the sea? *How* can you say my karma is like the sea?" He acted like he was ready to fight with me.

I replied, "Don't get so upset. What I have said is something that will definitely make you happy. You will certainly agree with me. When I said that the force of your karma is like the sea, not only should you not get mad at me, but you should thank me for wishing you good fortune."

He retorted, "Ha! That's really outrageous! You say the force of my karma is like the sea, and I should thank you? That doesn't make any sense."

I said, "I'll tell you the rest of the explanation later." This literally means "I'll continue explaining this in the next episode." That is, I'm not going to explain it to you now. Wait a while and I will tell you later on.

He demanded, "What are you going to explain?"

I said, "Do you know what the meaning of karma is?"

He said, "Karma is what people do."

I said, "There is good karma and bad karma. I meant the power of your good karma is like the sea. How do you feel now?" He stood there wide-eyed with surprise and had nothing to say. I continued, "I didn't say whether your good karma or bad karma was like the sea. Why did you get angry? My meaning was that your good karma is like the sea. Now what do you think?"

He said, "Oh, no problem. I'm sorry." He apologized, admitted he was wrong, which means he repented. Look how wonderful this is! Just one word made the difference. By adding the word "good," suddenly his extreme anger vanished. Don't you think this is strange? This is also called the wonderful Dharma. Do you understand? Being off by one word and not clearly saying the word "good," caused him to get angry. But when I added the word "good" to "karma like the sea," he was beside himself with joy. If you are off by one word, you can cause people to become happy or to get angry.

I told him, "Since I've said this to you, you should invite me to lunch."

He said, "Okay, okay!" Then he agreed to invite me for lunch.

Take a look at this. The minds of living beings are very strange. With the difference of one word, they can go from anger to joy. The power of karma is just like this.

There is another story that occurred also during the time that I was a Shramanera. One day I was carrying a roll of paper, and I met a person who was a real busy body. He liked to know about and meddle in other people's business.

He asked me, "What is it you have there? What are you carrying?"

I replied, "This is a bill of sale. I have just sold you."

He got angry. Because he would often get angry, I would occasionally do things that would get him stirred up. So this time I told him, "This is a bill of sale. I sold you."

He got angry and said, "How can you sell me? Huh? How can you sell me? What authority do you have to sell me?"

I said, "Of course I have the authority to sell you. And since I've sold you, you should be happy, because I wouldn't do so if you didn't like it. I actually have a special authority to sell you."

He got even angrier. "What kind of special authority?" He was really upset.

I told him, "If there is someone who wants to buy you, you should certainly be happy when I sell you."

He said, "That doesn't make any sense. If you sold me to someone, how could I possibly be happy about it? Explain yourself."

I said, "I'll explain it to you. I sold you to Shakyamuni Buddha so that you can be a monk forever."

He was dumbstruck. He stared at me with unblinking eyes.

I said, "Is this okay? Are you happy?"

He replied, "That's okay. You can do that."

When I was very young, I was really naughty. This is how naughty I was.

Look into this. The situation here is the same as the story above. I sold him just the same, but in the end he was happy. This is also the wonderful Dharma. Do not take it as just a joke.

"From all delusions, karma, and demonic states, within the worldly paths, I will attain liberation." I have explained "delusion" and "karma" in general, and now I will discuss "demon-states." If you do not cultivate the Path, demons will not come after you. But if you do cultivate, then demons will come after you. Why? When you do not cultivate you are like a poor person, and demons are just like bandits. Bandits do not rob poor people, because they know that poor people have nothing worth stealing. However, if you cultivate the Path, then you are the same as a rich person. If you are rich, then day and night the bandits will wait for the opportunity to rob you. They will try to steal your valuables. Thus there are demons when you cultivate the Path. It is said,

> *Demons polish the True Path;*
> *With the True Path, demons come.*
> *The more they polish, the brighter you become;*
> *When you become bright, it should be polished even more,*
> *Polished like the full moon in autumn*
> *Which shines in the sky upon the hordes of demons.*
> *Being revealed by the light, the demonic hordes retreat,*
> *And the original Buddha appears.*

"Demons polish the True Path." Only when you have a little bit of true sincerity, will the demons come to "polish" and test you. Therefore, the next line says, "With the True Path, demons come." If you truly cultivate, then there will be demons. "The more they polish, the brighter you become." The more the demon polishes you, the brighter you become. "When you become bright, it should be polished even more." The brighter you become, the more you should be polished. "Polished like the full moon in autumn." Demons test you until your light shines like the autumn moon. This is the autumn moon that shines radiantly in the sky during the fall. "Which shines in the sky upon the hordes of demons." In the sky it illuminates all of the hordes of demons. It means that if you have true wisdom, you can illuminate the hordes of demons. You will recognize all of them. When demons come, you will detect them. "Being revealed by the light, the demonic hordes retreat." Illuminating the demonic hordes refers to the light of your wisdom, which illuminates the demons so they are unable to find or exploit any weakness in you. "And the original Buddha appears." At that time the original Buddha comes forth.

When you cultivate the spiritual path and have some achievement, demonic obstacles will arise. For example, let us discuss keeping the moral precepts. You may not want to break the precepts, but you break them nonetheless. You do not wish to kill, but without being aware of it, you find yourself killing and breaking that moral precept. You do not wish to steal, but unbeknownst to you, you break this precept. You do not wish to break the precept against sexual misconduct, but without being aware of it, you find yourself breaking this moral precept.

What does it mean to do these things without knowing it? It means that you are confused, and then your ignorance comes forth. When ignorance arises you forget everything. For example, you might forget that you have taken the moral precepts or that you are vegetarian, and so you eat meat and break the moral precepts. Originally you do not intend to lie, but your ignorance comes forth and you lie. You do not intend to drink wine, but your ignorance arises and you take a drink. These are all situations in which your ignorance covers over your wisdom. And because you lack wisdom, you break the moral precepts. This is one scenario for breaking the moral precepts.

When you meditate and start to develop some power of meditative-concentration, you make a resolve. You realize that romantic relationships are unwholesome, so you think "I must change and refrain from this behavior." You have obtained a little bit of meditative-concentration, and from this concentration comes a little bit of wisdom. Therefore, you wish to put an end to sexual desire. Previously, when you did not want to cut off your sexual desire, nothing happened. However, as soon as you wish to cut if off, the "demons of lust" come. What do they do? Perhaps when you are asleep and dreaming, they may transform into different kinds of beautiful women. Not just one kind. They will appear as the kind you like the most and then try to seduce you. This is what happens with men. For women, they will manifest as various kinds of handsome men to tempt you. They challenge and test you in your dreams. If you do not have enough self-control, you will break the moral precepts in your dreams. When you do not have enough strength in your meditative-concentration, then you also do not have wisdom.

Perhaps this happens even when you're not dreaming, during ordinary times. If you have no concentration power and you lack wisdom, the demons will not bother you. However, if you wish to cultivate the path and make a resolve to practice, this kind of experience with a demonic obstacle can appear. For example if you are a man, your old girlfriend may come around, or if you are a women, your old boyfriend might come to see you. Then without realizing it, you break the moral precepts. Breaking precepts just shows a lack of the power of concentration. When you are without concentration, you are deluded, without any power of wisdom. This is an example of how ignorance covers over your wisdom and causes you to break the moral precepts. This is another kind of scenario for breaking the moral precepts.

Another situation is this. You say that you meditate all day long from morning to night. You investigate Dhyana and meditate. When you are meditating a demonic obstacle can arise. What demonic obstacle? Perhaps you see all kinds of states and experiences. Maybe you feel that you have spiritual powers or you feel that your body is the same as the void. You feel that you're as big as space. The *Shurangama Sutra* has a section on the 50 Skandha Demons. All types of these demonic states can appear. These are all demonic states.

In the past there was an old cultivator who practiced Dhyana meditation and cultivated the Path. When he was just about to enter samadhi, he had a state. What was this state? He saw a large boulder weighing a few tons suspended over his head by a fine rope. A mouse was chewing on the rope. If the rope were to break, the large boulder would smash the old cultivator to death. If he had become frightened and tried to run away when he saw this state, he would have been possessed by a demon. The demon king would have his way with him. However, his mind was like still water, and he thought, "If you fall on my head and smash me to death, I won't pay any attention to you. Even if I die, I will still continue to meditate here." After this, he entered samadhi, and as a result, no large boulder smashed him to death. If he had become frightened, he could have been possessed by a demon.

Further, when Shakyamuni Buddha was just about to perfect the Path and become a Buddha, the demon king, Pāpīyāṃs and his multitudes became uneasy. The demon king said, "Prince Siddhartha Gautama is about to become a Buddha. We should prevent him from accomplishing the Path and becoming a Buddha."

At that time, the demon king was thinking back and forth trying to come up with a wondrous method. When he had come to the point where he knitted his brows in frustration and felt that there was no way to stop him, some of his demon daughters arrived.

They asked, "Father, why are you so distraught?"

The demon king answered, "Prince Gautama is about to become a Buddha. I don't want this to happen. If he becomes a Buddha, our retinue of demons will lose its power and influence. I'm trying to think of a way to stop him from becoming a Buddha."

His daughters said, "We can disturb his resolve for the Path and cause him to have thoughts of lust."

Then the demon women got ready to destroy Shakyamuni Buddha's karma of the spiritual path. These demon women were extremely beautiful. When they went to where Shakyamuni Buddha was, they appeared in various seductive ways, and used this cunning method to try to entice Shakyamuni Buddha to have thoughts of sexual desire. However, Shakyamuni Buddha was fundamentally "thus, thus unmoving" when encountering states like this.

Then he thought, "Now you think you are really beautiful. Yet actually in the future when you're old you'll have wrinkles on your face like a chicken and the hair on your head will turn as white as a crane. In the future, you will be very ugly."

When he made this contemplation, the demon women all of a sudden saw themselves becoming old. Their eyes could not see clearly and their ears had difficulty hearing. And they saw themselves looking old, frail and decrepit. They became very ashamed and ran off.

When talking about demonic states, they are quite numerous. No matter what state or experience we cultivators of the Path encounter, we must not be moved by them. If you are not moved or disturbed by them, just this is having the power of concentration or samadhi. If you have samadhi-power, you can overcome and transform a scattered and restless mind. Dhyana Samadhi transforms a mind that lacks concentration. If you don't have scattered thoughts, you cannot be possessed by a demon. This is called breaking up the states of demons.

Within the worldly paths, I will attain liberation. Right within the worldly paths, one is able to obtain liberation. One reaches a state of non-attachment and attains liberation. The worldly paths are the mundane paths of existence that we are in now. Within the dharmas or phenomena of the world you can transcend the world. How can you transcend the world while being in the world? Just don't be attached. If you can separate from your attachments, then you can obtain liberation.

SUTRA:

> This is like the lotus flower that is not sullied by the water,
> Or like the sun and moon that do not stay fixed in the sky.
>
> Completely eradicating all the suffering of the evil paths,
> And equally bringing happiness to all living beings,
> In this way passing through kalpas as numerous as particles in
>   a kshetra-land
> Always benefiting those in the ten directions without end.
>
> I always conform with all living beings,
> Exhausting all kalpas of the future.
> Always cultivating the vast practices of Samantabhadra
> Bringing to perfection the unsurpassed great Bodhi.
>
> May all who practice the same way as myself,
> In every place where we gather together,
> Our karma of body, mouth, and mind the same,
> Together we learn and cultivate all the same practices
>   and vows.
>
> All of the Good Teachers who benefit me,
> Who elucidate for me the practices of Samantabhadra,
> I wish that we will always gather together,
> And that they will always be happy with me.

COMMENTARY:

This is like the lotus flower that is not sullied by the water. What does it mean not to be attached or sullied? It means, "Although a person is in the mundane world, his mind is beyond the mundane. If a flower is planted in a well, it will not be sullied by the dust." Although this person is in the world, yet his mind transcends the mundane world. This is like a flower planted in a well that is not defiled by the dust. No dust particles can reach the flower. So the verse says, "Just as the lotus flower is not sullied by the water." This is like a lotus that comes forth from the mud, but is not defiled by the mud. Its roots are in the mud and its stem is in the water, but the flower is above the water. This is called, "coming from the mud, yet being undefiled." We people should not be attached to any of the dharmas of the world. This is like the lotus flower that is not defiled by the dust.

Or like the sun and moon that do not stay fixed in the sky. It's like the sun and moon in the sky. They do not remain in the same spot in the sky. Although the sun and moon are in the sky, they don't stand still there nor are they attached to the sky. They are without any attachments.

Completely eradicating all the suffering of the evil paths. To "completely eradicate" means to totally wipe out the suffering of all the evil paths. The three evil paths are the paths of the hells, the hungry ghosts, and the animals. **And equally bringing happiness to all living beings**. One equally bestows this kind of happiness upon all living beings. **In this way passing through kalpas as numerous as particles in a kshetra-land**. I will act in this way throughout kalpas that are so many that they are as numerous as the smallest atomic particles in a kshetra-land. **Always benefiting those in the ten directions without end**. I benefit all living beings throughout the ten directions, constantly without end.

I always conform with all living beings. I want to at all times comply with living beings, comply with all living beings in cultivating and studying ten great King of Vows of Samantabhadra. **Exhausting all**

kalpas of the future. Throughout all kalpas, exhausting the limits of future time, I never reach the end of the power or force of these vows. **Always cultivating the vast practices of Samantabhadra**. I constantly cultivate and study the vast and great doors of practice of Samantabhadra Bodhisattva. **Bringing to perfection the unsurpassed great Bodhi**. The roots of goodness from my unsurpassed great Bodhi are brought to perfection without anything lacking whatsoever.

May all who practice the same way as myself—all those people who with me cultivate the Ten Great Practices of Samantabhadra—**in every place where we gather together**, that is at any time we are able to gather together in one place. **Our karma of body, mouth, and mind the same**. Our three karmas of body, mouth, and mind are identical. **Together we learn and cultivate all the same practices and vows**. The practices and vows that we cultivate and learn together are also the same.

All of the Good Teachers who benefit me. All those Good Teachers who are beneficial to me, **who elucidate for me the practices of Samantabhadra**, and who teach me how to cultivate the doors of practice of Samantabhadra Bodhisattva, **I wish that we will always gather together**. Those who have affinities with each other can congregate together. However, it would be impossible to be together with those who do not have affinities with you even if you wanted to. Those who always gather together have made vows to work diligently at cultivating the path together in life after life. "In the same assembly" means being in the same Dharma Assembly. **And that they will always be happy with me**. Those people will always be happy with me.

If you do not have affinities with a person, then even if you treat him well when meeting up with him, he will not feel like he is being treated well. However, if you have affinities with someone, even if you scold him or hit him, he will be happy. Why? Because you have these affinities with each other. So the relationships that people have with one another are subtle and wonderful.

SUTRA:

> I vow to always see in person all the Tathagatas
> And the assembly of disciples of the Buddhas that
>   encircle them.
> I'll give vast and great offerings to all of them
> To the end of future kalpas without ever becoming weary.

COMMENTARY:

I vow to always see in person all the Tathagatas. I make a vow to always personally see all Buddhas and to go to all of their worlds throughout the ten directions to draw near to them. **And the assembly of disciples of the Buddhas that encircle them.** I will be together with all the great assemblies of all the Buddhas' disciples that have gathered together who circumambulate, praise, and make offerings to the Buddhas. **I'll give vast and great offerings to all of them.** I will bring forth a resolve to make vast and great offerings to all the Buddhas and all the disciples of the Buddha. **To the end of future kalpas without ever becoming weary.** Because of my resolve to make vast and great offerings, even after the kalpas of the future have come to an end, I will not become weary. I will never become weary or tired of doing this.

SUTRA:

> I vow to uphold the subtle and wonderful Dharma of
>   all Buddhas
> And illuminate and make known all the practices of Bodhi,
> And attain the ultimately pure path of Samantabhadra,
> Always practicing to the end of future kalpas.

Within all states of existence,
I cultivate blessings and wisdom, constantly and without end.
By concentration, wisdom, skill-in-means, and liberation,
I will gain an endless treasury of merit and virtue.

COMMENTARY:

I vow to uphold the subtle and wonderful Dharma of all Buddhas,
and illuminate and make known all the practices of Bodhi. I further
vow to receive and uphold the subtle and wonderful, extremely profound
Dharma of all the Buddhas of the ten directions and the three periods of
time. So it is said,

> *The unsurpassed, profound, subtle and wonderful Dharma*
> *Is difficult to meet in billions of kalpas.*
> *I now see and hear it, and receive and uphold it.*
> *I vow to understand the Tathagata's true and actual meaning.*

Do not think that it is easy to understand the Buddha-dharma. Not only
is it not easy to understand, it is extremely difficult to even encounter
the Buddha-dharma. Therefore it is said,

> *A human body is difficult to obtain,*
> *The Buddha-dharma is difficult to hear,*
> *And it's hard to meet a Good Teacher.*

It is difficult to be able to hear the Buddha-dharma, but now we have
heard it. A human body is difficult to obtain, but now we have already
attained a human body. It is difficult to meet a Good Teacher. We should
look for a Good Teacher.

I vow to uphold the subtle and wonderful Dharma of all Buddhas.
I wish to cultivate according to the subtle and wonderful Dharma doors
of all Buddhas. **And illuminate and make known all the practices of**

Bodhi. I wish to promote and extol Buddhas' teaching and cause the Way of Bodhi to emit a light that appears throughout the universe. This is called illuminating and making known all the practices of Bodhi, which includes all the practices of the path to enlightenment.

And attain the ultimately pure path of Samantabhadra. I will obtain ultimate purity, attain the state of Nirvana, and perfect Samantabhadra's great Way of Bodhi. **Always practicing to the end of future kalpas.** At all times I wish to cultivate all the practices of Samantabhadra to the end of future kalpas.

Within all states of existence. Within all states of existence in the Three Realms, **I cultivate blessings and wisdom, constantly and without end.** The blessings and virtue, as well as wisdom, that I cultivate at all times are inexhaustible.

> *If you wish to cultivate blessings, you should do good deeds.*
> *If you wish to cultivate wisdom, you should extensively study the*
> *Buddha-dharma.*

If you do many good acts of merit and virtue, you will have blessings. If you propagate the Buddha-dharma widely, turn the wheel of the great Dharma, and teach and transform living beings, your wisdom will be revealed. Then your blessings and wisdom will be inexhaustible.

By concentration, wisdom, skill-in-means, and liberation. One's powers of concentration and wisdom will be perfected so that concentration and wisdom are perfectly bright. Further one will be able to use clever expedient skill-in-means and also the Dharma doors of liberation. **I will gain an endless treasury of merit and virtue.** I will obtain an inexhaustible and endless treasury of merit and virtue. A treasury of merit and virtue means that one's merit and virtue is inexhaustible. It's as great as space and as immeasurable as the Dharma

Realm. This treasury of merit and virtue is infinite, so that to the ends of future time it will not be exhausted.

SUTRA:

> In one particle are kshetra-lands as numerous as particles.
> In each kshetra-land are inconceivable numbers of Buddhas.
> Every Buddha dwells in the midst of their assemblies,
> I see them always performing the practices of Bodhi.
>
> Everywhere throughout the ocean of kshetra-lands in the
>   ten directions,
> On the tip of every hair in the ocean of the three periods
>   of time,
> Throughout the ocean of Buddhas and ocean of lands,
> I cultivate in all of them passing through an ocean of kalpas.
>
> The speech of all Tathagatas is pure;
> Each word contains an ocean of all sounds,
> That conforms to what living beings like to hear.
> Each sound flows forth from the Buddha's ocean of eloquence.

COMMENTARY:

In one particle are kshetra-lands as numerous as particles. In the Buddha-dharma, the small manifests within the great, and the great also appears in the small. One minute particle is the smallest, but in one minute particle all the measureless and boundless Buddha-lands can appear. Furthermore, each minute particle in a world system is a Buddha-land. And within each of these Buddha kshetra-lands are Buddha-lands as numerous as measureless and boundless numbers of minute particles. **In each kshetra-land are inconceivable numbers of Buddhas.** And within each of these Buddha-lands are inconceivable numbers of Buddhas.

They are so numerous there is no way you can know how many Buddhas there are.

Every Buddha dwells in the midst of their assemblies. Each one of those Buddhas has a Dharma assembly where all Buddhas, Bodhisattvas, Shravakas, and Arhats venerate, surround, and praise them. **I see them always performing the practices of Bodhi.** I see the oceanic assembly of Buddhas and Bodhisattvas cultivating the practices of the Path and the practices of Bodhi, that is, the practices of Bodhi cultivated by Samantabhadra Bodhisattva.

Everywhere throughout the ocean of kshetra-lands in the ten directions. "Throughout the ten directions everywhere," means that one goes to the ocean of Buddha kshetra-lands of the ten directions. Why is it called an "ocean" of lands? This is because "ocean" means multitudinous. That is to say it is measureless and boundless. There is no way you can know the number of Buddha kshetra-lands. So they are called "the ocean of kshetra-lands," that is, the ocean of all Buddha kshetra-lands.

On the tip of every hair in the ocean of the three periods of time... On the tip of each hair appears the ocean of all Buddha kshetra-lands of the ten directions and three periods of time. The ocean of the three periods of time means that on the tip of each hair there appears all the Buddhas of the ten directions and the three periods of time. **Throughout the ocean of Buddhas and ocean of lands...** The number of all these Buddhas is so numerous they are like a vast ocean. "And ocean of lands" means all of their lands are so numerous that they are infinite. **I cultivate in all of them passing through an ocean of kalpas.** The amount of time I pass through while cultivating is also measureless and boundless. It is as deep and unfathomable, limitless, and boundless as the ocean. I have cultivated for that long a time.

The speech of all Tathagatas is pure. I hear all the Buddhas, the Tathagatas speaking the Dharma with a pure sound. **Each word contains an ocean of all sounds.** Every sentence of Dharma spoken by all Buddhas is replete with an ocean of all sounds, which is boundless, and measureless. This is like what is described about the Buddha in the *Earth Store Sutra*: He has "the Thunder Sound and the Great Thunder Sound, the Lion's Roar Sound and the Great Lion's Roar Sound." These belong to the ocean of all sounds. **That conforms to what living beings like to hear.** The ocean of sounds of all Buddhas complies with the wishes and delights of all living beings. **Each sound flows forth from the Buddha's ocean of eloquence.** Each sound flows forth with measureless samadhi and eloquence. So it is called "oceanic eloquence." There is a short verse about this:

The Buddhas proclaim the Dharma with one sound,
And each living being obtains understanding according to its kind.

When the Buddha speaks the Dharma, he does so in one language, but all the various different kinds of living beings understand it without requiring a translation. All of the many different classes of living beings hear and understand, each according to its kind. The Buddhas speaking of the Dharma is inconceivable, and so it is called an "ocean of all sounds."

SUTRA:

> All Tathagatas of the three periods of time
> With their inexhaustible ocean of languages
> Constantly turn the wonderful Dharma wheel of principles
>   and their tendencies.
> With the power of deep wisdom, I can enter them everywhere.
>
> I can deeply enter the future
> And completely pass through all kalpas in a single thought.

**Each and every kalpa of the three periods of time
In a single thought I enter them all.**

COMMENTARY:

All Tathagatas of the three periods of time. The three periods of time are the past, present, and future. In terms of empirical experience there are three periods of time, but from the point of view of the underlying principle of things, there is only one period of time. There is no past, no present, and no future.

Why? If you say something is in the past, it has already gone by. You may say something is in the present, but that present is already in the past. You may say something is in the future, but it has not yet come, so why talk about it? So the *Vajra Prajna Paramita Sutra says,*

*Past thought cannot be obtained,
Present thought cannot be obtained,
And future thought cannot be obtained.*

If you understand that these three thoughts ultimately cannot be obtained, then the Buddhas of the three periods of time are just the one underlying principle.

The Tathagatas of the three periods of time is speaking in all-inclusive terms. If you just talk about the past, then the present and future are not included. If you only mention the future, then the past and present are not included. If you speak of the three periods of time, however, then the past, present, and future are all included. This is a general way of speaking to represent the entirety of all the Tathagatas who are measureless and boundless. It can also be explained as meaning whichever Tathagata that you are able to personally encounter. **With their inexhaustible ocean of languages...** The words and languages of the Buddhas of the ten directions and the three periods of time have no end. They are so measureless and boundless that they are like a great ocean.

Constantly turn the wonderful Dharma wheel of principles and their tendencies... Buddhas constantly turn the Dharma Wheel of principle and its tendencies. "Principle" is in contrast to "phenomena." Principles are the explanation of theories. Tendencies are the manifestation of the principles in specific situations. For example, we explain the Dharma and lecture the Sutras by explaining the principles and tendencies. The principles and tendencies may be shallow or profound, broad or narrow. "Broad" means far-reaching and great; "narrow" means not very many. "The Wheel of the wonderful Dharma" is referring to this kind of subtle, wondrous, and inconceivable Dharma-door.

With the power of deep wisdom, I can enter them everywhere. I have profound Prajna wisdom, which comes from practicing deep Prajna. Therefore, with the power of profound wisdom, I can enter the ocean of all sounds of all Tathagatas everywhere.

I can deeply enter the future. Not only am I able to deeply enter into the ocean of all sounds, but I can also deeply enter the ocean of all sounds of the future. **And completely pass through all kalpas in a single thought**. What does it mean to exhaust all kalpas in a single thought? One is able to contain ten thousand kalpas in a single thought, and expand one thought so it becomes ten thousand kalpas.

It can also be said that all kalpas are just one thought, and one thought is all kalpas. This principle is not easily understood, so I will now relate a case history to illustrate this point.

In Hangzhou, China, there is a mountain peak called Inverted Lotus Flower located in Western Heavenly Eye, a division of the Five Heavenly Eyes mountain range. These "Five Heavenly Eyes" are called Eastern

Heavenly Eye, Western Heavenly Eye, Northern Heavenly Eye, Southern Heavenly Eye, and Middle Heavenly Eye. They are called Heavenly Eyes because on the mountain peaks are pairs of springs, which are like two eyes. Many people cultivate the path there.

Chan Master Gao Feng Miao went to the Western Heavenly Eye Mountain to cultivate the path. Why? Every time he sat down to meditate, he would fall asleep. During my lecture on the Heart Sutra when we covered the Four Noble Truths of Suffering, Origination, Cessation, and the Path we mentioned the affliction of torpor, which is one of the 26 afflictions. Why is torpor an affliction? If you have torpor when you cultivate the path, you cannot enter samadhi. If you cannot enter samadhi, your mind becomes scattered.

Chan Master Gao Feng Miao wanted to find a method to cure himself of torpor. What method did he come up with? He knew that he could go to meditate at Inverted Lotus Flower Peak on Western Heavenly Eye Mountain. If he became slothful and fell asleep, he would fall off a cliff thousands of feet high and splatter on the ground below. He decided to put his life on the line and go to Inverted Lotus Flower Peak to cultivate the path. He sat on the edge of a cliff, a precipice, next to a valley that was thousands of feet deep. If he fell asleep there, he'd fall to his death. So he went there to meditate.

He meditated for one day and did not sleep. Then for a second day he did not sleep. Three days went by, and still no sleep. But on the fourth day he couldn't take it and finally dozed off. As soon as he fell asleep, he fell off the cliff. As he was falling, he was startled awake. After he fell about half-way down, he stopped falling. For example if the valley was 10,000 feet deep, then 5,000 feet would be half-way. Then someone caught him and brought him back up.

After he was brought back up, he asked, "Who has saved me?"

His rescuer answered, "It is the Dharma Protector Wei Tuo.

When he heard that the Dharma Protector Wei Tuo Bodhisattva had saved him, he was very happy, and he began having arrogant thoughts. He asked, "Elder Wei, how many people in the world can cultivate like me? How many?"

The Bodhisattva Wei Tuo replied, "Ugh! People who cultivate like you are as numerous as the hairs on an ox. You are really shameless. I will not protect your Dharma for eighty thousand great kalpas." Bodhisattva Wei Tuo vowed not to protect his Dharma for eighty thousand great kalpas and then left.

When Gao Feng Miao heard that Wei Tuo Bodhisattva would not protect his Dharma for 80,000 great kalpas he thought, "This is terrible!" With shame and remorse, he cried bitter tears. Then he thought, "I am really not a cultivator of the path. When Bodhisattva Wei Tuo came to protect my Dharma, how could I have had such arrogant thoughts?"

With shame and remorse he cried for a long time. Then suddenly he thought, "Hey! Before, when I cultivated the path, I didn't know that Bodhisattva Wei Tuo was protecting my Dharma, but I cultivated nonetheless. I didn't think that I could only cultivate the path by depending on Wei Tuo Bodhisattva. Now that he has stopped protecting my Dharma, it doesn't mean I should quit. I should still cultivate the path as before!"

So he resolved to go back to the same place to meditate. This time he was even more vigorous. He said, "Even if I die, I will cultivate the path. I will continue to investigate Dhyana and meditate. If I have to give up my life, I still want to accomplish my karma of the path.

So he continued to meditate. He was able to sit for several days, and then fell asleep. When he dozed off he fell down the precipice again. When he had fallen about halfway, again someone caught him and brought back up. After he was rescued, he asked, "Who is protecting my Dharma?"

His protector answered, "Wei Tuo."

Chan Master Gao Feng Miao got angry, "Elder Wei, so you lie, huh? You said you would not protect my Dharma for eighty thousand great kalpas, but you have saved me again. Haven't you told a lie?"

Bodhisattva Wei Tuo said, "No, I haven't lied. The conditions that I had set for you were actually fulfilled. Because of your arrogance, I said I would not protect your Dharma. However, afterwards you had a mind of shame and remorse, which surpassed the offenses of eighty thousand great kalpas. Because of this, I came to protect your Dharma again."

This case history explains that all kalpas are but one thought. The text said, "I exhaust all kalpas in a single thought." With one thought of repentance and reform, Chan Master Gao Feng Miao was able to go beyond eighty thousand great kalpas. The principle in this story is the same as the one in the text.

Each and every kalpa of the three periods of time refers to all kalpas of the past, all kalpas of the present, and all kalpas of the future. **In a single thought I enter them all.** In one thought I can enter a time period as long as all the kalpas of the ten directions and the three periods of time.

SUTRA:

> **In one thought I see in the three periods of time,**
> **All the Lions Among Men,**

And also constantly enter the states of the Buddhas
And their liberation like an illusion, and their awe-inspiring
    powers.

On the tip of an extremely fine hair,
Appear the adorned kshetra-lands of the three periods of time.
On a hair tip are the kshetra-lands of the ten directions as
    numerous as particles.
I deeply enter, beautify, and purify them all.

All of the illuminating Lamps of the World of the future
Who accomplish the path, turn the Wheel of Dharma, and
    awaken living beings;
I go to visit and draw near to them all
As they complete the Buddha's work and manifest Nirvana.

I quickly complete the spiritual powers,
The power of thoroughly entering the Mahayana through the
    Universal Door,
The power of cultivating all merit and virtue through wisdom
    and practice.
The power of the awe-inspiring spirit to shield all with
    great kindness.

COMMENTARY:

In one thought I see in the three periods of time. In a period of time as short as a single thought, I see all the Buddhas of the ten directions and the three periods of time. **All the Lions Among Men** refers to all Buddhas. **And also constantly enter into the states of the Buddhas...** I always enter into the states of the Buddhas. What are the states of the Buddhas? They are inconceivable states. An inconceivable state means one in which one thought is myriad kalpas, and myriad kalpas are but one thought. Most people without wisdom or the roots of goodness cannot believe this. Because they lack wisdom, they cannot fathom these states.

And their liberation like an illusion, and their awe-inspiring powers.
Entering the Buddhas' state is just like entering samadhi which is like an
illusion. Samadhi which is like an illusion is also the samadhi of liberation.
One is liberated from everything, and everything is like an illusion or
a transformation. One has spiritual powers in which one can playfully
roam everywhere to purify Buddha lands and one teaches and transforms
living beings. This is the state of the Buddhas and Bodhisattvas, which
in general is an inconceivable state. This is the samadhi which is like an
illusion. If you say it is true, it is still like an illusion, and if you say it is
false, yet it contains something real. It is also a real state. The illusion-
like samadhi and liberation is accompanied by the awesome power and
great awesome virtue of spiritual powers.

On the tip of an extremely fine hair. On the tip of a hair within a minute
particle, **appear the adorned kshetra-lands of the three periods of
time**. Thus there is a saying,

> The kshetra-lands of the Jeweled King appear on the tip of a hair.
> Sitting on a minute particle, he turns the Wheel of Dharma.

This is the same kind of state expressed by these lines of the Sutra. That
is, there "appear the adorned kshetra-lands of the three periods of time."
These are the adorned kshetra-lands of the Buddhas of the three periods
of time.

**On a hair tip are the kshetra-lands of the ten directions as numerous
as particles.** All the lands of the ten directions as numerous as smallest
atomic particles in a kshetra-land can appear on the tip of one hair. **I
deeply enter, beautify, and purify them all.** And in these kshetra-lands
of the Jeweled King on each hair-tip, I turn the great wheel of Dharma.
By means of the power of the ten great king of vows of Samantabhadra

Bodhisattva, I deeply enter this state, adorn all lands, purify the Buddha lands, and teach and transform living beings.

All of the illuminating Lamps of the World of the future refers to all the Buddhas of the future. **Who accomplish the path, turn the Wheel of Dharma, and awaken living beings;** all the Buddhas attain the path, turn the Wheel of Dharma, and teach and transform all living beings. To "awaken living beings" is to teach and transform all sentient beings. **I go to visit and draw near to them all.** When each Buddha is about to enter Nirvana, I will go to his Bodhimanda and draw near to him. **As they complete the Buddha's work and manifest Nirvana.** After they have completed all of their work as Buddhas, they manifest Great Nirvana.

I quickly complete the spiritual powers[40]. They will cause me to quickly complete and perfect all of my vows and spiritual powers. **The power of thoroughly entering the Mahayana through the Universal Door.** I use the power of the practices and vows that manifest through the Universal Door to totally enter the ocean of all the teachings of the Great Vehicle. **The power of cultivating all merit and virtue through wisdom and practice.** This is the power of my wisdom, the practice of deep Prajna, and the power of my complete cultivation of all merit and virtue. **The power of the awe-inspiring spirit to shield all with great kindness.** My great awesome virtue and the power of great, kind, and compassionate vows shield all living beings everywhere.

---

40. In the Sanskrit text, "spiritual powers" is the word "ṛddhi," which refers to a special category of supernatural powers like walking on water, going through solid walls, flying, etc.

SUTRA:

> The power of supreme blessings to purify and adorn
>   everywhere,
> The power of wisdom that is unattached and without reliance,
> The awe-inspiring power of samadhi, wisdom, and
>   skill-in-means,
> The power to universally accumulate Bodhi,
>
> The power of purifying all good karma,
> The power of eradicating all afflictions,
> The power of subduing all demons,
> The power to perfect all of Samantabhadra's practices.
>
> I am able to adorn and purify everywhere the ocean of
>   kshetra-lands,
> And liberate the ocean of all living beings.
> I'm well able to discern all Dharmas, like an ocean,
> And can deeply enter into the ocean of wisdom.

COMMENTARY:

The power of supreme blessings to purify and adorn everywhere.
"Everywhere" means to pervade everywhere. Purify means to make pure.
It's the power of the supreme blessings that pervades everywhere and
purifies all that is cultivated. "Supreme blessings" distinctly surpasses
all others. Ordinary people do not possess these kinds of blessings. What
kind of blessings are these? These sorts of blessings transcend the three
realms of existence. They are the blessings and virtue of the Bodhisattvas
and those that are cultivated by the Buddhas.

Why do I say that the Buddhas and Bodhisattvas can possess this kind
of power of supreme blessings? With the exception of the Buddhas, only
the Bodhisattvas can possess these kinds of adornments and supreme

blessings that reach everywhere and purify everything. The Buddha's body is called the body adorned with both blessings and wisdom, and so is the Bodhisattva's body. The bodies of both are adorned or beautified with blessings and wisdom, which can only come about from cultivation for measureless numbers of kalpas. They cultivated all kinds of roots of goodness and did various kinds of good deeds throughout measureless numbers of kalpas, and so they can be adorned with superior blessings. Therefore, these kinds of adornments are the adornments of blessings and virtue.

The power of wisdom that is unattached and without reliance. Since blessings and virtue are supreme, wisdom should also be supreme. What kind of wisdom is supreme? It is the wisdom without any attachment. To have no attachments is to also be without any reliance. Dependence or reliance on something is attachment, and attachment is dependence. Being without attachment is the power of wisdom that is unattached and without reliance.

The intellect of ordinary people has attachments. Whatever state they perceive, they become attached to that state or experience. They cannot attain liberation. The wisdom of liberation is the wisdom of true understanding that is without any attachments. If you are attached, then you cannot truly understand, and you do not have real wisdom. Your inferior wisdom is called worldly eloquence and intelligence. This is a kind of intelligence that uses mundane wisdom to debate or argue with others. So there is attachment to things in worldly eloquence and intelligence.

The awe-inspiring power of samadhi, wisdom, and skill-in-means. If you do not have the power of samadhi, you cannot produce the power of wisdom; if you do not have the power of wisdom, your power of samadhi can't come forth. If you have the power of great wisdom, then you have the power of samadhi. If you have no samadhi, you cannot be one who has great wisdom. Where does the power of samadhi come from? It comes from the power of the moral precepts. If you do not hold precepts, then you cannot have the power of samadhi, and without the power of samadhi, you do not have the power of wisdom. To be without the power of wisdom is to be without the power of the moral precepts.

If you have wisdom, then you can hold the moral precepts. But those without wisdom cannot hold the precepts. Why is this? It is because of extreme ignorance. If one's ignorance is too severe, then one has no wisdom. If one is without wisdom and breaks the moral precepts, one feels that one has not broken them. One still believes that one has upheld the moral precepts. Why? This is because one is really foolish. One believes that one's violation of the moral precepts was not a violation. This is called transgressing without realizing one has transgressed. One does not recognize that one has broken the precepts.

What is the power of "skill-in-means?" The Dharma of skill-in-means is an unfixed Dharma. The Dharma of skill-in-means is to "contemplate and teach according to the conditions and speak the Dharma for the sake of individuals." This means to contemplate the potentials and conditions and then speak the Dharma appropriate to that particular person. So one contemplates the conditions of the listener and speaks the Buddha-dharma. Therefore, it is said, "One bestows the particular teaching to each individual; one prescribes the medicine that is suitable to cure his illness." You speak the Buddha-dharma specifically for that person. You prescribe the medicine for that illness. This is the meaning of the Dharma of skill-in-means.

If you have skill-in-means, you must also have "awe-inspiring spiritual powers." "Awe-inspiring" refers to awe-inspiring virtue. What is awe-inspiring virtue? It is that which causes awe in others. Spiritual powers means that for example, someone may lie to you and think he is very clever because he deceived you. However, with your spiritual powers he cannot cheat you. This is what is meant by awe-inspiring spiritual power.

The power to universally accumulate Bodhi. Everything whatsoever comes about because of progression. The great comes from the small; one goes from near to far; and one enters the deep from the shallow. Bodhi is also cultivated to accomplishment bit by bit; one does not achieve it in one day. Shakyamuni Buddha "cultivated blessings and wisdom for three great asamkhyeya kalpas." This is to accumulate Bodhi. "For one hundred kalpas he cultivated to attain the hallmarks and subsidiary features." This is also to accumulate Bodhi.

What does it mean to accumulate Bodhi? For example, all of you began to learn the Buddha-dharma at the beginning of last year. This is what is meant by learning Bodhi. To learn the Buddha-dharma is the same as learning Bodhi. And learning Bodhi is to accumulate Bodhi. To accumulate means to amass, to collect, or gather together. From the time you began your learning of Bodhi until the present, your Bodhi has increased day by day. And your understanding of the Buddha-dharma has also increased each day. When you first began learning the Buddha-dharma, you did not understand anything that I said. After a time you could understand a little. This is accumulating Bodhi. Then after having listened for a long time, you could understand everything that I said. You say, "Oh, originally that's the way it is!"

Why were you able to understand everything? Because you have accumulated Bodhi. You understand the Buddha-dharma. This is called accumulating Bodhi. In order to accumulate Bodhi, you must have strength and you need to have perseverance. It will not work if you accumulate Bodhi today but not tomorrow. When you do not continue for a day, then what you have accumulated will be diminished by a day.

If you learn Bodhi today, but not tomorrow, you will lose what you have learned, and you won't understand.

For example, our young novice here told everyone he would be gone for two weeks, but he did not return for six weeks. He was away three times as long as he said he would be. During those six weeks he lost a lot of Bodhi, but he does not feel this is the case. He doesn't know how he lost it. By not attaining it, one is actually losing it. Instead of studying the Buddha-dharma, he ran off and bounced around from one place to another. During this time he was not accumulating Bodhi, but caused it to be dispersed.

From this explanation, it is easy for all of you to understand the principle of accumulating Bodhi. If you learn the Buddha-dharma, you accumulate Bodhi. If you do not learn the Buddha-dharma, you lose Bodhi. Bodhi is enlightenment. So if you lose Bodhi, you are not enlightened. You are not enlightened to the fact that you are mistaken. And you are not enlightened to or aware that you have wasted all of your time. You had such a good opportunity to learn the Buddha-dharma, but you casually went running around from place to place. Wouldn't you say that this is foolish? Foolish people cannot accumulate Bodhi.

In order to accumulate the power of Bodhi, you must have the power of samadhi, wisdom, and spiritual powers that were previously mentioned. The power of Bodhi refers to the power of enlightenment. And enlightenment refers to understanding things you did not previously understand. For example, now you can say, "Before I didn't understand the Buddha-dharma, but now as soon as I hear it, I understand it, even to the point where I understand it without having heard it."

Fundamentally, cultivating the power of the moral precepts is very important. One must uphold the moral precepts. For example, to casually drink a little wine is not to maintain the moral precepts. To casually engage in improper behavior is to not uphold the moral precepts. To casually indulge in confused activities is to not accumulate Bodhi. If you transgress the precepts, not only do you not acquire Bodhi, you are actually losing Bodhi.

The power of purifying all good karma. When we do good things, why do we not become Buddhas? It is because our good karma is mixed with bad karma. We may do good deeds, but within the good we do there is some evil. Or we may do bad deeds, but within them there is some good.

What does it mean to do a good deed, which contains some bad? You may happen upon a poor person who has nothing to eat and no clothes to wear, and you decide to help him. After you have helped him, you try to take advantage of him. "I was good to him before. Now he should do some volunteer work for me, and I won't need to give him too much money." If you have helped someone, and then ask him to do something for you, of course he will feel embarrassed to ask you to pay him for his work. For example, he works for one day and should receive twenty dollars, and you give him ten dollars. Without it being readily apparent, it's ten dollars less expensive for you. This is an example of doing something good and yet harboring a selfish motive. Giving him ten dollars in this situation has no merit and virtue.

In general, you do good with an ulterior motive. That is, you want something. What do you want? You want to get extremely good rewards in the future for doing some good deed now. So the good karma you created is not pure, because the good karma is mixed with bad karma. It is impure. Whatever good things we do, for example when we help other people, should be done without any hope for benefit in return. If you want people to benefit you, then you're being selfish. Basically you are not helping others but are only helping yourself. If you were really helping others and not yourself, why would you hope that others would help you? Why do you want them to have a good impression of you? Explain that. Now you help others, and yet you hope they will be grateful to you, thank you, and help you in the future. Is this not greed? Having a greedy mind like this is not truly helping people.

The way to truly benefit others and to truly do good deeds is described in this saying,

> *When doing good for others, don't seek for a reward.*
> *Having given things to others, do so without regrets.*

Whenever you do something good for anyone, you should not seek for a reward. Others may return your favor in the future, but that is up to them. You should not hope for or cling to these conditions. Wishing for this is just clinging to conditions.

For example, some people who do good deeds like to make offerings to the Three Jewels. However, whenever they offer something, they make an announcement or put an advertisement in the newspaper. There is a person who visits our temple occasionally with some vegetables, fruit, or something else, which he has bought. Whenever he comes, it is certain that he will want everyone to see what he has brought. It's as if he's saying, "Look at me! I'm a Dharma protector. I'm a great Dharma protector! I've come to make offerings to the Three Jewels!" Take a look at this. This is not true goodness. There is another saying,

> *Good that you want others to see is not true good.*
> *Evil that you try to conceal from others is great evil.*

"When doing good for others, don't seek for a reward." Do not seek a recompense from anyone you benefit. " Don't regret good deeds you have done for others." After you have given someone something, do not think,

"That's really too bad. I shouldn't have given it to him." Once you have given something to others, that's it. The material things of this world should be used by the people in this world.

The verse I quoted says, "Good that you want others to see is not true good." If you do a good deed and want others to know about it, then it is not true good. Why? Because you are greedy for fame. You hope people will say, "That person is truly someone who does good deeds. I've seen him do good deeds." You want everyone to know about this. You wish to put an advertisement in the newspaper. This is not true goodness. It is false. However, even though it is false giving, it is a little better than doing nothing at all. You wish to do something that is false, but gradually it can become true. If you don't even do what is false, then that is worse.

"Evil that you try to conceal from others is great evil." To do bad deeds and fear that people will know about them is the greatest evil. To do good deeds that you would like others to see is not pure good karma.

You might ask, "If I should do good things without the desire to have people know about them, then should I do good in secret so that others will not know?" No. This is not necessary. You do not need to let others know, and you do not need to conceal your deeds from others. If you are determined to do good deeds in secret, you are still seeking for fame. You are seeking for recognition as a person whose good deeds are not known by others. It is seeking for fame just the same.

Then how should you be? The most important aspect of cultivating the path is right here. You should not purposely want to be seen by other people. You also do not want to purposely avoid being seen. Act as if not acting. When you do things, do them as if you were not doing anything. If you do things and tell people about your good activities, that is just wanting to have recognition or fame. However, to conceal your good deeds is another manifestation of desiring fame. You wish to be recognized as someone who does things without wanting people to know about them. This is the difficult aspect of cultivating the path. If you do good things and want people to know about them, then you have an attachment. If you don't want people to know about them, you also have an attachment. What should you do? Act as if nothing is going on. Do not be attached. Do not be particularly concerned whether other people know about your deeds or don't know about them. You should think, "I'm doing this deed as if I haven't done anything." If you haven't done anything, then how could you wish for fame or not wish for fame? You couldn't. There wouldn't be any such thought at all. Just that is pure, good karma. Pure good karma is pure Dharma. **The power of purifying all good karma** is especially great.

The power of eradicating all afflictions. "To eradicate," means to destroy or extinguish. What is destroyed? Your afflictions are destroyed. This is most difficult. You are capable of accomplishing just about anything. However, to destroy your afflictions is something you find most difficult to do. Afflictions are without end. Since they are endless, they are the hardest to destroy. Yet you still want to destroy them.

One of the Four Vast Vows is, "I vow to cut off the infinite afflictions." To vow to cut them off means to eradicate them. If you cut them off, where do they go? From where do you cut them off? How do you cut them off? How do you destroy them? If they are not produced, then they are destroyed. Not to give rise to afflictions in the first place is to eradicate them. If you give rise to afflictions, your afflictions have not been eradicated. If there is production, then there will be destruction. If there is destruction, then there will be production. If, however, you are without production or destruction, then you will be without afflictions, and just that is to eradicate all afflictions.

There are very many afflictions. Due to the constraints of time, we can say that they are greed, hatred, and delusion. These are the most fundamental afflictions. If your mind is without greed, hatred, and delusion, then you have the power to eradicate all afflictions.

We say that we vow to cut off afflictions. You can make another vow. What vow can you make? I *vow not* to cut off my afflictions. If you do not cut them off, then what is the purpose of keeping them? Keeping them can be very useful. If you cut off your afflictions, you cut off Bodhi as well. So I do not teach you to cut off your afflictions. "Afflictions are just Bodhi." What should you do with them if you do not cut them off? Change them. How do you change your afflictions?

This is the change that means to transform, as in the phrase "infinite changes and transformations." Everyone pay attention to "infinite changes and transformations." *The Doctrine of the Mean* says,

> *From movement there is change.*
> *And from change there comes transformation.*
> *Only a person with utmost sincerity in the world can bring about*
>   *a transformation.*

Therefore, you want to transform your afflictions. The important point is right here. The text says to cut them off. Now, I'm changing it to "change them." You want to change your afflictions, not cut them off. If you cut them off, then you cut off Bodhi. Why? Because afflictions are just Bodhi.

How can you transform your afflictions? Of course there is a method to do this. Nowadays science has advanced and chemistry[41] is well developed. Afflictions are Bodhi. Before we said they should be cut off, but now I'm

---

41. Chemistry in Chinese consists of the characters, 化學, which literally means "the study of transformations."

saying we should transform them. What's the method to transform them? Now I will use a metaphor. Afflictions are ice, and Bodhi is water. If you smash the ice and put it away, that is the same as cutting it off. When you do that with afflictions, then there is no Bodhi either. But if you take the ice and melt it in sunlight, then it will change to become water. Water is analogous to Bodhi. Therefore, the principle that afflictions are Bodhi is just like this. If you transform your afflictions, like changing ice to water, they become the inherently existent Buddha nature. This is Bodhi or the Way of Enlightenment.

This is a very simple principle and I have often explained this to you. However, you have not paid close attention to it, so you are not able to use it. If you strike someone on the head with a chunk of ice the size of a tea cup, it can fracture his skull and he will start bleeding. You could even kill him and quickly send him off to see King Yama. This is what can be done with a piece of ice. But if you melt the ice into water, and personally throw a bowlful of water with as much force as possible—even a thousand or ten thousand pounds of force—at someone's head, it will not harm him. He will feel the force of water on his head, but cannot be killed by it. This analogy shows that if you use the Bodhi mind to teach and transform living beings, they will be very happy to accept it. But if you use afflictions to teach and transform them, even at the risk of their own lives, they will refuse to accept your teaching. They would rather die than accept your teaching. Ice and water are basically the same thing, but when ice changes to become water, this minor transformation makes a big difference.

Therefore, we should transform our afflictions and not cut them off. If we cut them off, then we will be without Bodhi as well. If you throw away the ice, which can kill a person, then you will not have the water either.

Where do afflictions come from? They come from Bodhi. However, they have changed into ice. So we can say that ice is water and water is ice.

Afflictions are just Bodhi. If you are capable of using them, they are Bodhi. But if you are not capable of using them, they are afflictions. When you're capable of using them, it is inexpressibly wonderful. If you are not capable of using them, it is inexpressibly crude and meaningless. For this reason, I tell all of you not to cut off your afflictions, but to keep them.

The power of subduing all demons. "To subdue demons" means to prevent them from disturbing your cultivation of the path and even have them become your Dharma protectors. There are many ways to subdue demons. You can subdue demons with your own spiritual powers, subdue demons with your own strength of the path, or subdue demons with your own virtuous practices. You can subdue demons with your own samadhi-power, subdue demons with your own wisdom-power, or subdue demons with your own power of moral discipline. There are many different ways to subdue demons.

There is not just one kind of demon. There are heavenly demons, earthly demons, demons among people, weird ghostly demons, and *li mei and wang liang* ghostly demons. There are also the demons of states, sickness demons, and demons of your own mind. External demons which include heavenly demons, earthly demons, demons among people, ghostly demons, and *li mei* and *wang liang* ghostly demons are not hard to subdue. Only the demons of your own mind are difficult to subdue. The demons of your own mind are always present inside your mind. They cause you to engage in immoral behavior. The most difficult to subdue are the demons of your own mind. If your power of upholding the moral precepts is solid and strong, and you have the true power of the precepts, then even if all the demon kings came to challenge you, none of their demon king spells could shake or disturb your power of the moral precepts. If you have samadhi power, you will also be able to subdue all demons.

So it is said,

> If a great mountain collapses in front of you, you are not afraid.

Regardless of how big the mountain is, if it crumbles right before you, you're not frightened at all.

> If a beautiful woman appears before you, you are not moved.

The most difficult moral transgression for a person to resist is the demon of lust. Whether you are a man or a woman, it is difficult to remain steadfast when the demon of lust comes. The demon of lust may use the body of an ordinary person to challenge you, or it may manifest a transformation body to challenge you, or it may challenge you in your dreams. You may not move when it appears in a transformation body or as a person. However, in order to steal your treasures, it comes to bother you in your dreams. In your dream it appears as the most beautiful woman to seduce you. If you do not have enough samadhi power, you will be troubled by this demon of lust.

If you are a man, the demon of lust will appear as a woman. If you are a woman, it will appear as a man. When it manifests as a man, it will either appear as a very handsome man or as the person the woman most likes in ordinary life. At this point, if a woman's samadhi power is insufficient, she will be turned by this demonic state. If she does have enough samadhi power, she will not be moved by these demonic states.

To sum it up, there are many kinds of demons. And there are many ways to subdue these demons as well. If you have the power of wisdom, you can subdue demons. If you have the jeweled wisdom sword, then when any demon king comes, you can kill him. What kinds of people are moved by these demons? They are all people who are foolish and without any wisdom.

After all this discussion, ultimately what does "demon" mean? It refers to the Sanskrit term *Mara*. *Mara* translates into English as "killer." Demons specialize in destroying people. What kind of people do they destroy? Those who cultivate the path. If you wish to cultivate the path, demons will want to come and destroy your karma in the path. Now we are talking about "the power to subdue all demons." What else can you use to subdue demons? You can use the power of mantras to subdue demons. If you can successfully hold mantras, then you can subdue all demons. If you can skillfully recite Sutras, then you can subdue all demons. If you bow to Sutras to the point that you invoke a response, you can also subdue all demons. Therefore, there are many ways to subdue demons. Since there are many kinds of demon kings, there are many methods to subdue them. The important question is whether or not one can use them at the appropriate time.

Talking about holding mantras, the Shurangama Mantra is made up of five assemblies or sections. And these five assemblies correspond to five divisions. The middle division is the Buddha division. The eastern division is the Vajra Division. The southern division is the Jeweled Birth Division. The western division is called the Lotus Division. The northern division is called the Accomplishment Division. In the Buddha Division, in the center, Vairochana Buddha is the host. This is just Shakyamuni Buddha. In the Vajra Division in the East, Akshobhya Buddha is the host. Ratnasambhava Buddha is the host Buddha for the southern division. Amitabha Buddha is the host for the western Lotus Flower Division. Amoghasiddhi is the host for the Accomplishment Division in the north, which is also called the Karma Division.

The five directions with their five divisions have five kinds of dharmas.

The first is the *dharma for extinguishing catastrophes*, which can dispel and extinguish all kinds of disasters and difficulties.

The second is called the *dharma for increasing and benefiting*. When you recite the mantra, it will help to strengthen your resolve for the path and to increase your wisdom, so that everything you encounter will be beneficial. This is called the dharma for increasing and benefiting.

The third is the *dharma for subduing*. This refers to using the great spiritual power of the mantra to subdue you so that you are very well behaved and obedient. You must behave yourself. This is called the dharma for subduing.

The fourth is called the *dharma of hooking and summoning*. What is the dharma of hooking and summoning? If a demon is a thousand miles away, ten thousand miles away, a million miles away, or a billion miles away from you, even to the point that it is in another world or on another celestial body, when you recite the mantra you can hook and summon him like grabbing him with a hook and bringing him to you. It's impossible for this demon to avoid coming to you. This is called the dharma of hooking and summoning.

The fifth is the *dharma of accomplishment*. No matter what you do, when you recite this mantra, you will successfully complete your task. This mantra possesses these five kinds of powers. The Shurangama Mantra is wonderful beyond words and an inconceivable state. This is the meaning of, "the power to subdue all demons."

The power to perfect all of Samantabhadra's practices. The power of the practices of Samantabhadra Bodhisattva is the greatest. And the practices that he cultivates are foremost. In China this Bodhisattva dwells at Mount Emei in Sichuan. It is one of the four famous sacred mountains in China. Most cultivators like to make a pilgrimage there to bow and pay respects to Mount Emei. Mount Emei constantly has a golden light. You have to walk more than 30 miles to reach the top. It is very high and difficult to climb. Nevertheless, many people come from afar, traversing mountains and rivers, to bow to Samantabhadra Bodhisattva.

Why do people wish to bow to him? Because the Bodhisattva made a vow that those who make a pilgrimage to Mount Emei will receive his help and accomplish the Path. Therefore, many cultivators of the Path go there to bow to Samantabhadra Bodhisattva. Mount Emei is one of the four famous sacred mountains in China.

It is not easy to perfect the power of the practices of Samantabhadra Bodhisattva. For example, each of the ten king of vows he made that were discussed above must be cultivated to perfection. They should be cultivated to the point that even if the reaches of space, living beings, the karma of living beings, and the afflictions of living beings all cease to be, one will still continue to practice in accord with these vows. This is what the "power to perfect all of Samantabhadra's practices" means. One is able to perfect them all.

I am able to adorn and purify everywhere the ocean of kshetra-lands. I am able to adorn and purify all the Buddha lands everywhere in the ocean of kshetras. **And liberate the ocean of all living beings.** All of us living beings have our attachments. As long as we have attachments, we cannot obtain liberation. Without liberation, we have not attained true freedom. Why haven't we attained freedom? Because we have attachments.

Once a Bhikshu went to request Dharma instruction from a Good Teacher. He put on his robe and sash, knelt down, put his palms together, and asked the Good Teacher, "What method should I use to attain liberation?"

The Good Teacher said only one sentence in reply and this monk became enlightened. What did he say? He said, "Who has bound you up?"

The Bhikshu thought, "No one has bound me up. I have bound up myself." At that time, he suddenly became enlightened and attained liberation."

It is easy to liberate one living being or two living beings. However, to liberate all living beings is very difficult to achieve. Even though it is difficult, if you try to do it and succeed, then it is not so hard.

I'm well able to discern all Dharmas, like an ocean. "All Dharmas" include the Three Treasuries and Twelve Divisions of the Sutras. The Three Treasuries include the Treasury of Sutras, the Treasury of the Shastras, and the Treasury of the Vinaya. All the Sutras, all Shastras, and the Vinaya, which explains the moral precepts, make up the Three Treasuries.

The Twelve Divisions are:

1. Prose;
2. Reiterative verses;
3. Predictions of Buddhahood;
4. Interjections that stand alone;
5. Spoken without request;
6. Causes and conditions;
7. Analogies;
8. Events in past lives;
9. Events in the present life;
10. Expansive teachings (*Vaipulya*);

11. What had never been before;

12. Explanations.

Prose refers to one sentence after another in the prose sections of the Sutras. Reiterative verses are the verse sections like we are explaining now that restate the meaning of the prose. Interjections that stand alone are verses that have no relationship to the prose that comes before or after them. They are a few lines of verse that appear on their own.

An example of an interjection that stands alone is this verse from the *Vajra Prajna Paramita Sutra:*

All conditioned dharmas
Are like dreams, illusions, bubbles, shadows,
Like dew drops and a lightning flash.
Contemplate them thus.

This is an interjection of a verse that stands alone.

Spoken without request means that one speaks the Dharma on one's own and not as a response to anyone's request. For example, the *Amitabha Sutra* was spoken by the Buddha on his own without it being requested. Causes and conditions explain the different causes and conditions in the Sutras. Analogies, as in the Analogies Chapter of the Dharma Flower Sutra, are used to explain the Dharma. Events in past lives may be about the past lives of the Buddhas, the Bodhisattvas, or the Arhats. Events in the present life refer to the things that took place in the current life. Expansive teachings explain the teachings of vast extent. Then there is what had never been before and finally explanation of the commentaries. These are called the 12 Divisions of the Sutras.

These Twelve Divisions of the Sutras and the Three Treasuries comprise all Dharmas. The Twelve Divisions of the Sutras are further divided into

the Great Vehicle and the Small Vehicle, the Bodhisattva Vehicle, the
Vehicle of Those Enlightened to Conditions, the Vehicle of the Shravakas,
and the Buddha Vehicle. There are various differences like this. If you
are not aware of them, then even though you want to practice, you will
not know which vehicle or practice is the most suitable for you. So the
text says, "I'm well able to distinguish the ocean of all Dharmas." The
Buddha-dharma is just like a great ocean. If you can distinguish the true
reality of all dharmas, then you can cultivate in accord with the Dharma,
and can deeply enter into the ocean of wisdom. You should be able to
deeply enter the ocean of wisdom. If you can distinguish the ocean of all
dharmas, then you can deeply enter all dharmas. When one deeply enters
all dharmas, one attains wisdom that is as measureless and boundless
as the great ocean.

SUTRA:

> I am able to purify everywhere the ocean of all practices,
> And perfect the ocean of all vows.
> I draw near and make offerings to the ocean of all Buddhas,
> And cultivate without weariness for an ocean of kalpas.
>
> All Tathagatas of the three periods of time,
> And the practices and vows of most supreme Bodhi,
> I make offerings to them all as I perfect and cultivate
>   these practices.
> Relying upon Samantabhadra's practices, I awaken to Bodhi.
>
> All Tathagatas have an elder disciple
> Whose name is the Venerated Samantabhadra.
> I now transfer all my roots of goodness,
> And I vow that all my wisdom and practices will be identical
>   to his.

COMMENTARY:

I am able to purify everywhere the ocean of all practices. All the methods of cultivation are like a great ocean. When I cultivate the Path, I should be concentrated, without any admixture, and I should single-mindedly cultivate pure practices. I cannot allow the least bit of defilement in the midst of these pure methods of practice. Therefore the text reads, "I can purify the ocean of all practices everywhere."

And perfect the ocean of all vows... To cultivate, it is necessary to make vows. After making vows, you must fulfill them. When vows are fulfilled, they can be called perfected. I make all kinds of vows and fulfill all kinds of vows. When I cultivate the ten king of vows of Samantabhadra, my vow power must equal that of Samantabhadra Bodhisattva. In this way I perfect all the numerous vows, which are as vast as the ocean. Therefore it says, "And perfect the ocean of all vows."

I draw near and make offerings to the ocean of all Buddhas. All the Buddhas of the ten directions are measureless and boundless in number, just like a great ocean. I wish to draw near to this ocean of all Buddhas and make offerings to them. **And cultivate without weariness for an ocean of kalpas.** I cannot become weary in my cultivation. Passing through measureless numbers of kalpas, I will never tire or become lazy. I must always be vigorous. Although an ocean of kalpas refers to numerous kalpas and is such a long duration of time, I certainly will never become weary.

All Tathagatas of the three periods of time. That is, all the Buddhas of the ten directions and the three periods of time, **and the practices and vows of most supreme Bodhi.** I cultivate the most supreme and wonderful path to enlightenment and its practices and vows. **I make offerings to them all as I perfect and cultivate these practices.**

All the Buddhas, Tathagatas, of the ten directions cultivate the most supreme Bodhi and all practices and vows. I should at the same time, make offerings to them and perfect the cultivation of these practices in the same manner as them. **Relying upon Samantabhadra's practices, I awaken to Bodhi.** When I cultivate Samantabhadra's great kings of practices and vows, I awaken to Bodhi, the path to enlightenment.

All Tathagatas have an elder disciple. All of the Buddhas, Tathagatas, of the ten directions have an eldest son. Who is this eldest son? The text says, **whose name is the Venerated Samantabhadra**. He is called the Venerated Samantabhadra, Samantabhadra Bodhisattva. **I now transfer all my roots of goodness.** I now dedicate all the roots of goodness that I have obtained through cultivation to the ten great king of vows of Samantabhadra Bodhisattva. **And I vow that all my wisdom and practices will be identical to his.** I vow that my wisdom and methods of practice will be identical to those of Samantabhadra Bodhisattva.

SUTRA:

> I vow that my body, mouth, and thought will always be pure
> And that all of my practices and all kshetra-lands will also be
>   the same.
> Wisdom such as this is called Samantabhadra.
> I vow in all ways to be the same as he is.

COMMENTARY:

I vow that my body, mouth, and thought will always be pure. I make a vow that all my body, mouth, and thought karma will be pure. I will not create the evil karma of killing, stealing, or sexual misconduct with my body; my mouth will not create the evil karma of irresponsible speech, false speech, harsh speech, or divisive speech; and my thought will not create the evil karma of greed, anger, and delusion. My three karmas of body, mouth, and thought will always be pure.

And that all of my practices and all kshetra-lands will also be the same... All of the methods of practice that I cultivate and all of the lands will be pure. **Wisdom such as this is called Samantabhadra.** This wisdom is great like Samantabhadra Bodhisattva, as are these pure methods of practice, and the Pure Lands. **I vow in all ways to be the same as he is.** I vow that in all aspects, I will be the same as Samantabhadra Bodhisattva. That is, I vow to learn from Samantabhadra Bodhisattva, to cultivate his practices, to cultivate his Dharma of the ten great king of vows, and to perfect his wisdom and the wonderful application of his inconceivable spiritual powers. In every way, I wish to be the same as Samantabhadra Bodhisattva.

SUTRA:

> I will wholly purify Samantabhadra's conduct,
> And all the great vows of Manjushri.
> I will complete all of these activities without remainder.
> Throughout all kalpas of the future, I'll never tire.
>
> All of the practices I cultivate are without measure,
> And I attain measureless merit and virtue.
> Amid measureless practices I peacefully dwell,
> And thoroughly understand all spiritual powers.

COMMENTARY:

I will wholly purify Samantabhadra's conduct. This is spoken by one who cultivates the practices of Samantabhadra. He says, "When cultivating the practices of Samantabhadra, I want to completely purify them, which means that I perfect his practices and vows. **And all the great vows of Manjushri...** Manjushri is called "Wonderful Virtue," or

"Wonderful Auspiciousness." Not only should one perfect and wholly purify the practices of Samantabhadra, but one should also perfect all the great vows of Manjushri Bodhisattva.

I will complete all of these activities without remainder. I will be the same as both Samantabhadra Bodhisattva and Manjushri Bodhisattva in the way they cultivate their practices and vows, and in their accomplishment of their tasks of merit and virtue. **Throughout all kalpas of the future, I'll never tire.** In my cultivation of the great king of vows of Samantabhadra Bodhisattva, throughout infinite kalpas of the future, I will never grow weary. There will never be a time when I will grow tired or become lazy.

All of the practices I cultivate are without measure. The methods of practice that I cultivate are immeasurable and boundless in number. **And I attain measureless merit and virtue.** Since the methods of practice I cultivate are without measure, the merit and virtue I obtain is also measureless and limitless.

Amid measureless practices I peacefully dwell. I peacefully dwell in and remain unmoving in immeasurable methods of practice and measureless Dharmas. Amid all these practices I constantly cultivate. **And thoroughly understand all spiritual powers.** I have a thorough understanding of and skill in all spiritual powers.

SUTRA:

> Manjushri has courageous wisdom.
> Samantabhadra's practices and wisdom are also the same.
> I now transfer all roots of goodness,
> To constantly cultivate with and learn from them all.

All Buddhas of the three periods of time praise
Such supreme and great vows as these.
I now transfer all roots of goodness,
In order to attain the preeminent practices of Samantabhadra.

I vow that when my life approaches its end,
All obstacles will be completely dispelled,
I will personally see Amitabha Buddha,
And be immediately reborn in his Land of Peace and Bliss.

COMMENTARY:

Manjushri has courageous wisdom. Manjushri Bodhisattva has the greatest wisdom. And amongst all Bodhisattvas, he has the most seniority. In the past he was Shakyamuni Buddha's teacher. Now in this present life Shakyamuni Buddha has become a Buddha, and Manjushri Bodhisattva comes before the Buddha to help him to propagate, teach, and spread the Buddha-dharma. Therefore, his wisdom is most courageous and brave. Courageous wisdom is great wisdom.

Samantabhadra's practices and wisdom are also the same. Samantabhadra Bodhisattva's wisdom as well as the vows and practices he cultivates are especially great and also extremely courageous.

Manjushri Bodhisattva lives on Wu Tai (Five Peaks) Mountain in China. This mountain has five peaks: the central peak, the eastern peak, the western peak, the southern peak, and the northern peak. It is a very cold place, and even in the summer there is snow on its peaks. Manjushri Bodhisattva has established a Bodhimanda there on Wu Tai Mountain.

I now transfer all roots of goodness. Now I dedicate all the roots of goodness I have gained from cultivating the ten great kings of vows. What do I transfer them to? **To constantly cultivate with and learn**

from them all. I transfer roots of goodness because I wish to follow Manjushri Bodhisattva in practice and learning. I wish to also forever follow Samantabhadra Bodhisattva in constantly cultivating and learning the Buddha-dharma.

All Buddhas of the three periods of time praise... These two Bodhisattvas have been praised by all the Buddhas of the past; they are being praised by all the Buddhas of the present; and they will be praised by all Buddhas of the future. All Buddhas of the three periods of time together in unison praise Manjushri Bodhisattva and Samantabhadra Bodhisattva. **Such supreme and great vows as these...** As was spoken of previously, these ten great king of vows are most supreme. **I now transfer all roots of goodness.** Now I transfer all of the roots of goodness that I have **in order to attain the preeminent practices of Samantabhadra**. I do so to complete the ten great king of vows of Samantabhadra Bodhisattva, which are most supreme and preeminent methods of practice.

I vow that when my life approaches its end... I wish that in the future at the time of death, that is, when my life is about to come to an end, **all obstacles will be completely dispelled**. I will have eradicated all my obstructions. All obstructions include the obstructions of retribution, karmic obstructions, and obstructions of afflictions. I vow that these three obstructions will be destroyed, so that when my life is about to come to its end, I will not need to undergo the suffering from the results of karma in the present, nor will I receive the karmic retribution of rebirth. Further, I will be without the obstruction of afflictions and my ignorance will be cut off. "All obstructions will be completely eradicated."

I will personally see Amitabha Buddha. I will personally see the Buddha of the Land of Ultimate Bliss, Amitabha Buddha. Amitabha is a Sanskrit word that means "measureless life" and also "measureless light." Since Amitabha Buddha's lifespan is without measure, he is called the Buddha of Measureless Life. Further, since his light is without measure, he is called the Buddha of Measureless Light. This Buddha is the lord of the Western Land of Ultimate Bliss. He has affinities with the living beings of the Saha World and with living beings of the lands of the ten directions. Whether this land or that land, or this world or that world, he has affinities with all living beings in all of the measureless Buddha-lands.

Why does Amitabha Buddha have affinities with living beings? It is because in the past on the causal stage of practice he made vows:

> When I become a Buddha, my land will be the Land of Ultimate Bliss. None of the other worlds of the ten directions will be as blissful as my land. No world will be as blissful as my world. If living beings of the ten directions wish to be born in my country, all they must do is hold my name. They should recite my Buddha-name, and I will accept them so that they may become Buddhas. If they do not become Buddhas, I will not become a Buddha. I will not attain the Proper Enlightenment.

Amitabha Buddha made forty-eight vows to rescue living beings. Therefore, any living being of the ten directions who recites the name of Amitabha Buddha can be born in the Land of Ultimate Bliss.

This is especially the case for those that practice the ten great king of vows of Samantabhadra Bodhisattva. At the very end it says that the merit will be transferred to going to the Land of Ultimate Bliss. One vows to be reborn in the Land of Ultimate Bliss. The Land of Ultimate Bliss in the West belongs to Amitabha Buddha, and according to the Secret School classification, his is the Lotus Flower Division.

Akshobhya Buddha is in the Vajra Division in the East. The Vajra Division focuses on cultivating the Vajra Unmoving Dharma. The most important aspect of the Vajra Dharma is taming and subduing as well as hooking and summoning. What happens when you hook and summon a demon? The

Powerful Vajra Lords act like police and issue a summons for the demons to appear. And they must appear. This is the hooking and summoning Dharma. In the Dharma of taming and subduing, the Powerful Vajra Lords display the frightening appearance of Vajra, which causes all the goblins, demons, and strange ghosts to be terrified. This is the taming and subduing Dharma in the East.

What Dharma does Amitabha Buddha cultivate? The Dharma of gathering in. Gathering in means to use the power of kindness and compassion to guide living beings to his land. When subduing you, he does not allow you to recklessly engage in misbehavior again. You must abide by the rules, but you are still allowed to go wherever you wish. In the Dharma of gathering in, Amitabha Buddha has made a vow to lead you to his land to cultivate with him. When looking at the two Buddhas, Amitabha and Akshobhya, one uses kindness and compassion to teach and transform living beings, and the other uses awesome virtue to teach and transform living beings. One subdues and the other gathers in. These two Buddhas teach and transform living beings in this Saha World and amongst all Buddhas have the strongest affinities with living beings here.

And be immediately reborn in his Land of Peace and Bliss... I go to the Western Land of Ultimate Bliss and see Amitabha Buddha in person. I am immediately reborn in the peaceful and happy land.

SUTRA:

> After I'm reborn in that land,
> I will then accomplish these great vows.
> All of them will be completely perfected without remainder,
> Bringing benefit and happiness to the realms of all beings.
>
> All in that Buddha's assembly are pure.
> At that time I will be born from a supreme lotus flower,

I'll personally behold Measureless Light Tathagata,
Who will appear and bestow upon me a prediction of Bodhi.

After receiving this prediction from the Tathagata,
With countless hundreds of kotis of transformation bodies,
My vast wisdom power that pervades the ten directions
Brings benefit everywhere to the realms of living beings.

COMMENTARY:

After I'm reborn in that land... If you can recite the name of Amitabha Buddha, by means of the power of his vows he will lead you to the Land of Ultimate Bliss. The one who cultivates the ten great king of vows of Samantabhadra Bodhisattva says, "After I'm reborn in that land." "Reborn" here refers to being reborn in the Land of Ultimate Bliss. **I will then accomplish these great vows.** When I'm reborn in the Land of Ultimate Bliss, I will perfect the cultivation of the ten great king of vows. **All of them will be completely perfected without remainder.** I will completely cultivate and fully perfect all these Dharmas, all practices, and all vows without remainder."

"Without remainder" means nothing is left out in the slightest bit, which means it is fully perfected. All of my practices and vows are complete and perfect. At that time, I will be **bringing benefit and happiness to the realms of all beings**. My ability in cultivation has reached perfection, and I'm completely capable of using all the wonderful functions of spiritual powers. I can also go to the worlds of the ten directions to bring happiness and benefit to all the realms of living beings. I want to rescue all living beings so that they can become Buddhas. Why? I have obtained peace and happiness, and so I want all living beings to obtain peace and happiness as well. Therefore, I will bring benefit and happiness to the realms of all living beings.

All in that Buddha's assembly are pure. In the ocean-like Lotus Pool assembly in Amitabha Buddha's Land of Ultimate Bliss the great Bodhisattvas and the entire ocean-like assembly of Bodhisattvas are all pure. **At that time I will be born from a supreme lotus flower.** At that time I will be born from a supremely wonderful lotus flower. I'll see the Buddha in person. As soon as the lotus opens, I will see the Buddha in person. " **I'll personally behold Measureless Light Tathagata.** I'll personally see the Buddha of the Land of Ultimate Bliss, that is Limitless Light Buddha, who is also known as Limitless Life Buddha. **Who will appear and bestow upon me a prediction of Bodhi?** When I see Amitabha Buddha in person, he will immediately bestow a prediction upon me. He will give me the specific name I will have when I realize Bodhi and tell me when I will become a Buddha.

After receiving this prediction from the Tathagata... After I have received the prediction that Amitabha Buddha has bestowed upon me, **with countless hundreds of kotis of transformation bodies**, I will then be able to create by transformation numberless division bodies, that is billions of transformation bodies. In fact the transformation bodies will number in the trillions. **My vast wisdom power that pervades the ten directions...** At that time my wisdom will also be vast and great. It will be the same as the Buddha's wisdom. It will fill up all places throughout the ten directions and it **brings benefit everywhere to the realms of living beings.** What do I do with my great wisdom? What use is it? It is to rescue all living beings and cause them all to realize Buddhahood.

SUTRA:

> To the ends of space or world-systems,
> To the ends of living beings, their karma, or their afflictions,
> But all things such as these have no end,
> So too my vows ultimately will never end.

Suppose in all the boundless kshetra-lands of the
ten directions,
One uses their multitude of jewels as adornments and
offerings to the Tathagatas,
And gives the most supreme peace and happiness to gods
and humans
Throughout kalpas as many as the smallest atomic particles in
all kshetra-lands.

Suppose another person hears this king of supreme vows,
And as they pass by his ear but a single time is able to give rise
to faith,
And his mind thirstily seeks supreme Bodhi,
The merit and virtue he gains will surpass that of the
first person.

COMMENTARY:

To the ends of space or world-systems. Space is basically endless, as
are world systems, living beings, the karma of living beings, and the
afflictions of living beings. They are all endless and inexhaustible. Let's
suppose that they could come to an end. Even if they did, the power of
my vows will never end

In fact none of these can come to an end. Worlds have periods of creation,
dwelling, decay, and emptiness. Although we say it has creation, dwelling,
decay, and emptiness, yet it is not truly empty, nor does it come to an end.
And its decay does not come to an end. Everything goes in a continuous
cycle like this. This is the same as birth, dwelling, change, and extinction.
We people have a period of birth and growth for twenty years. Then we
live for a period of twenty years where we are in a state of stasis at this
time of our lives. After this period of about twenty years, we enter the
period of change or decay where our body changes but still subtly in

moment after moment without cease. After this period of change and transformation there comes extinction of our life, which does not last for just one day but takes place over a period of twenty years. These four periods total eighty years. Birth and growth, dwelling, change, and extinction are the same as creation, dwelling, decay, and emptiness.

When we talk about worlds, we say one period of increase and one period of decrease is called a kalpa. A period of "decrease" is when people's average lifespans reach 84,000 years and then they begin to decrease by one inch in height and one year in their lifespan every one hundred years. In our case, this period of "decrease" continued like this until the time that Shakyamuni Buddha appeared in the world. At that time the average human lifespan was about eighty years. Because this period of "decrease" has continued, now the average lifespan is around sixty years worldwide.

Some people say that there are people who live for ninety or even one hundred years. That is correct, but some people die after being alive for about ten years or a little over twenty years. Sixty years refers to the average lifespan. Some people live a little longer, and some live for a little less time, but the worldwide average lifespan is around sixty years.

The average lifespan will continue to decrease until it reaches thirty years, at which time a plague will start to spread. This plague will be fatal for anyone who contracts it, because no medicine will be able to cure this disease. It will reach the point where eighty percent of the population of the entire world will die. The only people who will survive will be those living in the mountains, in the countryside, or in distant places where there are not many people where the toxic vapors of the disease cannot reach. When the average lifespan reaches about twenty-five or twenty-six years, the disaster of fire will erupt. Right now don't we have a single sun? At that time seven suns will appear in the sky.

Why will seven suns be able to appear? They will appear as retribution brought about by the force of living beings' karma. Now we are beginning to journey into outer space. This process of exploration is just an invasion of outer space. Without any reason, we humans do not stay in our own world. Rather we wish to forcibly take over and occupy the worlds of others. In the future this kind of invasion of outer space will decimate the moon, and then there will be more suns. Eventually seven suns will appear in the sky. At that time, the whole world will have volcanoes. All the rivers, lakes, and oceans will dry up, as this world is destroyed and burned dry. How far will this fire reach? It will reach up to the heavens of the First Dhyana. This disaster of fire will be the first disaster.

When the average lifespan is twenty years, the second disaster, the disaster of water, will strike. After the disaster of fire comes the disaster of water. When everything is burned, then there is no more water. In this world when something is totally destroyed, it can reappear again. One may ask, "But isn't it the case that there was no water at all?" In the atmosphere water vapors will continue to circulate, and gradually water will take over. As a result of this, the world will change to become an entire world of water. First, it became a world of fire, and then it transformed to a world of water. The disaster of water will reach up to the heavens of the Second Dhyana. Even the gods in the heavens of the Second Dhyana will drown. At this time, very few human beings will survive.

After the water disaster, when the average lifespan is between fifteen and twenty years, there will be another disaster. What will that disaster be? It will be the disaster of wind. And this disaster will be even more severe. It will blow away everything up to the heavens of the Third Dhyana.

Therefore, it is said, "the Six Heavens of Sensual Desire have five marks of decay." The Six Heavens of Sensual Desire are:

1. The Heaven of the Four Kings;
2. The Trayastrimsha Heaven;
3. The Suyama Heaven;
4. The Tushita Heaven;
5. The Bliss From Transformations Heaven;
6. The Mastery Over Others' Transformations Heaven.

In each of these Six Heavens of Sensual Desire, when these five marks of decay appear, the gods there will die.

What are the five marks of decay?

1. Gods wear a flower crown made from naturally grown flowers. When the five marks of decay appear, the flowers fall off and the crown wilts and falls apart. Then the flowers on the crown dry up.

2. The clothing of the gods is extremely fine, delicate, and unsoiled. When the five marks of decay appear, the clothing of the gods gets soiled.

3. Gods do not perspire, regardless of how hot it is. However one of the five marks of decay is that their armpits begin to perspire. The bodies of the gods always emit a pleasant fragrance. According to Buddhism, people who are skilled in cultivation emit a fragrance from their bodies. However, once Upasaka Vimalakirti reprimanded some cultivators whose bodies smelled fragrant. He said, "Don't emit such a strong fragrance! When you have such a good fragrance, living beings will become attached to you as soon as they smell it. They will become greedy for your scent. So don't emit such a fragrant aroma anymore!"

4. The bodies of the gods are always fragrant. Not just one god is fragrant, but all of the gods have bodies that emit a fragrant scent.

A sign of the five marks of decay is that they lose their fragrance. A foul odor enters their bodies and it gives off a stench. This is the fourth mark of decay.

5. What is the fifth? They are no longer able to sit still in their seats. The gods always appear as if sitting in dhyana samadhi. They are not like humans who resemble monkeys who from morning until night run hither and tither doing this or that. On the contrary, gods always sit in meditation and appear as if they are in dhyana samadhi. Moreover, they do not talk very much, unlike humans who like to talk all day long. We never stop talking with each other. The gods don't talk very much at all. However, when the five marks of decay appear, the gods cannot sit still anymore. Even when they try to meditate, they are always moving about in one way or another. They are unable to sit still. Once this occurs they become confused. When they get confused, they fall. Then they die.

When gods are about to die the five marks of decay appear. Thus there is the saying, "In the Six Heavens of Sensual Desire, there are five marks of decay." "The heavens of the Third Dhyana have the disaster of wind." Even if you have cultivated to the heavens of the Third Dhyana and are reborn there, when the disaster of wind comes, you'll be blown into oblivion.

It is said, "If a person is able to cultivate to the state of Neither Cognition Nor Non-Cognition," that is if you are able to cultivate to reach the Heaven of Neither Cognition Nor Non-Cognition, "That is not as good as going to the Western Land and then coming back." That is not as good as going to the Land of Ultimate Bliss in the West. One is reborn in the Land of Ultimate Bliss and then afterwards if you wish, you can return to this world to teach and transform living beings. Therefore, it's better to be reborn in the Western Land where you have more certainty and less risk.

There will be very few people left after the wind disaster. At that time the human population will increase very rapidly. When the average human lifespan is ten years, a severe plague will strike, and most people will die leaving few survivors. After this plague is over, the period of increase will begin. Every one hundred years, the average height will increase by one inch, and the average human lifespan will increase by one year. This rate of increase will continue until the average human lifespan reaches 84,000 years.

One such period of increase and period of decrease is called one kalpa. One thousand of these kalpas is called a small kalpa. Twenty small kalpas constitute one middle-sized kalpa, and four middle-sized kalpas equal one great kalpa (Maha-kalpa). After the time of emptiness, a world begins to be created again. How long does it take to go through the process of creation? Twenty small kalpas. One thousand kalpas make up one small kalpa, and twenty small kalpas make up a middle-sized kalpa. The period of creation lasts for twenty small kalpas, the period of dwelling lasts for twenty small kalpas, the period of decay lasts for twenty small kalpas, and the period of emptiness lasts for twenty small kalpas. Creation, dwelling, decay, and emptiness make up one cycle of a world system. After a world is in a state of emptiness, it will be created again, and after that it will be in a state of dwelling. Then it will decay and finally be in a state of emptiness. Our world systems constantly goes through the cycle of creation, dwelling, decay, and emptiness without end, just as people are born and die, are born and die, are born and die again and again. Our world goes through the same process endlessly. Creation, dwelling, decay, and emptiness continues without end.

To the ends of living beings, their karma, or their afflictions. The number of living beings is also without end, and the power of living beings' karma has no end. Further, the afflictions of living beings are also endless. Suppose all of these were to end, yet the power of these vows will never end. **But all things such as these have no end.** There will never be a time when any of them will come to an end. **So too my vows ultimately will never end.** The power of my vows will ultimately never end.

Suppose in all the boundless kshetra-lands of the ten directions, one uses their multitude of jewels as adornments and offerings to the Tathagatas. Throughout all the boundless Buddha lands of the worlds of the ten directions, with all the myriad jewels of the worlds of the ten directions, one adorns and makes offerings to all Tathagatas, thus generating the greatest amount of merit. **And gives the most supreme peace and happiness to gods and humans.** One gives the most superior and wondrous happiness to gods in the heavens and people in the world.

Throughout kalpas as many as the smallest atomic particles in all kshetra-lands. I make offerings for as many kalpas as there are minutest particles in all the kshetra-lands throughout the ten directions.

Suppose another person hears this king of supreme vows… If there is a person who can hear of the supreme and wonderful practices of these ten great king of vows of Samantabhadra Bodhisattva, **and as they pass by his ear but a single time is able to give rise to faith, and his mind thirstily seeks supreme Bodhi,** if one sincerely seeks wonderful superior Bodhi as earnestly as a thirsty person craves a drink of water, then **the merit and virtue he gains will surpass that of the previous person.** If one's mind has just a single thought of seeking for Bodhi, then his merit and virtue will surpass the merit of one who makes offerings of a multitude of jewels as numerous as the grains of sand in the Ganges River to the Tathagatas and adorns all their worlds as mentioned before. His merit and virtue is greater than that of the previous person.

SUTRA:

> Always separating far from bad teachers,
> And leaving forever all unwholesome paths.
> Quickly seeing the Tathagata Measureless Light,
> And perfecting Samantabhadra's most supreme vows.

> This person well obtains a superior lifespan,
> And is well able to attain rebirth in the human realm.
> Before long this person will accomplish
> These practices of Samantabhadra Bodhisattva.

> In the past, owing to a lack of wisdom power,
> I have done the five Avīci offenses of extreme evil,
> By reciting the great kings of vows of Samantabhadra
> In one thought they will all be wiped away.

COMMENTARY:

Always separating far from bad teachers. It is said,

> *When people are close to crimson, they become red.*
> *When we are close to black ink, we become black.*
> *If we contact brown, we become brown.*
> *And if we touch yellow, we become yellow.*

You learn to be like the people with whom you associate. In China the saying, "The mother of Mencius selected good neighbors," concerns the same concept.

Mencius' family first lived nearby a cemetery where many people were put in caskets and buried. Following tradition their relatives would come to offer pigs and sheep as sacrifices to their deceased ancestors. When Mencius was a child he observed what people were doing, and he would mimic them in his play. So as a little child he would make people out of clay, put them in little fake caskets, and bury them in the ground. Then he made little clay pigs and sheep as sacrifices, and then he'd bow to the ground.

When his mother saw this, she thought, "What good is it for my child to learn these kinds of things? How will he develop in the future?" With that, she moved to another neighborhood.

Where did they move? This time Mencius' family found themselves next to a slaughterhouse where pigs, sheep, and so forth were killed. Where upon Mencius began to learn and mimic this kind of behavior. When his mother saw this, she disapproved and moved again.

This time they moved next door to a school where Zisi, the grandson of Confucius, was teaching. He taught a group of students who came to the school to study and then returned home for their meals. When his students entered the school, they bowed in veneration to the sacred plaque to Confucius and paid their respects again when they left the school. Thus they performed proper etiquette when entering and leaving the school. When Mencius observed the students, he began to emulate their way of study and respect.

When his mother saw this she said, "It is right to live in a place like this; we should live here," and she sent Mencius to school to study.

As a young child, Mencius studied for a few days, and then lost interest and didn't want to study anymore. When his mother was weaving at home on a loom, Mencius told her that he was not going to study anymore. His mother did not say a word, but took out a knife and cut the thread in the middle of the cloth she was weaving.

When Mencius saw what she had done, he knew something was wrong. He knelt before his mother and said, "Why have you gotten angry? Did I do something wrong? Please tell me."

Mencius' mother replied, "Stopping your study is just like my cutting the threads before finishing the weaving of this fabric. Do you understand? If you don't study, you won't accomplish anything in the future."

Mencius thought, "If that's the way things are, then I had better continue to study." Later he became a great sage. In China he is second only to Confucius. How was he able to become a sage? Because his mother educated him well. She moved three times until she moved to a place where Mencius could have the opportunity to study. Then afterwards he was able to successfully complete his studies. In the beginning, if his mother had not moved when they were living next to a cemetery, Mencius would have grown up to be a cemetery worker. He would have watched over the graves and performed rituals of worship and sacrifice. If they had remained next to the slaughterhouse, Mencius would have grown up to be a butcher who kills sheep and pigs. In the end they moved next to a school, and he became a famous scholar.

The story of Mencius' education is an example of what is meant by being far apart from bad teachers and drawing near to good teachers. This is the meaning of what I said previously.

> *When people are close to crimson, they become red.*
> *When we are close to black ink, we become black.*
> *If we contact brown, we become brown.*
> *And if we touch yellow, we become yellow.*

So it all depends on what color you draw near to. When you draw near to good teachers, the same principle applies. On the other hand, if you meet with bad teachers, they will only teach you bad things. They will teach you to harm people wherever you go. They will always teach you to be jealous of others and to obstruct others. This is the way bad teachers are. So you don't want to draw near to bad teachers but stay far away from them. Keep your distance from them. Therefore the text reads, "Always far apart from bad teachers." They do not teach you to cultivate good things. Rather they teach you unwholesome things.

And leaving forever all unwholesome paths. If you stay far away from bad teachers, then you can forever leave all the evil paths of existence. If you do not keep far away from bad teachers, then you can fall into the evil paths of existence. Now that you're able to stay far away from bad teachers, you are able to leave all the evil paths of existence. What are the evil paths of existence? They are the hells, hungry ghosts, animals, and asuras. These are the four evil destinies, which are also called the evil paths of existence. The beings in these evil paths of existence undergo the suffering that is a result of their offenses.

Why does a person undergo the suffering that is a result of their offenses? Since you learned all kinds of evil from bad teachers, you created evil offenses. And having created evil offenses, you fall into the evil paths of existence. Now you are apart from bad teachers, so you can be far apart from all evil paths of existence.

Quickly seeing the Tathagata Measureless Light. When you leave all evil paths of existence, you can go to all the good paths of existence. If the things that people encounter in the world are not evil, then they are good. If you are not doing evil things, then you are doing good things. If you do good, you will have good karma. If you have good, then you can attain good results. What are good results? You'll be able to quickly see the Buddha. So the Sutra says, "Soon to see the Tathagata Measureless Light." You will be able to quickly see and to personally behold Amitabha

Buddha of the Land of Ultimate Bliss who is known as Measureless Light Buddha and Measureless Life Buddha.

And perfecting Samantabhadra's most supreme vows. When you reach the Land of Ultimate Bliss of Amitabha Buddha, you will be able to completely perfect the most supreme ten great king of vows of Samantabhadra Bodhisattva. **This person well obtains a superior lifespan.** This person will quickly obtain the most supreme lifespan, which means that he will have a long life.

Buddhism speaks about not being attached to the appearance of a lifespan, but now the text mentions a supreme, long lifespan. Is this not the appearance of a lifespan? This appearance of a lifespan being talked about here is not something that the person sought to attain. This was attained because he stayed far away from all bad teachers, forever left all the evil paths of existence, and saw Amitabha Buddha. In this case even if one did not want a long life, he would still definitely obtain one.

This is not like the situation in our world in which we wish for a long life, but do not attain it. Or we want to have happiness, but do not attain true happiness. When you go to the Land of Ultimate Bliss, your lifespan is measureless and your light is measureless. Amitabha Buddha has a measureless lifespan, and so do we. Amitabha Buddha's light is measureless, and if we are born in the Land of Ultimate Bliss, our light will be measureless as well. Therefore, the text says, "This person well obtains a supreme lifespan." "Well obtains" means that this is a result of your good karma, not because of your attachments.

And is well able to attain rebirth in the human realm. If this person wishes to teach and transform living beings, then he can return and be reborn among people. And when he's born among people, everything he does will be perfect. This is called "coming back again according to your vows." If he does not want to come back, he does not need to. However, if he does want to come back, he can do so very naturally. This is true freedom where you can do as you wish.

Before long this person will accomplish these practices of Samantabhadra Bodhisattva. This person refers to the person who cultivates the ten great king of vows of Samantabhadra Bodhisattva. Before long he accomplishes all of the merit and virtue of these vows. The practices he perfects are the same without any difference as those perfected by Samantabhadra Bodhisattva. The power of Samantabhadra Bodhisattva's practices is the greatest. These practices that you have cultivated and perfected are the same as his.

In the past, owing to a lack of wisdom power. "In the past" means long ago in the distant past. Earlier, the text said,

All the evil karma I have created in the past,
Caused by beginningless greed, hatred, and delusion,
Produced in body, speech, and thought,
I now fully repent and reform of it all.

"All the evil karma I have created in the past, caused by beginningless greed, hatred, and delusion…" Why do we have greed, hatred, and delusion? Because we do not have wisdom, and we are without the power of Prajna. Why do we do evil? Because we do not have any wisdom, we create all kinds of evil karma. One with true wisdom does not create evil karma. Therefore, because one lacks wisdom, **I have done the five Avīci offenses of extreme evil.** We people are the subjects, which means that we are the ones who are creating or doing. Karma is the object or that which we create.

Who creates bad karma? Whoever does not cultivate good dharma cultivates evil dharmas. Whoever cultivates evil dharmas is the one who creates evil karma. If there is a doer, then karma will be created. Therefore, there is a subject and object. When karma is created, then the creator who made it must undergo the results of what he has done. Therefore, the text mentions, "extreme evil."

What is extreme evil? There are five actions that are classified as the most evil:

1. Killing one's father
2. Killing one's mother
3. Killing an Arhat
4. Creating a schism in the harmonious Sangha
5. Spilling the Buddha's blood

In the world, people are basically incapable of killing their fathers, but there is a type of person who is capable of doing this. This type of person can commit the ten evil karmas and the five rebellious acts.

The next one is killing one's mother. In truth, the world has had many instances of people murdering their fathers but very few instances of people killing their mothers. Nevertheless, it still happens. A few months ago the newspaper reported the story of a child who had killed his mother. This happened in the United States, and the child was 15 or 17 years old. I do not know if you saw this story. The boy's mother was a widow and had been raising her son alone for over ten years. He was her only child and was attending high school.

One day the mother told her son she wanted to paint a picture of him in the nude, and she asked him to take off his clothes. The son did not want to do this, but his mother insisted. The son was very obedient, however, and so at her urging, he took off his clothes and modeled for his mother. She painted all day, from ten in the morning until ten at night, but still had not finished.

Now his mother was not just focused on painting all this time, but at times she was also eyeing her son. Eventually she went up to him and hugged him. Then she tried to force him into having sexual relations with her. The son became extremely frightened and adamantly refused to do this. At this point the mother took out a handgun from her pocket and told him, "If you don't shoot and kill me, I must have you." Then she gave the gun to her son and told him to shoot her. Her son was mentally confused by this situation and shot and killed his mother.

After the killing, he reported it to the police who brought him to court and charged him with murder. Then, later at a hearing, he confessed the whole affair in great detail. In the end, I do not know what the result of this case was. This is an example of killing one's mother. When this kind of incident occurs, it is often due to some special circumstances.

Killing an Arhat means to kill one who has realized the fruition of an Arhat. This is also one of the five rebellious acts. Another of the five rebellious acts is creating a schism in the harmonious Sangha. The Sangha is called a harmonious assembly. The Sangha is harmonious in six ways, and Sangha is not just one or two people. There must be at least four people to be a Sangha.

The Sangha is harmonious in six ways.

(1) Harmonious in body, they dwell together. Members of the Sangha do not fight or argue with each other.

(2) Harmonious in speech, there is no contention. When the Sangha is together, they do not argue or gossip about rights and wrongs, and they do not gossip about others or themselves. Being harmonious in speech they do not contend with each other. The *Vajra Sutra* discusses the Samadhi of Non-Contention. Those who have renounced the life of a householder and live together should not

contend. They should attain the Samadhi of Non-Contention. As soon as you contend, you have the appearance of a self and others. When you have the appearance of self and others, there is right and wrong. If there is right and wrong, then there is a winner and a loser. When there is a winner and a loser, there is the appearance of living beings, and from the appearance of living beings, comes the appearance of a lifespan. Having these four appearances prevents you from gaining true samadhi-power. This is what is meant by "harmonious in speech they do not contend."

(3) Harmonious in thought, they are happy together. One's mind should also be harmonious. You should not think that you have your own thoughts and I have mine, and that my thoughts need not be harmonious with yours, and yours need not be harmonious with mine. Everyone should have harmonious minds and be happy together. In this way everyone is very happy and joyful.

(4) Being harmonious with respect to benefits, each gets his share. When there are good things, they should be enjoyed by everyone together. It is not that one person alone enjoys them. When there are benefits, everyone is treated equally. You get some good from it and I get some benefit from it as well. This is called "being harmonious with respect to benefits, each gets his share."

(5) Harmonious in views, they have a common understanding. The viewpoints of everyone should be the same. For example, when studying the Buddha-dharma, everyone should agree and share a common understanding. Their views must be harmonious.

(6) Harmonious in the moral precepts, they cultivate together. Everyone cultivates and upholds the moral precepts together.

These are the six kinds of harmony, and when these six kinds of harmony prevail it is called a harmonious Sangha. However, if you sow discord and create mischief that will create disharmony in the Sangha. As a result, you are displeased with me and I'm displeased with you. And you are jealous of me and I create obstructions for you. This causes the Sangha assembly to be in disharmony. This is called creating a schism in the harmonious Sangha.

To spill the Buddha's blood is another of the five rebellious acts. Some people say that since we have been born after the time of the Buddha, we cannot spill the Buddha's blood. However, whatever you do that harms Buddhism can be called spilling the Buddha's blood. If you destroy the jewel of the Buddha, this is spilling the Buddha's blood. What is destroying the jewel of the Buddha? For example, smashing a Buddha statue. Although it is an image, it is the same as spilling the Buddha's blood. Or perhaps one burns a picture of the Buddha. This is also called spilling the Buddha's blood. There is also the jewel of the Dharma. All the Sutras are the wisdom-life of the Buddha's Dharma-body. The Brahma Net Sutra says, "Wherever there are Sutras, there is the Buddha." This refers to the Buddha's Dharma body. Therefore, if you burn or destroy the Sutras, that is also called spilling the Buddha's blood.

Members of the Sangha cultivate according to the Buddha's teachings so that in the future they will become Buddhas. If you create discord in the Sangha, that is also called spilling the Buddha's blood. To be disrespectful to the Three Jewels and to do harmful damage to them is also called spilling the Buddha's blood. It is not necessarily the case, then, that a Buddha must be in the world for you to spill the Buddha's blood. Now the Buddha has already entered Nirvana, but all of the Buddha's teachings still exist. If you do not protect the Buddha's teachings, but rather do harm to them or do the same to a particular monastic, then you have spilled the Buddha's blood. These are all classified under the five rebellious acts and are all considered to be extreme evil.

"The five Avīci offenses of extreme evil I have done." "Extreme evil" means that there is no evil that is greater than this. The retribution for doing acts of extreme evil is to fall into the Avīci Hell. Avīci is Sanskrit, and means "uninterrupted," and there are five ways this hell is "uninterrupted." The first is "uninterrupted with respect to time" or "uninterrupted with respect to kalpa." Kalpa is also Sanskrit and it means "division of time." What is meant by uninterrupted with respect to time? From the first day to the last day that one enters the Uninterrupted Hell, there is not a single moment in which the pain and suffering cease. The suffering continues without interruption, and so it is said to be uninterrupted with respect to time.

The second is "uninterrupted with respect to form," referring to bodily form. When one falls into this hell, one sees one's body filling up the entire hell. Even if there are many people in the hell, one still fills up the entire hell, as do the others, without obstructing one another. You have your hell, and I have mine, and everyone sees himself filling up his own hell. This is the meaning of uninterrupted with respect to form.

The third meaning of Avīci is "uninterrupted suffering." This refers to the suffering undergone when you fall into this hell. In this hell, there is also the Hell of the Mountain of Knives, the Hell of the Pot of Boiling Oil, the Hell of the Iron Trident, the Hell of the Iron Hammer, the Hell of Saws, the Axe and Chisel Hell, the Iron Net Hell, the Iron Donkey Hell, the Iron Rope Hell, the Iron Horse Hell, and so forth. All of these different hells cause one to undergo suffering. And because this suffering never stops, it is called "uninterrupted suffering."

The fourth meaning is "uninterrupted retribution." It does not make any difference whether you are Chinese or any other nationality. Whoever goes to this hell, must undergo the retribution of that hell. You must undergo that kind of retribution of suffering. This is called "uninterrupted retribution."

The fifth is "uninterrupted life." When you fall into this Avīci hell, you undergo myriad births and myriad deaths in a single day and night. How is it that each day and night one is born a myriad times and one dies myriad times? In this hell you undergo the retribution of suffering to such an extreme that you die. After you die, a wind called the "clever wind" blows on you, and you come back to life again. In this way, in a single night and day you are able to die and be reborn myriad times. This is "uninterrupted life."

By reciting the great king of vows of Samantabhadra, in one thought they will all be wiped away. If you are able to recite this Chapter on the Great King of Practices and Vows of Samantabhadra Bodhisattva, then in a single thought you can destroy all of your offenses. They will all be wiped away very quickly. All of the five uninterrupted offenses will be simultaneously eliminated.

SUTRA:

> His clan, family, race, or skin color,
> His appearance and wisdom are all perfect.
> All demons and those of heterodox paths cannot destroy him,
> And for those in the three realms, he can become worthy
>   of offerings.
>
> He will quickly advance to the great Bodhi-tree king,
> And seated there subdue the horde of demons,

> Realize the Equal and Right Enlightenment and turn the
>   Wheel of Dharma,
> And benefit all living beings everywhere.

COMMENTARY:

His clan, family, race, or skin color. "Clan" refers to your ethnicity
and "family" refers to your family name or surname. "Race" means the
race of people to which you belong. And "color" refers to whether you
are a white person, a yellow person, a black person, or a red person. **His
appearance and wisdom are all perfect.** Your physical characteristics
and appearance are beautiful, dignified, and complete, and your wisdom
will also be complete and great. Therefore, the text reads that they "are
all perfect."

All demons and those of heterodox paths cannot destroy him. None
of the heavenly demons or adherents of heterodox paths have any method
to give you trouble. Why? Because the inconceivable power from the
ten great king of vows of Samantabhadra Bodhisattva will support and
protect you.

And for those in the three realms, he can become worthy of offerings.
You can become one who should receive the offerings of those in the
three realms of existence, that is, the Realm of Sensual Desire, the Form
Realm, and the Formless Realm. This means that you have realized the
level of attainment of an Arhat and the position of one who is "worthy
of offerings."

He will quickly advance to the great Bodhi-tree king. You will very
quickly go to the base of the Bodhi Tree and become a Buddha, and
sit in the great Bodhimaṇḍa. **And seated there subdue the horde
of demons.** At that time, beneath the Bodhi Tree you will be able to
vanquish all demons and others such as these. **Realize Equal and Right**

Enlightenment, turn the Wheel of Dharma. You will accomplish the Unsurpassed, Right and Equal, Proper Enlightenment, and turn the great wheel of Dharma **and benefit all living beings everywhere**. You will benefit all living beings universally.

SUTRA:

> If a person with respect to these vows of Samantabhadra,
> Reads, recites, receives, upholds, and explains them,
> One's reward can only be known by the Buddha,
> And one will certainly attain the path of supreme Bodhi.
>
> If a person recites these vows of Samantabhadra,
> I'm only speaking about a small portion of one's roots
>   of goodness
> In a single thought, everything will be perfected.
> And one can accomplish the pure vows of living beings.
>
> I practice the supreme conduct of Samantabhadra
> And transfer all of its boundless and superior blessings,
> Vowing that all living beings everywhere, who are sinking and
>   drowning,
> Will quickly go to the kshetra-land of Measureless
>   Light Buddha!

COMMENTARY:

If a person with respect to these vows of Samantabhadra... Suppose you are able to cultivate the ten great king of vows of Samantabhadra Bodhisattva and one **reads, recites, receives, upholds, and explains them...** if you're able to read and recite them, or to receive and uphold them, or explain them for others, then **one's reward can only be known by the Buddha**. Only the Buddhas can verify and know this kind of reward. **And one will certainly attain the path of supreme Bodhi.** For sure you will obtain the great path of Bodhi.

If a person recites these vows of Samantabhadra... Suppose someone can read and recite the ten great king of vows of Samantabhadra Bodhisattva. **I'm only speaking about a small portion of one's roots of goodness.** I'm only speaking about a very small amount of one's roots of goodness. **In a single thought, everything will be perfected.** In a single thought, everything that one seeks for will be fulfilled. **And one can accomplish the pure vows of living beings.** One will be able to accomplish the vows made by all living beings.

I practice the supreme conduct of Samantabhadra. I cultivate the practices of Samantabhadra, which are the most excellent, subtle, and wonderful practice. **And transfer all of its boundless and superior blessings.** I transfer all the measureless and boundless, and wondrous rewards of blessings from this practice, to all living beings of the Dharma Realm. **Vowing that all living beings everywhere, who are sinking and drowning...** I vow to rescue and liberate all living beings everywhere who are sinking and drowning in the ocean of suffering. So that they **will quickly go to the kshetra-land of Measureless Light Buddha!** They will very quickly go to the Land of Ultimate Bliss of Amitabha Buddha, Measureless Light Buddha.

Epilogue

SUTRA:

At that time, after Samantabhadra Bodhisattva, Mahasattva, had finished speaking before the Tathagata these pure verses on the great king of vows of Samantabhadra, the youth Sudhana was overwhelmed with boundless joy. All the Bodhisattvas were extremely happy as well. And the Tathagata praised him, saying, "Very good! Very good!"

At that time, this supreme Dharma of the inconceivable state of liberation was spoken in the presence of the World Honored One and the Sagely Bodhisattvas, Mahasattvas with Manjushri Bodhisattva as their leader.

Also present were all the great Bodhisattvas and the six thousand Bhikshus who had matured in their practice, with Maitreya Bodhisattva as their leader and all the great Bodhisattvas of the Worthy Kalpa who were led by Immaculate Samantabhadra Bodhisattva.

COMMENTARY:

At that time refers to the time after Samantabhadra Bodhisattva had finished speaking these pure verses. Thus the text says, **Samantabhadra Bodhisattva, Mahasattva.** Samantabhadra Bodhisattva is a great Bodhisattva among Bodhisattvas, **while before the Tathagata,** the Buddha, **finished speaking these pure verses on the great king of vows of Samantabhadra.** Samantabhadra Bodhisattva was in front of Shakyamuni Buddha and he explained the vast and great king of vows of Samantabhadra that he made himself. The ten great king of vows are as follows:

The first is to worship all Buddhas;

The second is to praise the Tathagatas;

The third is to extensively cultivate making offerings;

The fourth is to repent of karmic obstacles and reform;

The fifth is to follow and rejoice in the merit and virtue of others;

The sixth is to request the turning of the wheel of Dharma;

The seventh is to beseech the Buddhas remain in the world;

The eighth is to always follow and learn from the Buddhas;

The ninth is to constantly conform with living beings;

The tenth is to transfer all merit and virtue.

After he finished speaking these pure verses on the great king of vows, **the youth Sudhana was overwhelmed with boundless joy**. After the youth Sudhana had heard about these ten great king of vows, he jumped for joy. **All the Bodhisattvas were extremely happy as well**. Not only did the youth Sudhana become so happy that he jumped for joy, all the Bodhisattvas were happy too. **And the Tathagata**, Shakyamuni Buddha, **praised** Samantabhadra Bodhisattva, saying, "**Very good! Very good!**" He said, "It's truly good that you have explained this Dharma. This is really the best!"

At that time, this supreme Dharma of the inconceivable state of liberation was spoken in the presence of the World Honored One, Shakyamuni Buddha, and all the **Sagely Bodhisattvas, Mahasattvas** and all the great Bodhisattvas. They heard the inconceivable state of liberation that was previously spoken. **With Manjushri Bodhisattva**, also known as "Wonderfully Auspicious" Bodhisattva, **as their leader.** He was a leader among those Bodhisattvas.

Also present were all the great Bodhisattvas and the six thousand Bhikshus who had matured in their practice. There were all the great Bodhisattvas and also six thousand Bhikshus in the Dharma Assembly,

with Maitreya Bodhisattva as their leader. He was the leader of the Bhikshus and great Bodhisattvas. Maitreya is a Sanskrit word that means someone who belongs to the clan named "Kindness." It also means "invincible" or "Ajita."

And there were also **all the great Bodhisattvas of the Worthy Kalpa.** This kalpa of ours is called the Worthy Kalpa. Why is it called the Worthy Kalpa? It's because many sages and worthies will appear in this world at this time. All these great Bodhisattvas **who were led by Immaculate Samantabhadra Bodhisattva.** The Bodhisattva named Immaculate Samantabhadra Bodhisattva was at the head of the great assembly.

SUTRA:

Assembled together were also all the great Bodhisattvas who will succeed to the position of a Buddha in one life and who were at the position of Anointment of the Crown, as well as all the remaining Bodhisattvas, Mahasattvas from the various different worlds of the ten directions, who were as numerous as the smallest atomic particles in an ocean of kshetra-lands, gathered together.

All the great Shravakas were headed by the greatly wise Shariputra, Mahamaudgalyayana, and others. Also present were all the people, gods, and all the rulers of the worlds, as well as heavenly dragons, yakshas, gandharvas, asuras, garudas, kinnaras, mahoragas, humans, non-humans, and so forth. Upon hearing what the Buddha had said, all in the entire great assembly were extremely happy, faithfully accepted it, and put it into practice.

COMMENTARY:

Assembled together were also all the great Bodhisattvas who will succeed to the position of a Buddha in one life. What is meant by "will succeed to the position of a Buddha in one life." He is called a Dharma Prince and is at the position of Dharma Prince. In our Saha world, Shakyamuni Buddha is the Dharma King. When his Buddha-dharma passes into extinction, the one who will succeed to the position of the Buddha is Maitreya Bodhisattva. Maitreya Bodhisattva, in one life, will be the next Buddha.

Maitreya Bodhisattva lives in the inner palace of the Tushita Heaven. Each Bodhisattva who is about to succeed to the position of a Buddha lives in the inner palace of the Tushita Heaven. For example, before Shakyamuni Buddha became a Buddha, he lived in the inner palace of the Tushita Heaven. After that he descended from the Tushita Heaven, entered the womb, left the womb, renounced the life of a householder, realized the Path, turned the wheel of Dharma, and rescued living beings.

When Shakyamuni Buddha was in his mother's womb, he also turned the wheel of Dharma, but most people could not perceive this kind of state. They thought that he just spent his time in the womb without doing anything else. Actually he spoke Dharma for all the ghosts and spirits while in his mother's womb.

Maitreya Bodhisattva will succeed Shakyamuni Buddha. Amitabha Buddha is the Teaching-Master in the Land of Ultimate Bliss. When he retires, Guan Shi Yin Bodhisattva will be his successor as the Buddha in one life. When Guan Shi Yin Bodhisattva steps down, Great Strength Bodhisattva will follow him in becoming a Buddha in one life. This is the meaning of "succeed to the position of a Buddha in one life."

And, who were at the position of Anointment of the Crown... When a Buddha becomes a Buddha, his head must be anointed. The emperors of the past, when they were about to succeed to the throne, similarly did the ritual of having their head anointed. After they did the ritual of

Anointment of the Crown, they became the Sons of Heaven (i.e. emperor). When the Buddha is about to become a Buddha in one life, it is the stage where one will "succeed to the position of a Buddha in one life." It is also called the position of "Anointment of the Crown."

Anointment of the Crown occurs when one is about to become a Buddha. All the Buddhas of the ten directions anoint with sweet dew Dharma-water the crown of the head of the one who is about to become a Buddha. When Shakyamuni Buddha came into the world, nine dragons came to anoint his head. This is also called the ritual of Anointment of the Crown. When one dwells at the stage where one will succeed to the position of a Buddha in one life or the position of Anointment of the Crown, one is about to become a Buddha. One will become a Buddha in one's next life.

"The great Bodhisattvas" are those who will succeed to the position of a Buddha in one life and occupy the position of Anointment of the Crown. There are not just one or two who are like this. There are many, many Bodhisattvas from all the worlds of the ten directions who are going to become Buddhas. They are those who will succeed to the position of a Buddha in one life. These Bodhisattvas who are at the position of Anointment of the Crown are quite numerous.

As well as all the remaining Bodhisattvas, Mahasattvas from the various different worlds of the ten directions, who were as numerous as the smallest atomic particles in an ocean of kshetra-lands... They all came to the Saha world to listen to Shakyamuni Buddha explain the *Flower Adornment Sutra* and to hear Samantabhadra Bodhisattva speak the Chapter on the Practices and Vows of Samantabhadra. They came from Buddha-lands as numerous as the smallest atomic particles in a great ocean of kshetra-lands. They were so numerous that one could not say just how many there were. "All Bodhisattvas Mahasattvas" means that there were also a lot of great Bodhisattvas.

All the great Shravakas were headed by the greatly wise Shariputra, Mahamaudgalyayana, and others. There were both Mahamaudgalyayana and the one of great wisdom, Shariputra. Shariputra was foremost in wisdom. How do we know this? When Shariputra was in his mother's womb, he enabled his mother to defeat her brother in debate. Before she was with child, she could not defeat him regardless of what principles she presented. Her brother defeated her every time they debated. But when Shariputra's mother was carrying him, she never lost a debate with her brother. He always lost after that.

Her brother told her, "The child in your womb must be exceptional. He certainly has great wisdom. It is only due to his help, that you are able to win in these debates. You never had such great wisdom before, so it's certain that you are carrying a very wise child in your womb."

He thought that when his sister has this child, he will be his uncle. If an uncle were defeated in debate by his nephew, he would lose face and be humiliated. Therefore, he decided that he would travel widely to study the classics and works of heterodox teachings.

How diligently did he study? He did not cut his hair or shave his beard. In fact he did not even have time to cut his fingernails. Why? It was not that he did not want to cut his hair or shave, or cut his nails, but rather that he did not have time to tend to such things. He was constantly studying the literary works of heterodox teachings. His fingernails grew so long that they grew into curls, and people called him "the Long-Nailed Brahmin." Brahmin is one who cultivates pure practices. He was so busy he did not even have time to cut his fingernails. Just imagine how great his devotion to learning was.

Why did he study so hard? He wanted to be able to return home and defeat his nephew, the child of his younger sister. That was his wish.

After he studied for over ten years, he returned home and told his sister that he wanted to debate her son. Who would have known, but his sister's child was not there. He asked, "Where is your son?"

She replied, "He has already become a monk with Shakyamuni Buddha."

When the uncle, whose name was Kaushthila, heard this, he became angry. "How can he become a monk with the Buddha? What kind of spiritual virtue does the Buddha have that the child would become a monk with him? He is better off learning the spiritual path with me. My learning and virtue are the highest. Why did he want to renounce the householder's life to become a monk with Shakyamuni Buddha?"

Then Kaushthila went off looking for Shakyamuni Buddha in order to bring his nephew back. However, he could not get him back without a reasonable excuse. He decided that when he met Shakyamuni Buddha, he would challenge him to a debate. He specialized in studying how to debate and was a master at it.

When he found Shakyamuni Buddha, he asked him, "On what basis have you taken my nephew as your disciple? What special abilities do you have to do this?"

Shakyamuni Buddha replied, "I don't have any special abilities at all. He wanted to become a monk with me, so what else could I do?"

The uncle said, "Well, I've come here to debate with you. Let's set up a topic to debate."

Shakyamuni Buddha replied, "What shall we debate? You go ahead and begin."

The uncle said, "My tenet is that I don't accept anything. This is my principle. No matter what you say, I won't accept it."

Shakyamuni Buddha then responded, "Your tenet is that you don't accept anything. Well then, do you or do you not accept your view of this tenet that you don't accept anything?"

Kaushthila thought, "If I accept this view, I will violate my original tenet, because I said that I don't accept anything. However, if I do not accept this statement, I am rejecting my own tenet. It will be invalidated because I don't accept it. If I accept it, I will be defeated, and if I don't accept it, I will still be defeated. What am I going to do?"

Before Kaushthila began the debate with Shakyamuni Buddha, he had made a bet. He had said, "If I lose, I will give you my head," and if Shakyamuni Buddha lost, he would return Kaushthila's nephew to him. He'd have to return Shariputra to his uncle. In the beginning they had made this agreement. And now he realized his own principle would not stand up. He decided to run away. He ran for almost two hours. How far can you run in two hours? Not too far.

Then he thought, "I'm a man, not a woman. How can I not keep my word? If I said I would give my head, then I will give my head. Why make such a big deal out of it? I definitely should keep my word." So he ran back to see Shakyamuni Buddha.

Shakyamuni Buddha said, "Why have you returned?"

He answered, "Give me a knife."

"Why should I give you a knife?"

"Because I want to cut off my head and give it to you!"

Shakyamuni Buddha said, "Why do you want to cut off your head to give to me?"

"Because I said I would." The uncle admitted that he had lost the bet. "I said clearly that if I were defeated, I would give my head to you."

Shakyamuni Buddha replied, "It would be useless to cut your head off to give to me. What can I do with a head? But if you don't cut if off, it might still be of some use. If you keep it on your shoulders, you can consider yourself the same as being dead, and then you can leave the life of a householder and become a monk. Wouldn't that be better? Why cut off your head? Your head is now mine, and I don't want you to cut it off. I want it kept on your body. Just shave your head and become a monk, then that will be enough. Shaving your head is equivalent to cutting it off."

Kaushthila said with relief, "Oh! That's okay!" He then left the life of a householder and became a monk with Shakyamuni Buddha.

Shariputra's name means "the son of Shari." His name came from his mother's name, which was Shari. *Putra* means "son." The *shari* is a name of a type of bird. In India it's called *shari*. In English it is an egret. That bird's eyes are expressive and beautiful. Shariputra's mother's eyes were as beautiful as an egret's, so she was called Shari. And her son was called the son of Shari, Shariputra.

Maudgalyayana. Maudgalyayana, also Sanskrit, means descendent of those who eat "radishes" or who "harvest beans." When his ancestors cultivated the spiritual path, they ate these foods. This name commemorates his ancestors.

Amongst the disciples of the Buddha, Maudgalyayana was foremost in spiritual powers. Both he and the greatly wise Shariputra were at the head of the assembly of **all the great Shravakas**. They were their leaders. "Shravakas" are those who become enlightened by hearing the Buddha's teachings. They hear the Dharma of the Four Noble Truths—suffering, accumulation, cessation, and the path—and become enlightened. They understood that adventitious afflictions cause trouble and thus became enlightened.

Also present were all the people, gods, and all the rulers of the worlds. "Also present" means that there were not only Bodhisattvas, Shravakas, and Those Enlightened to Conditions in the assembly, but that there were others as well, including people, all the gods in the heavens, spirits of the heavens, and all world rulers, who were kings of countries, **as well as heavenly dragons.**

There are many kinds of dragons. There are dragons in the heavens, dragons in the oceans, dragons that guard valuable treasures, and those dragons that form the clouds and make it rain. How do they become dragons? In the past they were quick and intense with the Vehicle, but loose with the moral precepts. So they became dragons. To be quick and intense with the Vehicle means that they cultivated and were able to uphold all kinds of mantras. They were also able to recite Sutras and sit in Dhyana meditation. They were capable of learning any Dharma very quickly. What was the one exception to this? They did not hold the moral precepts. What moral precepts did they not uphold? They did not uphold the moral precept against killing, against stealing, against sexual misconduct, against lying, and against taking intoxicants. They did not keep the Five Moral Precepts, and so they took a fall and received the body of a dragon. What is more, their thoughts of anger are very severe. Dragons have a lot of anger. Why did they fall and take on the body of dragons? Just because they had too much anger.

Those who study the Buddha-dharma should be sure to keep in mind to not be lazy. In monasteries, in the early morning the wooden boards are hit at four o'clock. A wooden mallet is used to strike a wooden board that produces a sharp sound. When the people hear this, they should all get up. Then the bell is rung. Once the bell is rung, if you stay in bed and sleep, you might become a dragon in the future. People who do not honor the rules of a monastery can become dragons. In fact, the best scenario is that you will become a dragon, and the worst scenario is that you will become a snake. So do not think that being a little lazy is of any good. If you do not get up in the morning when you hear the bell, you can become a snake. But if you do not rest after hearing the evening bell and drum, you may also suffer a fall.

Dragons become dragons because they misbehave and don't follow the rules. Take a look at how crooked the shape of a dragon is. When he travels down the road or does things, he is always crooked. This is the way one looks when one misbehaves.

There are many kinds of **yakshas**: flying yakshas, heavenly yakshas, yakshas that travel on the earth, and yakshas that dwell in the water. Yakshas and dragons are among the eightfold pantheon of ghosts and spirits. What is the main food of dragons? Dragons are big worms that eat things like fish and eat just about everything else. However, they are also eaten by others. Who eats them? I'll tell you about who eats them later on.

Yaksha is Sanskrit; it means "speedy ghost." Yakshas travel very fast, and they look quite frightening. One yaksha may have ten heads, or ten yakshas might share one head. Is this not strange? One yaksha may have ten legs, or ten yakshas might share one leg. That's how weird they are. They have an especially bizarre appearance. They may have three or five legs. It's not fixed. They might also just be a head or just two legs. They can be extraordinarily weird freaks. If you do not know about them, and you see one, it can scare you to death.

Gandharvas are the musical spirits who play where the Jade Emperor lives. These spirits are also known as "incense-sniffing" spirits. As soon as the Jade Emperor lights his aloeswood incense, they smell it and rush to that place. They very joyfully go there to play music. They are very skilled musicians. They are the incense and music spirits for the Jade Emperor.

Asura is a Sanskrit word that means "ugly" or "not upright." It is also translated as "one without wine." Not upright means that they are extremely ugly. And being without wine simply means that they do not have any wine to drink. They have the blessings of the gods, but do not have the virtue of the gods. This means that they have the reward of blessings like gods, but they lack the virtuous practice of the gods.

Asuras are of many kinds, and they can be found among the gods, humans, ghosts, and animals. In general there are asuras in all the paths of existence. What are asuras? They specialize in fighting with people. They like to fight with words, with their bodies, and with their minds. They like to fight with the three karmas of body, mouth, and mind.

However, female asuras are most beautiful. In fact, they are incredibly beautiful. Not only can humans fall in love with them, but also when the Jade Emperor saw the daughter of the asura king, he became desirous of her. The Jade Emperor has some samadhi power, but when he saw the asura king's daughter, whose name was Shezhi, he lost it all. At that time he decided to ask the asura king if he could marry her. The asura king approved of the Jade Emperor's request and gave his daughter to him in marriage. The Jade Emperor was quite delighted to have such a beautiful heavenly maiden, and so he invited the asura king for a feast. To show the utmost respect, he had his heavenly army welcome the asura king and also escort him back to his home.

The asura king was very mistrustful and liked to fight. He thought, "Oh, you Jade Emperor, you want to show off your strength to me, so you have sent out your army to frighten me. This is ridiculous!" Although in his heart he was very unhappy with the Jade Emperor, he felt there was no reason to express this openly. So for the time being he patiently restrained himself.

The Jade Emperor liked to go to the world to hear an accomplished immortal explain the classics. This immortal lectured the *Classic on the Wonder of the Jade Emperor's Mind Seal* including the following section:

> *There are three kinds of supreme elixir, the spirit, vital energy, and*
> *reproductive essence.*
> *Elusive and intangible,*
> *Remote and unclear,*
> *Supporting nothingness and also maintaining existence;*
> *Very soon you will be successful.*
> *Mixing them together like the turning wind.*
> *It will be efficacious after one hundred days of practice.*

He lectured this classic and the Jade Emperor went every day to listen to the immortal teach.

One day the daughter of the asura king got jealous. She asked the Jade Emperor, "Where do you go every day? You're never at home."

He answered, "I go to the realm of people to listen to the classics. There is a person who lectures the *Classic on the Wonder of the Mind Seal*, so I go to listen to him."

The asura woman said, "I'd like to go with you. Let's go together to hear these lectures."

The Jade Emperor said, "You are a woman. You can't go there to listen to the lectures. An immortal lectures the classics in that place, and he doesn't want any women to come."

The asura woman had more doubts and said, "You don't want me to go? You are certainly carrying on with other women."

The asura woman had spiritual powers, and so when the Jade Emperor went off in his cart to hear the classics lectured, she used a kind of magic technique to make herself invisible. So although she accompanied him, he could not see her. She hid her body and rode off with him to listen to the classics too.

When the Jade Emperor got out of the cart, the asura woman became visible again, and the Jade Emperor said, "What are you doing here?"

She replied, "I've come to listen to the classics, of course."

The Jade Emperor took out his whip and hit her, and she cried out. The immortal heard her, and had never heard a woman cry out like this before. He then opened his eyes to take a look at her. When he saw how beautiful she was, he had thoughts of desire. This experience influenced him so that his sensual desire was aroused. Thus, he was no longer able to lecture the classic and his karmic achievement in the spiritual path was lost. Because of this, the Jade Emperor got even more upset, and so he returned home.

After they returned, the asura woman went to see her father and said, "The Jade Emperor has been cheating on me. He goes out and has affairs with all sorts of women. He told me he was going to listen to the classics, and so I went with him to check it out. He said what I did was wrong and hit me."

When her father heard this, he got very angry. "This time I'm going to do battle with you!" he said, as if talking to the Jade Emperor. Then he assembled his asura army. He planted his feet on the bottom of the ocean and with one hand toppled the heavenly palace.

The Jade Emperor did not have the spiritual powers to deal with the asura king, and so he went to beseech Shakyamuni Buddha to rescue him.

Shakyamuni Buddha replied, "Don't worry. Go back and tell your army to recite 'Maha-Prajna-Paramita,' and everything will be fine."

The Jade Emperor returned to his army, and told them what to do. As a result as soon as they recited "Maha-Prajna-Paramita," the asura army was defeated and fled. Why? Because Maha-Prajna-Paramita is wisdom, and the asuras are rooted in ignorance. Once they saw the light of wisdom, they were defeated. This is the general meaning of asuras.

Garudas are the great golden-winged *p'eng* birds. They only eat dragons. Their bodies are huge and with a wing-span that is so big it extends for three hundred and sixty yojanas. Garudas can flap their wings to fan aside the water in the ocean. When the water is gone, the dragons are exposed, and the p'eng birds can eat them just like humans eat noodles. They slurp up the dragons just like they are noodles, a mouthful at a time. In one mouthful, a great golden-winged *p'eng* bird could swallow up from ten to twenty dragons. Since their wing-span is three hundred and sixty yojanas, the diameter of their beaks must be at least one hundred yojanas wide. It is easy for them to consume a few thousand dragons at a time. This can cause the dragons and their young to be eaten to extinction.

Then the elder dragons went to Shakyamuni Buddha and asked him to save them. "We dragons and our offspring are almost all eaten up by the great golden winged *p'eng* birds," they said. "What can we do? We dragons are now on the verge of extinction."

Shakyamuni Buddha said, "Don't worry. I'll give you a Kashaya robe. Give each one of your dragons and offspring a thread from this robe to hide under. Then when the great golden winged *p'eng* birds come looking for you, they won't be able to find you."

The elder dragons took the robe back and tore it up and gave each dragon a thread of the robe, which they tied to themselves. As a result the golden-winged *p'eng* birds had no way to find the dragons and eat them. They had heard from others that Shakyamuni Buddha had saved the dragons, so they too went to the Buddha and complained, "You've saved the dragons, but now we have nothing to eat. We're going to starve to death. The great golden-winged *p'eng* birds will all become extinct! The Buddha's kindness and compassion is not impartial. You saved the dragons, so now you have to save us too."

Shakyamuni Buddha said, "Fine. If today you take refuge with the Three Jewels, that is the Buddha, the Dharma, and the Sangha, and if you uphold the moral precept against killing as well as the other Five Moral Precepts, I will tell my disciples to give you seven grains of rice each time they have a meal. After this, you should not kill." Then the great golden-winged *p'eng* birds took refuge with the Three Jewels and became vegetarians and no longer ate dragons. However, although they stopped eating dragons, they had eaten so many dragons prior to that time that there are few dragons today. Therefore, at the present time we do not see dragons. This is the explanation of garudas.

Kinnaras are called "doubtful" spirits, and they also perform music for the Jade Emperor.

Mahoragas are great pythons.

Humans, non-humans, and so forth and all the gods. **Upon hearing what the Buddha had said, all in the entire great assembly.** All of those in the Dharma assembly, **were extremely happy, faithfully accepted it, and put it into practice.** All were exceedingly happy and believed in this inconceivable Dharma. They followed this Dharma and carried it out in their practice.

This year I've lectured the Chapter on the Practices and Vows of Samantabhadra during this first six-week summer session. The principles have not been explained completely, due to the limitations of time. I have not been able to explain these principles in detail, but have only discussed these ideas in general. If you want to truly understand the meaning of this Sutra, you should earnestly use a lot of effort, and then you can truly understand it. The Buddha-dharma is inconceivable, and so it is called "wonderful Dharma." This Chapter on the Practices and Vows of Samantabhadra is an inconceivable chapter. If I were to explain the principles completely, it would take a very long time. I have just given a simple explanation. If you want to investigate the Buddha-dharma further, you should work hard on your own and look into it more deeply.

I don't know whether I have explained the Sutra well or not. I do not have any wish for it to be good or bad. What does this mean? I have explained as if I have not explained, and you should have listened as if you have not listened. To be without listening and without explaining is the true wonderful Dharma. Therefore, you should realize that it is unnecessary to explain and unnecessary to listen. Once you understand this wonderful Dharma, then you will have not wasted your time during these six weeks.

What happens when one has not wasted one's time? Eating is still eating, wearing clothes is still wearing clothes, and sleeping is still sleeping. That's the way it is.

VERSE FOR
TRANSFERRING THE MERIT

May the merit and virtue
    accrued from this work
Adorn the Buddhas' Pure Lands,
Repaying the
    four kinds of benefactors
And aiding those suffering in
    the three paths.
May all who see and hear of this
Aspire to awaken to the Truth,
And when this life is over,
Be born together in
    the Land of Ultimate Bliss.

Namo Dharma Protector Weituo Bodhisattva

DHARMA REALM BUDDHIST ASSOCIATION BRANCHES

USA

**Dharma Realm Buddhist Association
The City of Ten Thousand Buddhas**

4951 Bodhi Way

Ukiah, CA 95482 USA

p 707.462.0939
f 707.462.0949
www.drba.org
www.cttbusa.org
cttb@drba.org

Buddhist Text Translation Society

4951 Bodhi Way, Ukiah, CA 95482 USA

www.bttsonline.org
www.dharmaradio.org

**Instilling Goodness Elementary School
Developing Virtue Secondary School**

2001 Talmage Road

Ukiah, CA 95482 USA

p & f 707.468.3847 (girls)
p & f 707.468.1138 (boys)
www.igdvs.org

Dharma Realm Buddhist University

4951 Bodhi Way, Ukiah, CA 95482 USA

p 707.621.7000
www.drbu.org
info@drbu.edu

The International Translation Institute

1777 Murchison Drive
Burlingame, CA 94010-4504 USA

p 650.692.5912
f 650.692.5056

**Institute for World Religions /
Berkeley Buddhist Monastery**

2304 McKinley Avenue

Berkeley, CA 94703 USA

p 510.848.3440

f 510.548.4551

www.berkeleymonastery.org
paramita@drba.org

The City of the Dharma Realm

1029 West Capitol Avenue

West Sacramento, CA 95691 USA

p 916.374.8268
f 916.374.8234
www.cityofdharmarealm.org
cdr@cityofdharmarealm.org

Avatamsaka Vihara

9601 Seven Locks Road
Bethesda, MD 20817-9997 USA

p & f 301.469.8300
www.avatamsakavihara.org
DharmaMaster@avatamsakavihara.org

**Blessings, Prosperity, and
Longevity Monastery**

4140 Long Beach Boulevard
Long Beach, CA 90807 USA

p 562.595.4966

www.bplmonastery.org

Gold Mountain Monastery

800 Sacramento Street
San Francisco, CA 94108 USA

p 415.421.6117
f 415.788.6001
www.goldmountainmonastery.org
www.drbachinese.org/branch/GMM

Gold Sage Monastery

11455 Clayton Road

San Jose, CA 95127-5099 USA

p 408.923.7243

f 408.923.1064

drbagsm.org/en;drbagsm.org/zh

Gold Summit Monastery

233 1st Avenue West

Seattle, WA 98119 USA

p & f 206.284.6690

www.goldsummitmonastery.org

goldsummit@drba.org

Gold Wheel Monastery

235 North Avenue 58

Los Angeles, CA 90042 USA

p 323.258.6668

f 323.258.3619

www.goldwheel.org

Long Beach Monastery

3361 East Ocean Boulevard

Long Beach, CA 90803 USA

p & f 562.438.8902

www.longbeachmonastery.org

CANADA

Gold Buddha Monastery

248 East 11th Avenue

Vancouver B.C., V5T 2C3 CANADA

p 604.709.0248

f 604.684.3754

www.gbm-online.com

drba@gbm-online.com

Avatamsaka Monastery

1009 4th Avenue S.W.

Calgary, AB, T2P OK8 CANADA

p 403.234.0644

f 403.263.0637

www.avatamsaka.ca

AUSTRALIA

Gold Coast Dharma Realm

106 Bonogin Road, Mudgeeraba

Queensland 4213 AUSTRALIA

p 61.755.228.788

f 61.755.227.822

www.gcdr.org.au

TAIWAN ROC

Dharma Realm Buddhist Books Distribution Society

85 Chung-hsiao E. Road

Sec. 6, 11th Floor,

Taipei City, 11575 TAIWAN, ROC

p 02.2786.3022

f 02.2786.2674

www.drbataipei.org

www.fajye.com.tw

fajye@drbataipei.org

Amitabha Monastery

126 Fuji Street, Chih-nan Village,

Shou-feng, Hualien County

97445 TAIWAN ROC

p 03.865.1956

f 03.865.3426

MALAYSIA

Dharma Realm Guan Yin Sagely Monastery

161 Jalan Ampang, 50450 Kuala Lumpur

WEST MALAYSIA

p 03.2164.8055

f 03.2163.7118

Fa Yuan Sagely Monastery

1, Jalan Utama, Taman Serdang Raya
43300 Seri Kembangan, Selangor
Darul Ehsan, WEST MALAYSIA

p 03.8958.5668

Lotus Vihara

136, Jalan Sekolah
45600 Batang Berjuntai, Selangor
Darul Ehsan, WEST MALAYSIA

p 03.3271.9439

**Malaysia Dharma Realm Buddhist
Association Penang Branch**

32-32C, Jalan Tan Sri
Teh Ewe Lim, 11600 Jelutong
Penang, WEST MALAYSIA

p 04.281.7728
f 04.281.7798

Prajna Guanyin Sagely Monastery

Batu $5^1/_2$ Jalan Sungai Besi
Salak Selatan, 57100 Kuala Lumpur
WEST MALAYSIA

p 03.7982.6560
f 03.7980.1272